Romantic Weekends

Virginia, Washington D.C. & Maryland

D1089356

*R*omantic *W*eekends

Virginia, Washington D.C. & Maryland

Norman & Kathy Renouf

HUNTER
PUBLISHING

Hunter Publishing, Inc.
300 Raritan Center Parkway
Edison NJ 08818
Tel (908) 225 1900
Fax (908) 417 0482

164 Commander Boulevard
Agincourt, Ontario
Canada
Tel (416) 293 8141

ISBN 1-55650-702-X

Cover photo: *Sunset at Oxford, MD*
Superstock

Maps by Kim André

Contents

Maps

This guide is for lovers everywhere who believe that romance can begin with a glance and last a lifetime.

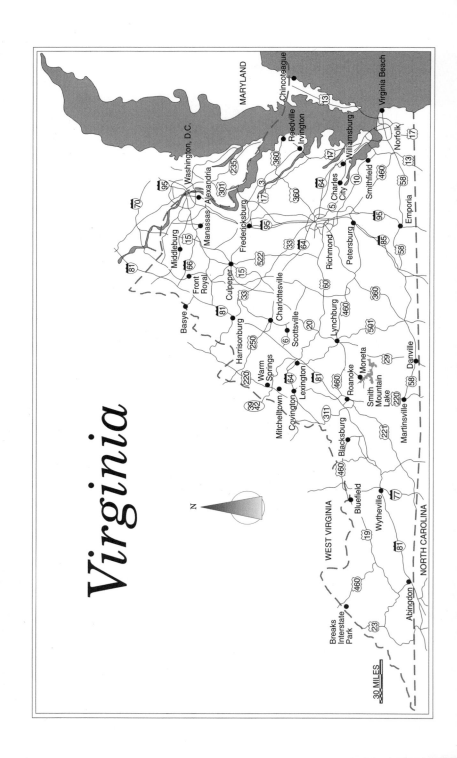

Introduction

The impetus for this guide is pure and simple: romance. If it weren't for romance – our own romance, that is – it wouldn't have been written. It was 21 years ago that we first met, fell in love and married. For reasons that even we don't fully understand, we separated shortly afterward. Leading our separate lives on different continents, we had no contact for over 17 years. A totally unrelated trip across the ocean and a meeting that occurred despite incredible odds led to a friendship that, through many twists and turns, sparked something we thought we had lost forever. On March 4, 1995, we remarried in the same church where we had wed nearly 20 years before.

Like everyone else, we enjoy getting away for the weekend. When both of you work (one of you at home) and there are two teenaged boys and their friends always around, it is difficult to find those quiet – and very necessary – moments to enjoy each other. We decided this time that we owed it to ourselves, and to those around us, to keep our romance strong and fresh. To do this, we needed to devote at least one weekend a month exclusively to each other. That meant getting away from the normal routine and the pressures of "regular" life.

We began to scour the bookshops for guides that offered interesting suggestions about unique and romantic adventures for couples. We had hoped to find one that was easy to read and entertaining as well. It should come as no surprise that we looked in vain. We realized that we had stumbled on a major gap in the market. Given Norman's extensive travel-writing experience, we did the only logical thing – we wrote it ourselves.

The right accommodations are a very important ingredient in an enjoyable weekend. You'll find in these chapters an eclectic mix ranging from secluded log cabins tucked away in the mountains to grand hotels in major cities. Of course, location alone doesn't ensure a romantic experience. In our travels through Virginia, Washington D.C. and Maryland, we have searched for areas that offer not only interesting accomodations, but fun and romantic things to do and, of course, enticing restaurants. Some of the areas we have chosen will, of course, be familiar. In these instances, we have suggested fresh alternatives that we hope will appeal. And that has been our primary goal: to ferret out spots that most people wouldn't have the time or resources to find themselves.

There are some tokens of romance that are just about universal. A dozen long-stemmed red roses, a limousine ride, a gift of fine lingerie, a tour in a horse-drawn carriage, a chilled bottle of champagne – all speak the language of love. In each chapter, we have included information on where to find (or arrange for) these special touches.

In many cases, what one person considers romantic may not appeal to another. So we have taken great care to include options that will suit couples of all ages and interests. Once you realize how many wonderful choices are available, the two of you may just get adventurous and try something new.

Throughout the text the following icons will be used:

Lodging   Dining   Sightseeing

In closing, we hope you have as much fun on these trips as we had researching them. There are lots of things to discover out there, but the most important of these is your continued discovery of each other.

Central Virginia

Richmond
Where Southern Grace
& Progress are Confederates

This is a city with attractions so diverse that it literally has something for everyone. Not the least of these charms is an especially delightful location on the falls of the James River.

So taken were early settlers with the beauty of this spot that they wasted no time starting a colony here. Its similarities to a particular Thameside village were so striking that they named it in that village's honor; hence, Richmond. Thanks to its strategic location, the settlement developed quickly into a political and economic power. The way you see the town today is, for the most part, the way it was laid out as far back as 1737. The natural gathering place of those in colonial power, it played an important role in the development of events leading up to the Revolutionary War. It was here, at St. John's Church a month before the hostilities, that Patrick Henry cried, "Give me liberty or give me death!" The following decades were prosperous ones for the city, with the coal, flour, furniture, textile and tobacco industries all flourishing. However, the Civil War violently interrupted this growth, changing the face of Richmond forever. As the capital of the Confederacy, the city and its environs were the site of numerous costly battles. In 1865, when it became apparent that Richmond would fall, the retreating Confederate Army set it ablaze. Large portions of the city were destroyed. However, the spirit of Richmond's residents ultimately triumphed; both they and the city rebounded quickly. Prosperous and growing once again, Richmond is now home to such major companies as Reynolds Metals, Ethyl Corporation and the well-known Philip Morris.

Roots go deep here. Interdependence in times of upheaval and a wealth of local traditions have bound Richmonders together with a strong sense of local pride. In years past, this has made Richmond a very insular society. It is only during the past two decades that the city has reached out socially and culturally as it always has commercially. "Old Richmond" is still alive and well in the hearts of its natives, but now it's tempered with dashes of cosmopolitan flavor and open-mindedness that have undoubtedly made it a more attractive place to live, work and visit.

Not all of the changes are positive. The advent of the shopping mall has had a devastating effect on what was once the core of the city. Once-omnipotent downtown department stores such as Miller & Rhoads and Thalhimers stand boarded up on Broad Street. The center of gravity has shifted down to the financial district, and the area that immediately surrounds it. There, in the Shockoe Slip – and slightly farther east, in Shockoe Bottom – is an eclectic mix of specialty shops, bars and trendy restaurants that cater to divergent tastes. Another hub of activity lies a couple of miles to the west. Called the Fan District, this is an unusual residential area sprinkled with neighborhood businesses and enlivened by students from Virginia Commonwealth University.

In conclusion, modern-day Richmond is an intriguing mix of history, politics and culture bound together by the genteel manners and easygoing informality peculiar to the Southern conservative tradition.

If you are history lovers, there is much here to explore. Places to include on your itinerary are the state capitol; the White House and Museum of the Confederacy; St. John's Church; The Valentine Museum; the Virginia Museum of Fine Arts; the John Marshall House Museum; the Black History Museum and Cultural Center of Virginia; and the Edgar Allan Poe Museum – and these are just the most important. Rather than giving sketchy details of each, we recommend you pay a visit to the Bell Tower Visitors' Center, (804) 648-3146, located in the west corner of the delightful Capitol Square. Hours are 9 a.m. to 5 p.m. from Monday to Saturday, and noon to 5 p.m. on Sunday. If you prefer to plan your schedule in advance, give them a call; they will be happy to send all the information you require. For a general overview of the history and main points of interest, you may want to make time for the guided city tour, "Old Richmond Today," run by Historic Richmond Tours, (804) 780-0107. The company's 24-seat mini-bus arrives at your hotel around 9:45 a.m.; from there it takes you on a two-and-a-half-hour drive around town, the highlight of which is the historic state capitol. The cost is $16 per person, and reservations are required.

Because of its prominence, Richmond and its key attractions are fairly well-known and easy to research through area publications. That said, we've decided to offer a more lighthearted, innovative and slightly maverick approach to the city. As this is our home, we feel justified in taking a few liberties. So buckle your seat belts and get ready to hit a home run in a town where sports lovers can really play the field.

Richmond's claim to fame may not be sports, but for a city of its size, it is actually quite sports-oriented. Its minor league teams in both baseball and ice hockey won their respective championships during the 1994 and 1994/95 seasons. **The Richmond Braves** – who play in baseball's class AAA International League – serve as the "farm team" for the Atlanta Braves. Call the Richmond Braves' ticket office at (804) 359-4444 and plan to spend a delightful afternoon or evening watching America's favorite pastime at the team's beautifully designed stadium, The Diamond.

During the winter months (and well into the spring, when they are having a successful season) an evening at The Coliseum watching the **Richmond Renegades** is always lively. It can be difficult to get tickets for major league ice hockey; when you can get them, they often seat you so far away from the action that you lose track of the game. No such problem here. Although the East Coast Hockey League is not quite as skilled as the NHL, the action is fast and furious. With a little advance planning, you may get down close to the rink. Once there, it won't take long to develop a keen appreciation of this fast-paced, demanding game. A schedule and tickets may be obtained by calling (804) 643-7825.

There is one "major league" sport that comes to Richmond for two weekends – one in March and one in September. The action takes place in a stadium that boasts the largest seating capacity of any Virginia sports complex. Good thing, too, because this two-day event generally draws crowds in excess of 130,000, making it the largest spectator event in the Old Dominion. The sport is **NASCAR racing**. The first day's race is the NASCAR Busch Series Grand National, while the second day's race (the most important of the two) is a leg in the NASCAR Winston Cup Series. The stadium – located on the Virginia State Fairgrounds, just northeast of the city limits – is the Richmond International Raceway (RIR). Here, 81,184 permanent seats encircle the ¾-mile "D"-shaped oval. Average lap speeds are in the 125-mile-per-hour range. On the September weekend, when the weather is warmer, night racing is held and the whole affair is preceded by a NASCAR SuperTruck Series. In addition to NASCAR racing, the fairgrounds hosts several other events throughout the year (including a nationally-sanctioned steeplechase each spring). Information and tickets may be obtained by phoning (804) 345-RACE (7223). Be advised, though, that you must make your plans early to see the Winston Cup Races. Despite the number of seats, tickets for this event are sold out many months in advance.

Of course, this huge influx of people creates an equally huge traffic jam. If you don't fancy getting stuck in it, you might consider going over it! The quickest (and most exciting) way of getting to the raceway is by helicopter. Locally-based **HeloAir Inc.**, (804) 226-3492, will shuttle you to and from the stadium for $90 a person. So add an extra thrill to your day, and schedule a flight.

The sport of racing appeals to both sexes; both men and women undoubtedly fantasize about getting behind the wheel of a race car. Wouldn't the chance to fulfill such a dream be the perfect gift for your partner? Imagine the thrill you'd both have watching a video of him or her speeding around the track in a genuine NASCAR vehicle. **The Buck Baker Racing School**, (704) 366-6224, (800) 529-BUCK or fax (704) 596-8931, comes to the RIR three times each year for that express purpose. Both three-day ($2,000) and one-day ($795) sessions are offered. On day one, you begin by walking the track to learn the safe and proper travel pattern (known by the drivers as the "line"). This is followed later in the morning with instruction designed to familiarize you with the race car itself. After lunch, you take a ride in the passenger seat while your instructor demonstrates how the "line" actually works. The next step is to trade seats. Now you must show the instructor that you are sufficiently familiar with the concept of the "line" to go it alone. Last but not least comes your big moment: a solo performance, with five other "greenhorns" on the track. For those who continue on to days two and three, there is more of the same, with your instructor evaluating your progress each morning. You will learn more advanced techniques (such as "sling shot" passing and making pit stops), both in a classroom and on the track. E. W. "Buck" Baker, the man who oversees this operation, is a legend in the sport of Winston Cup Racing. Small wonder: he boasts two championships, 46 Winston Cup victories and a place in no fewer than four racing halls of fame. When he retired from racing, he recognized the need for a "real time" racing school that would give the professionals an opportunity to hone their skills, racers looking to move up to Winston Cup competition a chance to test their talents, and corporate groups and fans a place to experience the adventure of a lifetime. He and his instructors have been successful in all three regards since the school's inception in 1980. In addition to their engagements at the RIR, these schools are offered in Atlanta, Georgia and Rockingham, North Carolina. While we concede that finding the money for this treat may be a trick, your partner is sure to "lap" it up.

Accommodation is particularly scarce here on racing weekends, but then Richmond can be busy during many times of year. We'll recommend a cross-section of places, ranging from a huge Five-Diamond hotel to an intimately beautiful bed and breakfast.

The town's grandest, most historic and most unusual
hotel is **The Jefferson,** (804) 788-8000 or (800) 424-
8014. Located at the junction of Franklin and Adams
Streets – about a dozen blocks from the financial district
– this hotel first opened its doors on October 31, 1895. It
was the brainchild of millionaire Major Lewis Ginter,
who was born in New York of Dutch immigrant parents
and came to Richmond in 1842 at the tender age of 18.
Before the Civil War – during which he served with
distinction in the Confederate Army – he made his first
millions as an importer of fabrics. Following the war, he
moved back to New York, where he made his mark in the
field of banking. Upon his subsequent return to Richmond, this "business tycoon" became a civic leader and
one of Richmond's wealthiest citizens. He was a classic
Jeffersonian – sophisticated and widely-traveled, having
crossed the Atlantic more than 30 times and gone around
the world on several occasions. So impressed was he by
the grand hotels of Europe, he was determined that
Richmond have the "finest hostelry in America." To this
end, he commissioned a renowned architectural firm in
New York to build a startlingly beautiful hotel which
was a combination of Renaissance and other styles of
architecture Ginter particularly admired. It was a lavish
endeavor, with the overall cost estimated at between $5
and $10 million. The centerpiece for the hotel's upper
lobby was The Palm Court, which featured a life-size
sculpture of Thomas Jefferson executed in Carrara marble. (It took the artist two years to complete, and cost
$12,000.) No expense was spared, either, for the comfort
of guests. The hotel featured billiard rooms, a library,
ladies' salons, a grill room, Turkish and Russian baths
and every contemporary convenience of the time. These
included electric lights, electric elevators, hot and cold
running water in all 308 rooms, and a Telesme (the
predecessor of the telephone) for room service.

Not surprisingly, The Jefferson soon became the hub of
Richmond's social life. Unfortunately, Major Ginter lived
only long enough to enjoy it for a couple of years. Had he
lived a few years more, he would have witnessed the
destruction of nearly three-fifths of the hotel by fire. The
only casualty in the 1901 tragedy – which was blamed on
a fault in the electrical wiring – was the statue of Jeffer-

son. It was dropped during the evacuation and, hitting the floor, decapitated. In due time, the statue was recovered from a neighboring front yard, repaired and returned to the hotel. The surviving 100 guest rooms were re-opened just 14 months after the fire; extensive renovations begun in 1905 restored the hotel to its former glory. A total of 220 new rooms were added, along with what are perhaps the hotel's most recognizable and celebrated features: the grand staircase and the mezzanine. It was up a replica of these wide, red-carpeted steps that a drunken Rhett Butler carried a reluctant Scarlett O'Hara for a night of passion in the movie *Gone With The Wind.* If walking up those stairs doesn't put you in a romantic mood, you had better check your pulse. The Palm Court was also renovated. And when the enlarged hotel was reopened in 1907, it had some permanent residents. The fountains had been removed and live alligators came to live in the pool. These became a source of much interest. And while the alligator tales are not extinct, the creatures you see today will offer no threat; the last live one died in 1948.

The new hotel continued in the footsteps of its predecessor and, once again, became the heartbeat of Richmond society. Among the distinguished guests: nine presidents (from Harrison to Reagan), other high-ranking notables, and numerous celebrities. One of the world's most famous dancers, Bill "Bojangles" Robinson, was "discovered" here waiting tables in the dining room. (His statue now stands at the entrance to Sixth Street Marketplace.) Sadly, seven people died and 20 more were injured when a second blaze tore through the hotel in 1944. Ensuing years saw The Jefferson undergo a slow and painful decline until it finally closed in 1980.

Fortunately, this was not the end of the story. In 1983, a local developer with vision organized a group of investors who initiated yet another reconstruction. Three years of work (and $34 million) were spent on restoration and modernization. Every effort was made to bring back the best of a bygone era, while adding the modern amenities required by discriminating travelers. The unveiling of this masterful mix came on May 6, 1986 when The Jefferson re-opened for business. Historic Hotels Inc., a Richmond-based group of investors, acquired the hotel in 1991. They further upgraded the facilities, redecorating each of the guest rooms and suites – as well as refurbishing the Palm Court and The Rotunda – at a price of $4.5 million. Even if you decide to stay elsewhere, you can experience the ambiance of The Jefferson by paying a visit to its extraordinary public rooms. The Palm Court is now the registration area; it features the original bellman's desk and nine of the original stained glass windows, dating from 1907. The real place of honor, however, is reserved for the original marble statue of Thomas Jefferson. The stone statesman now keeps watch over the bustle of activity from his post beneath a stunning domed skylight. A walk down either side of the legendary marble staircase will bring you into The Rotunda. Here, tall faux marble pillars support a soaring ceiling embellished with multi-color and gold-leaf designsand crowned by a striking skylight. An Axminster carpet of gigantic proportions and graceful period furniture create a lush setting in which you may relax and dream of a bygone age. The atmosphere lends itself perfectly to intimate conversation. Beverage service is offered here six nights a week, and the wine-by-the-glass menu is extensive. You'll even enjoy light classical piano if you visit in the early evening or during the Sunday champagne brunch.

Today, The Jefferson has 274 guestrooms. This includes 26 suites of varying sizes, the most luxurious of which are the Presidential and Governor's Suites. Spacious and finely appointed, each opens onto a large private balcony. The latter even has a baby grand piano. Just imagine this scene: you return to the hotel after a delightful dinner and make the long climb, arm in arm, up those famous stairs. You enter your suite. The room is bathed in the gentle glow of candlelight. A blaze of red roses draws your eye to the piano, where the musician you have hired is playing "your" songs. The champagne is chilled and the night is young... now **you** write the ending.

Admittedly, the suites are not within everyone's price range (the Presidential Suite rents for $825 a night.) There are, however, more manageable options. If you choose the Romance Package, you'll be welcomed by a complimentary bottle of champagne and a Jefferson Hotel memento. The following morning, a full American breakfast will be delivered to your room. Prices per night are $185 for a deluxe room or $250 for a standard suite. Another option is the Bed & Breakfast Package. At $140 per couple, this includes one night in a deluxe room and a full breakfast buffet for two in Lemaire, The Jefferson's signature restaurant.

The Lemaire – which currently enjoys a Four-Diamond rating from the AAA – seats 118 in seven separate and intimate rooms. It is named in honor of the maitre d'hotel who served Thomas Jefferson in the White House and introduced Americans to the art of cooking with wine. Featured on the menu are selections from Lemaire's legendary recipes, all distinguished by the use of wine, light sauces and garden-fresh herbs and vegetables. The chef here is the award-winning Mark Langenfeld, who has served in many prestigious establishments, including The Grand Hotel Victoria-Jungfrau in Interlaken, Switzerland.

The Jefferson was one of only five hotels in the world to be awarded the coveted AAA Five-Diamond award for the year 1994. It is also listed in the National Register of Historic Places and the Virginia Historic Landmarks Register.

Three blocks east on Franklin is another hotel that is impressive in its own fashion, although not so imposing in size. A row of Greek Revival houses dating from 1847 forms the facade of the **Linden Row Inn**. Behind this is a unique and fascinating layout featuring a brick-walled garden with footpaths and a fountain, and an unusual collection of buildings housing both public areas and other rooms.

Equally fascinating is this inn's history. In 1811, Elizabeth Poe, an actress who was performing with a traveling company at the Richmond Theatre, became ill and died. She left behind two young children, one of whom – Edgar Poe – was taken in by a Mr. & Mrs. John Allan (who gave him the middle name, Allan). The family moved to England, where they lived for five years before returning to Richmond. Here they took up residence across the road from Linden Row, with Mr. Allan's business partner, Charles Ellis. Mr. Ellis planted, on the present site of the hotel, a

garden that was renowned for its beautiful roses, jas-
mine and lindens. Edgar Allan and the Ellis children
spent many a day playing happily in these gardens;
legend has it that this was the "enchanted garden" Poe
mentions in his famous poem, "To Helen."

The properties were used for a variety of purposes before
their donation to the Historic Richmond Foundation in
1979 by the late Mary Wingfield Scott, one of Richmond's
pioneer preservationists. After much consideration, the
trustees decided that redevelopment by the private sec-
tor – within guidelines set by the foundation – would be
in Linden Row's best interests. Various plans were rejected before the foundation agreed to one that would
ensure the retention of the original interior, with its
molded plaster cornices, ceiling medallions, marble man-
tels and intricate woodwork. In 1986, the buildings were
sold to Southeastern Historic Properties which, in conjunction with Great Inns of America, began the arduous
process of renovation. The hotel was opened in 1988 with
71 guest rooms (including seven suites), as well as numerous public rooms furnished with authentic period
antiques. The intent was to retain and enhance the
19th-century ambience, while offering up-to-date amenities such as individual climate control, remote control
cable TV, and AM/FM radio. This marriage of old and
new has been so beautifully accomplished that the inn
merits the AAA Four-Diamond award. When making a
reservation, call (804) 783-7000 or (800) 348-7424, or fax
(804) 648-7504, and ask for one of the seven parlor
suites. Spacious and elegant, these feature "gasoliers"
and handsome mantel and pier mirrors, most of which
were collected by Mary Wingfield Scott for use in these
very rooms. Depending upon the season, these suites
rent for $114-$157 a night. Regular rooms are in the
$74-$107 range.

Linden Row is famed for its Southern hospitality, and
you will be enchanted by the evening wine and cheese
reception in the parlor. The dining room features Southern cuisine and other American favorites; in good
weather, light dining and refreshments are served on the
patio. Guests may also enjoy the use of the nearby YMCA
Fitness Center and pool, compliments of the manage-

ment. Valet parking is available, as is free transportation downtown and to the neighboring business districts. If you prefer to take a stroll, the inn is within walking distance of most of the main attractions in downtown Richmond.

We have already mentioned Shockoe Slip, located down by the business center. If you're attracted by its social whirl, you should consider either of the next two options.

If you really want to impress your partner, book the Governor's Suite in **The Berkeley Hotel**, (804) 780-1300, on the corner of Twelfth and Cary Streets. This hotel opened in August 1988, and has already been given AAA's Four-Diamond rating. For $400 a night, you get a key to this luxurious suite where the bedroom and living room area are divided by something that is rarely found in Richmond hotels: a jacuzzi. Valet parking, twice-daily maid service, and access to a nearby fitness center are complimentary. Fine dining is also just around the corner. Thanks to chef Jay Frank, **The Dining Room at the Berkeley Hotel** – where reservations are preferred but not required – has developed a formidable reputation. Innovative dishes are prepared and presented in Continental fashion, in an atmosphere of understated elegance.

Just across the road at 100 South 12th Street is the much larger **Omni Richmond Hotel**, which is both Four-Star and Four-Diamond-rated. Located in the fashionable James Center – a combination of offices, banks, specialty shops and cafés – this hotel has 363 guest rooms. Well over 200 of these offer king-sized beds, with all of them well-appointed and equipped with the usual amenities (including in-room movies and a mini-bar). Request a room on one of the higher floors if you'd like a magnificent view of either Capitol Square or the James River. For exercise or relaxation, the on-site Capital Club features an indoor/outdoor pool with a sundeck; squash and racquetball courts; and Nautilus equipment. For your dining pleasure, the Gallego Restaurant and Wine Bar specializes in Angus steaks. The Café Gallego, adjacent to the inside mall, serves a variety of foods in a more informal atmosphere. It is open throughout the day, and remains so for late-night snacking.

The Omni offers a choice of two enticing packages. The Bed & Breakfast Package, at $99 a night, includes accommodation in a king-bedded deluxe room, breakfast buffet for two the following morning, and a welcoming bottle of champagne. The Good Life Package offers a king-bedded deluxe room and dinner at the Café Gallego for an affordable $109. Additional information and reservations may be obtained by calling (804) 344-700 or Omni Reservations at (800) THE-OMNI.

An insider's tip: the Christmas season is a beautiful time to visit The James Center. Hundreds of life-sized reindeer fashioned from grape vines and wrapped in thousands of white lights "graze" in the courtyards and "drink" from the gurgling stream running through the lobby. The surrounding trees have traded their foliage for gowns of twinkling lights, while a profusion of poinsettias add a splash of holiday red. This is a wonderland, and we come here every year to walk hand-in-hand, remembering Christmases past.

You will recognize the **Radisson Hotel Richmond**, (804) 788-0900 or (800) 333-3333, by its unusual shape. Located a few blocks west, it resembles a large slice of cheese. Actually, this design represents a very clever use of a difficult space, as the plot on which the hotel sits is wedged tightly between Canal Street and the Downtown Expressway. An easygoing mood prevails here. The public rooms are furnished in an understated elegance and there is a pleasant leisure complex that features an indoor pool. The rooms to ask for are the "point" rooms, whose unique layout is dictated by their position at the sharp narrow end of the building. These rooms are spacious, neatly decorated in a rather modern style, and boast magnificent panoramic views of both the river and downtown Richmond. The cost is $150 night. The *pièce de la resistance*, however, is the Penthouse Suite. Located on the 13th and 14th floors, this room is really special; it is certainly the accommodation of choice for many visiting celebrities. The huge downstairs floorspace is furnished with contemporary pieces, including an impressive modern glass dining table. A spiral staircase leads to the bedroom, which occupies a loft overlooking the downstairs. Incidentally, this room is one of the very few we have found in this city that features a jacuzzi. It goes without saying that the views are spectacular. You can add your name to the list of those who slept here for $500 per night.

Come with us now to a different area of the city and a smaller, more intimate venue. Many southern cities have one particularly elegant boulevard, lined by ancient trees and grand mansions that bespeak days past. This is typically the one section of town that played host to the wealthy of that day; here, the virtues and dignity of a gentler time seem more than a distant memory. For a true taste of "Old Richmond," drive down **Monument Avenue.** Laid out in 1889 between Lombardy and Belmont Streets, Monument is lined on both sides by a particularly diverse blend of properties, most of them constructed in the "classic revival" style. As its name implies, the avenue has another claim to fame: the magnificently grand statues of the South's Confederate heroes. Whether mounted or on foot, these serve as a reminder to passersby of the esteem in which these men were – and often still are – held. Five of these were erected between 1890 and 1929, in a post-Civil War exercise to glorify "The Lost Cause." Monument Avenue made headlines in 1995, when the city council debated whether to honor tennis star Arthur Ashe by placing a statue of the Richmond native on this avenue.

At 2036 Monument Avenue – on the north side and almost at its mid-point – stands **The Emmanuel Hutzler House**, (804) 355-4885 or (804) 353-6900. Built in 1914 by the youngest son of a prosperous dry goods merchant, it now functions as a most delightful bed and breakfast. Emmanuel Hutzler's status in early 20th-century Richmond is immediately apparent from the stunning use of natural mahogany paneling, the beautiful leaded glass windows, impressive interior columns and coffered beam ceiling. In 1991, this 8,000-square foot home was restored and converted to a delightful four-room bed and breakfast. The first three rooms – Henrietta's Room, Isaac's Suite and Marion's Room – are beautifully furnished. In addition, each boasts a private bath with tub and shower. However, the ideal choice for a romantic interlude would be the Robinette Suite. This 16-foot by 20-foot room, which overlooks Monument Avenue, is both bright and airy. The sleeping area is equipped with a four-poster queen-sized bed and cherry Sheraton dresser. You may also enjoy relaxing in the sitting area with its antique sofa, side chair and table, in front of a working fireplace. The adjoining nine-foot by 13-foot tiled bathroom – also over-looking the avenue – has a four-foot by six-foot jacuzzi tub and separate shower. Rates range from $85–$135 per night. All four rooms have telephone and cable tele-vision; central air-conditioning cools the house in the summer months. The genteel character of this turn-of-the-century area is reflected in the public rooms down-stairs. These provide a marvelous place to sit, relax and converse with other guests. A light breakfast is included in the tariff, and is available each morning in the dining room. A full breakfast may be had on request, and for an extra charge. Lighted off-street parking is provided, but be advised that smoking is prohibited in the house. To sum it all up, staying here gives you the opportunity to enjoy all that the city has to offer, but in a more relaxed, classically beautiful atmosphere.

 Every couple who visits Richmond should set aside Sat-urday morning for a trip to **Capitol Square**. Richmond became Virginia's third capital city when legislators voted to relocate here from Williamsburg in 1779. Their first meeting place was a warehouse on the corner of 14th and Cary Streets, in the Shockoe Slip. It was not until 1788 that the two legislative branches and the governor's office were moved into the new capitol build-ing. The original red brick structure, yet another design by the multi-talented Thomas Jefferson, was covered in stucco in 1880. It was not unusual to see livestock graz-ing on the sloping lawns before 1818, when the 12 sur-rounding acres were fenced in. Today this government complex is dominated by the historic Capitol building. Tucked behind and to one side is the governor's mansion, the country's oldest continually-occupied governor's house; as well as a park that serves as a delightful green oasis in the hustle and bustle of the city. Fountains encircled by rose bushes, graceful statues and the in-triguing bell tower (now a visitors' center) are all con-nected by brick-paved walkways dotted with old-fashioned park benches. When you go, be sure to take along bread or other such goodies for the squirrels.

It is time now to continue down the hill and cross Bank Street to Main, following a route that is by now familiar to those staying at either The Berkeley or the Omni. Trace 12th Street to its junction with East Cary, and the beginning of the Shockoe Slip. Among the restaurants, microbreweries, cafés and specialty shops is one boutique that will definitely appeal to the lady in your life. Of course, the really romantic man will call ahead at (804) 643-GIFT, and make arrangements for a gift certificate to be waiting in the hotel room. Be prepared to be rather generous. It's unlikely that you'll regret it; few things make a woman feel more pampered than exquisite lingerie. Pamela Brumbaugh understands this better than most. Her intriguing **My Romance**, located at 1206 E. Cary Street, is the area's exclusive carrier of La Perla intimate apparel. This premier Italian design house hand-crafts each piece with the finest laces and most luxurious fabrics from around the globe. Not that these are the only items you are likely to find enticing; suffice to say that you are unlikely to leave My Romance empty-handed.

For a surprise that will give you a permanent reminder of your special weekend in Richmond, make an advance appointment with **Robert Thomas Photography,** (804) 266-5458, at 5809 Lakeside Avenue, Suite G1-C. The object: a romantic photography session for your partner, or for both of you. Patti Short will professionally arrange hair and makeup for $30 and $50, respectively. Depending upon the number of shots, the sitting fees range between $25 and $50. Any additional cost depends entirely upon your whims. Choose a wall portrait, an album that will hold a variety of your favorite poses, or perhaps a calendar; the choices are limited only by your imagination and your pocketbook. Sittings may be booked for either Saturday and Sunday, and Robert's schedule is flexible enough to fit almost any time constraints. If you've visited My Romance beforehand, then maybe your partner will pose in her new lingerie – or even less!

Selecting a restaurant in Richmond is no easy business. A recent proliferation of such establishments enables Richmond to rival much larger cities with regard to the number of options. There is one restaurant, however, that has become a Richmond institution. A chance to dine here shouldn't be missed. **The Tobacco Company Restau-rant,** located at 12th and Cary Streets, was a trailblazer when Shockoe Slip was in its infancy some 25 years ago. It is just as popular now as it was then. The building that houses the restaurant was used as a tobacco warehouse in the mid-19th century. The ensuing renovations have been so innovative that they alone make a visit here worthwhile. Large double doors with beautiful leaded glass panes usher you into the main level. This is comprised mostly of lounge areas accented by a large, ornately carved bar and a lovely three-story atrium.

After relaxing here with a before-dinner drink, ascend in an antique glass elevator to the formal dining areas on the floors above. These are tastefully furnished with antiques, the prize of which is a gigantic brass chandelier that once hung in the lobby of Cincinnati's Federal Reserve Bank. Muted flower arrangements and baskets of lush ferns suspended from the rafters contribute softness and warmth. Each floor offers a slightly different decor and ambience. Dining may be formal or informal. The restaurant's contemporary American-style cuisine – the preparation of which is overseen by award-winning chef Mark Kimmell – is outstanding. In keeping with the general atmosphere, it is served in a friendly yet unobtrusive manner.

The lovely Victorian Lounge with its cozy fireplace is a perfect place to enjoy quiet conversation and after-dinner coffee. Alternatively, live entertainment is offered in the atrium. For a bit more action, take to the dance floor in the Tobacco Company Club, located on the basement level. Clearly, there is something for everyone, and a delightful evening is virtually assured. It is wise, however, to make a reservation; call (804) 782-9431 well in advance.

Coinciding with the increasing popularity of "The Slip," several new restaurants have sprung up around the outermost perimeter of the area. One of these, **The Frog and the Redneck,** at 1423 E. Cary Street, (804) 648-FROG or fax (804) 782-0910, has rapidly developed a very formidable reputation. The main dining room is rather large and open, with contemporary furnishings and a unique cartoon mural adding a splash of color from the walls. The menu is not extensive – partly because it changes daily – but it is interesting. Both fish and shellfish are prominently featured in mouth-watering selections that are tastefully enhanced with intriguing combinations of herbs, vegetable, sauces and cheeses. Entrées at The Frog and Redneck range from $17 to as much as $26.50 (for jumbo lump crabcakes). You won't go away hungry, as the portions here are very generous. An innovative option available only by the table is the "Chef's Choice" tasting menu, at $35 per person.

Such fine food calls for equally fine wines, and this restaurant's regular list is extensive. It is cleverly divided into two categories: Frog (French) wines and Redneck (domestic) wines. If this list fails to please, check out the Reserve List, which also offers a nice selection of vintage port. Those who really appreciate good food will testify that there are few things that round out a fine meal better than a glass of great port.

A few blocks away – just past the old Main Street railroad station – is the area known as Shockoe Bottom. The character here is quite different. By day, this area's centerpiece is the colorful Farmer's Market. The blocks that surround it are comprised of a strange mix of restaurants and bars intermingled with small supermarkets and various specialty shops. At night the area really comes alive and one place in particular stands out from the rest. **Havana '59**, (804) 649-CUBA, at 16 North 17th Street, offers its patrons a revolutionary concept in eating and drinking. Set in an old building that has obviously seen better times, this restaurant – unlike others of its kind–has never been renovated or restored. Rather, in keeping with its theme, cracks in the plaster are left untouched and tables (each with its own pack of playing cards) are jammed tightly into every nook and cranny. The decorations are designed to recreate a festive atmosphere reminiscent of the city for which it is named. Particularly noteworthy are the large metal shutters designed as a security measure in the past. On those hot sultry nights so common to summertime Richmond, this allows Havana '59 to open up right onto the sidewalk.

Dishes are prepared on a wood-fired grill and freshly squeezed juices – from pineapple to lime, both sweetened with sugar cane – are blended with the typical Cuban fare. The Havana '59 experience is really atypical; if you are looking for something different and fun, this is it. Even if you eat someplace else, it's worth a trip just to sit at the bar and soak up the atmosphere.

Beer lovers might want to pop around the corner for a quick brew. At the **Cobblestone Brewery & Pub**, (804) 644-BREW, located at 110 North 18th Street, you'll find plenty of choice. Apart from their own selections, they keep a wide number of national and international selections on draft. As they like to say, "Our beers are 100 years behind the times."

The locals here adore Italian food, and one restaurant in this genre is a cut above the rest. About two miles from downtown Richmond is Carytown, a trendy area that mixes both residential and commercial. In the heart of this area, at 3343 West Cary Street, is the **Amici Ristorante**. With an emphasis on authentic Northern Italian cuisine, the award-winning menu features homemade pasta, fresh seafood, wild game and nightly specials. These are brilliantly accompanied by selections from the Amici's wide-ranging wine list. The Amici Ristorante offers fine European service in an intimate setting with a casual and friendly atmosphere. During warm weather you may choose to have cocktails or dinner served on the outdoor patio. After dinner, be sure to linger over a capuccino or espresso. And save room (if you can) for one of their delightful desserts, prepared daily on the premises. Space here is limited, so reservations are recommended. Call (804) 353-4700.

Many native Richmonders choose to celebrate their special occasions by taking a cruise along the James on the *Annabel Lee,* a convincing replica of an old-fashioned paddlewheel river boat. This is a tradition that deserves some consideration. She sets sail from Intermediate Terminal on Dock Street, just a few minutes' drive from downtown Richmond. Her normal route is a round trip to Drewery's Bluff, incorporating approximately 10 miles of lovely scenery each way. A premier dinner cruise leaves at 7 p.m. on Saturdays, while a champagne brunch cruise (with complimentary champagne) departs at 1 p.m. on Sundays. Expect a delicious buffet meal, freshly prepared on board. There's also a cabaret-style show, followed by live music that'll get you on your feet, whether you prefer to boogie or dance cheek-to-cheek. For a little fresh air, stroll the outside decks, where you may admire the view (and each other). Boarding begins a half-hour prior to sailing time, and reservations are necessary. Call (804) 644-5700.

Another great idea for Sunday is the champagne brunch – held between 11:30 a.m. and 3 p.m. – at the **James River Wine Bistro,** (804) 358-4562. Located at 1520 West Main Street, this is a neat combination of bar and restaurant that prides itself on the number of wines available by the glass. Indeed, they advertise over 120 – one of the largest such selections in the state.

Theater lovers will certainly want to visit the **Carpenter Center for the Performing Arts** at 600 East Grace Street. A showcase for various Broadway companies – as well as recording artists, the symphony, the ballet and the opera – this theater is also notable in its own right. Built in 1927, when it opened under the name Loew's Theater, it has been described as "the ultimate in 1920s movie palace fantasy design, both inside and out." As the movie-going population migrated to the suburbs, the theater suffered a serious decline in popularity. (It had become downright seedy before its glorious restoration in the 1980s.) This is truly a marvelous place in which to see a show. The decor is breathtakingly ornate and the facilities are wonderful for a theater of its size. By the way, be sure to look up after you are seated. The ceiling is painted to resemble the night sky and you will see wispy clouds literally drifting across a field of twinkling stars. Information on the schedule and ticket availability may be obtained by calling (804) 782-3900.

Even in a city the size of Richmond, traffic can be hectic. And no couple wants to spend their precious hours trying to find a parking place. If you prefer to leave the driving to someone else, there are at least two interesting and romantic options. One is very traditional and the other is an innovative twist on a classic idea.

Let's be traditional first. What lady or gentleman wouldn't be impressed by a tour around town in a turn-of-the-century carriage, drawn by two freshly-shampooed horses and accompanied by a driver and footman in period costume? Go on (it's well worth the expense) and call **Jim Hundley** at (804) 743-9233. The initial charge of $200 covers the first hour or so, but every subsequent hour is charged at the much-reduced rate of $50. Sunday morning, with its minimal traffic, would be an ideal time to see the highlights of the city. We'd like to suggest a path that follows Monument Avenue and winds down The Boulevard towards Byrd and Maymont Parks, returning to downtown via the historic Hollywood Cemetery. The latter is the final resting place for two United States presidents (James Monroe and John Tyler), Confederate President Jefferson Davis, and literally thousands of Confederate soldiers. It also offers some of the best views of the James River, and the ever-growing city skyline.

For those who prefer the more modern luxury of limousine transport, you might as well milk the evening for all it's worth. Besides the traditional choices, **Stewart's Limousine Service** at (804) 264-1129 offers the use of Limoooosine, the "Cow Print Limo." Believe it or not, this vehicle is painted to resemble a cow. It has Stewart's "S" brand on its side, a license plate that reads LIMOOO, cushions and pillows printed with cows, and, yes, you've guessed it – a horn that "moos." It is still navigated by a uniformed chauffeur, and features the usual limo luxuries of a bar, TV, telephone and stereo. The price tag is $85 for the first hour, with additional hours at a lower rate, inclusive of tip. This should steer you both in the right direction and put you in the moo-d for love.

Oh, don't forget the roses. After all, what lady's weekend would be complete without them? **Vogue Flowers and Gifts** will oblige you with anything you want and deliver it to your preferred destination. They'll also provide champagne and wine baskets, as well as exotic silk flower combinations. Call them at (804) 353-9600, (800) 923-1010 or fax (804) 353-0699.

Hanover County
A Railroad Town
Sets the Stage for Romance

Located about 15 miles north of Richmond and 85 miles south of Washington, D.C. is a county both rich in history and typically Virginian.

The history of this area's original inhabitants is recalled by the Pamunkey River on the county's northern boundary. It was named for the Indians who still maintain a reservation on the lower part of the river in neighboring King William County. In the late 17th century, English colonists patented this land and developed warehouses here to house the area's tobacco crop. During the 18th century, Hanover County was at the very center of Virginia's "Great Awakening," which was led by the Reverend Samuel Davies, founder of the Hanover Presbytery. During this period – in 1749, to be exact – Newcastle was incorporated as Hanover's first town. (It only narrowly missed becoming the state capital!) The county was also the birthplace of two great orators – Patrick Henry and William Clay – both of whom who helped shape this country's early history. Hanover's strategic location just north of Richmond made it the site of numerous battles and skirmishes during the Civil War. After that, the residents settled down to a quiet, rural life – until the coming of the railroad opened up the area.

In 1836, the Richmond, Fredericksburg & Potomac Railroad (RF&P) laid a single track from Richmond to the South Anna River, passing through an area of "slashes," or low swampy areas of slash pines. To fuel its engines, the railroad typically purchased much of the forested land along its right-of-way. In 1836, the RF&P purchased a 462-acre tract of land in central Hanover County. The first development in the area came in 1845, when the railroad built "Slash Cottage," a long, low building with a large room suitable for balls, picnics, and other gatherings. The plan was to run excursions out from Richmond to the new "resort." The railroad company sold lots on each side of the tracks to homeowners and businesses seeking to capitalize on the area's growth. And grow it did. By 1854, a new town was incorporated there and named **Ashland**. It derived its name from the Kentucky home of Henry Clay, a native of the town and the "mill boy of the slashes." By 1858, the first Ashland Hotel had opened and an accommodation (commuter) train regularly transported people between Ashland and Richmond. The ensuing Civil War brought economic depression to Ashland, which led to the closing of the hotel and all resort facilities. In 1868, Randolph Macon College purchased the hotel building and moved it from its southside location in Boydton to Ashland. Between 1872 and 1879, the historic campus – located on the site of the original RF&P building – was expanded by the addition of three buildings: Washington Franklin Hall, Pace Hall, and the Duncan Memorial Chapel. Many of the town's lovely old houses date from the turn of the century, when Ashland's population numbered around 1,000 and the town was a commuting suburb of Richmond.

In 1923, the RF&P Railroad commissioned a well-known local architect, W. Duncan Lee, to design a new station. The times being what they were, he had to take into consideration the practice of segregation. His solution: a symmetrical floor plan with a "white" waiting room on the north end and a "colored" one on the south, each with a window to the central ticket office. With the proliferation of cars came a decline in rail travel; this led to the closing of the station in 1967. It was abandoned and remained so until 1983, when it was donated to the town. Now it serves a dual purpose: as a railroad station for a limited number of Amtrak services, and as the home of the **Hanover Visitor Information Center**, (804) 752-6766. The latter is open from 9 a.m. to 5 p.m. daily.

Less than a decade ago, Ashland was no place for a weekend break. While there were numerous sights of interest both in the town and its environs, it was too sleepy and conservative to welcome tourists. Perhaps this was a holdover from its roots. After all, one of the provisos of the RF&P was that "no spiritous liquor, nor mixture thereof" be sold on the property without that organization's approbation! Recently, however, things have changed considerably. While Ashland has retained the more pleasing points of its character, and is by no means "touristy," its current atmosphere is more open and easygoing. An interesting inn and a restaurant full of character have opened almost next door to each other and enthusiastically welcome visitors.

The Ashland Hotel was opened around 1876 and burned down in 1905. On its original site was constructed a long structure in the Georgian Revivalist style, consisting of a three-story central portion and side wings with two stories. This, the Henry Clay Inn, was also destroyed by fire in 1946. Meticulously recreated in 1992 and standing only a half-block away at 114 North Railroad Avenue is the new **Henry Clay Inn**, (804) 798-3100 or (800) 343-4565. This establishment sits incongruously among its surroundings, its warm atmosphere immediately felt as you step onto its delightful country-style front porch. Here you will most likely be greeted by guests who have already made themselves comfortable in its rocking chairs. The lobby is spacious and impressively − yet invitingly − furnished. An imposing staircase leads to an open parlor on the second floor. This in turn leads out to the balcony portion of the double front porch. The inn's 15 rooms include one two-room suite with a king-sized bed and jacuzzi; one suite with a queen-sized bed and jacuzzi; and 13 standard rooms, 10 with queen-sized beds, two with two double beds, and one with a pair of twin beds.

You'll awake each morning to the aroma of coffee brewing and the smell of the freshly baked breads that accompany the other breakfast fare. Breakfast is only served between the hours of 8 a.m. and 9:30 a.m. on the weekends. If you just can't wait for that first cup of coffee, persuade your partner to slip out into the second floor parlor and retrieve one from the sideboard. Later in the evening, marvelous dinners are served in the same restaurant. The chef here is trained in classical French cooking, but chooses to improvise and has developed a culinary style all his own. You'll certainly have noticed the large collection of original works by local artisans in the gallery just off the lobby. Take a few minutes to enjoy these and to browse in the gift gallery across the lobby. The latter offers an assortment of unique specialty items for both house and garden.

There is no shortage of hotels in Ashland, as Interstate 95 passes just east of the town. However, there is nothing either romantic or unusual about those near the highway's junction with Route 54. When traveling Interstate 95, take the Route 54 West exit (England Street) and continue 1½ miles into historic Ashland, turning right at the railroad tracks. The inn will be in plain view across the tracks. However, since it's located on a one-way street, you must go up a little further, cross the tracks, and double back.

If you fancy slightly more unusual places to eat, then you won't have to go very far. But don't be too late, as closing hours are still fairly early in Ashland.

The first option is just across England Street at 100 South Railroad Avenue, within easy walking distance of the inn. The **Ironhorse Restaurant**, (804) 752-6410, occupies a building originally constructed in 1900 as a department store. Indeed, that was its function until the store's closing in 1960. In 1991, the restaurant took up residence. The low, wide window spaces – which once beckoned to passersby with goods of every sort – now display large, elegant potted plants. The plentiful floor space has been used wisely as well. Just to the right of the entrance is a bar/lounge where you will be entertained on weekends by local musicians. Overlooking this is a large moose head hanging from the wall. To the left is the dining area. Here the tables are adorned with fresh flowers and spaced at comfortable intervals, allowing for intimate conversation.

The menu changes monthly and is limited to just six to seven contemporary entrées, augmented nightly by a couple of specials. The food is innovatively presented and very tasty indeed. You won't be bored with your surroundings, either. The clientele is an eclectic mix, and there is more entertainment if you wander to the rear of the dining room. There you may chat with the chef as you watch your food being prepared in the open kitchen. Altogether a delightful experience, though not inexpensive. Oh, and don't be surprised when the "Iron Horses" thunder by on the tracks just a few feet away!

For a different, more casual dining experience, head back towards I-95 and turn right at the junction with U.S. Route 1. Very shortly, you will come to a restaurant that has become an Ashland institution since its opening in 1978. **The Smokey Pig**, located at 212 South Washington Highway, (804) 798-4590, is owned and operated by the Jeffers family. That this was originally intended as a barbecue restaurant is evident in the numerous pig ornaments, artifacts and photographs. Though the menu has expanded greatly since then, all of the dishes are still prepared on the premises and mixed by hand from old family or local recipes. Especially filling and delicious is the Pig Sampler, a combination of all the restaurant's appetizers.

Service here is courteous and comprehensive; so much so, that if you should happen to catch a wild turkey (they're plentiful in the area) they will even smoke it for you. Failing that, order some pit-cooked barbecue to enjoy back home.

If you want to learn more about this town, set aside an hour and follow the self-guided walking tour detailed in the brochure "Ashland Virginia, A Turn of the Century Railroad Town." This is available from the visitor information center at the inn's front doorstep.

You will probably be curious about one of the area's most famous citizens, Patrick Henry. Born on May 29, 1736 at Studley, in Hanover County, this amazing gentleman was influential in politics at both the local and national levels until his death 63 years later. He loved to hunt and fish and was an accomplished musician, playing the violin, the flute and the pianoforte. He was married twice and fathered 17 children. A successful lawyer and a member of the House of Burgesses, he is best remembered for his "Give me liberty, or give me death" speech at St. John's Church in Richmond in 1775. He was also the first commander-in-chief of the Virginia forces, as well as the first governor of the independent commonwealth of Virginia, elected on June 29, 1776.

Should you visit Ashland between April and October, take the nine-mile drive through undulating countryside to see Patrick Henry's home during his most active political years. Travel along Route 54 through town (where the speed limit is strictly observed) until you reach the junction with 685. Take a right here. After a short while, **Scotchtown**, (804) 227-3500, will appear on the left. The surrounding 9,976 acres were deeded to one Charles Chiswell of Williamsburg on July 15, 1717. Because the property had to be occupied within two years, the house – thought to be one of the oldest of the Virginia plantation type – is believed to have been built about 1719. The December 28, 1769 issue of the *Virginia Gazette* contained a notice of sale for the plantation. Patrick Henry bought it, along with 960 acres, at an auction held at Hanover Courthouse the following September. He, his wife Sarah, and six of their children moved to Scotchtown in April, 1771. It was their home until 1778.

The house has now been restored and furnished with 18th-century antiques. It is open from 10 a.m. to 4:30 p.m. daily from April to October, except on Sundays, when the hours are from 1:30 p.m. to 4:30 p.m. The first Friday, Saturday and Sunday in December are special days at Scotchtown. On the Friday and Saturday evenings there is a traditional candlelight tour and re-enactment play. On the Sunday, there are three seatings for a special 18th-century "groaning board" lunch. Scotchtown also hosts central Virginia's Scottish Festival and Games on the fourth weekend in May.

Still on Route 54 – but this time to the east of Ashland, at its junction with Route 301 – is a complex of rare historical importance. The **Hanover Tavern** was built in 1723 and very quickly became an important inn and stagecoach stop. It played host to many notable personalities of the day, among them Thomas Jefferson, George Washington and the Marquis de Lafayette. In 1781, Lord Cornwallis made the tavern his headquarters for 18 days; he reportedly left without paying the bill. The owner, John Shelton, later became the father-in-law of Patrick Henry, and the statesman actually lived and worked here for four years. In fact, it was from here, in 1763, that he was called to the **Hanover County Courthouse** just across the road. There he made his first public attack on the policies of King George III, while representing defendants in "The Parson's Cause." The courthouse was built in 1735, and in 1774 local citizens met and adopted the "Hanover Resolves." An early 19th-century jail and clerk's office complete the complex.

By 1953, the tavern was in a poor state of repair indeed. Seeing its immense potential, six young actors transformed it into what is now known as the **Barksdale Theater at Hanover Tavern,** (804) 730-4860. The first regular season of professional theater took place there the following year, making the Barksdale the oldest not-for-profit theater in the country. Unlike many local theaters, this one has not only survived, but prospered. Marvelously varied productions are staged here in an intimate theater that seats 199 people. None of the seats are more than 21 feet from the stage. But don't just go there for the entertainment. In the tavern's romantic candlelit dining rooms, you may enjoy a delicious pre-show meal catered by Richmond's highly respected Bull & Bear Club. Curtain time is at 8:30 p.m., Wednesday through Saturday, and dinner is served beginning at 7 p.m. This is certainly something to add to your agenda.

End your visit on a high note by making the short journey down Interstate 95 to the Atlee Road Exit. Head east (past the 7-Eleven) to Route 813, and then follow the signs to the Hanover County Airport. Located by an industrial estate, the airport is home to two companies that offer a different perspective on the area.

Barnstormers Airshows, Inc., (804) 798-8830, in operation for more than 20 years, offers a balloon adventure that will take you where the wind blows. Upon your arrival at the Balloonport there will be a pre-flight briefing by an FAA-certified commercial pilot. Then you'll be hoisted aloft for an hour to an hour and a half. Upon landing, the ground crew – who have been in radio contact with the pilot –

deflate and pack up the balloon. Then they return you to Barnstormers Hanover Balloonport for the post-flight festivities. There you will receive a certificate commemorating your flight, followed by a picnic of cheese, sausage, seasonal fruit and hot sausage biscuits, all washed down by champagne. At this point you may just be celebrating your return to *terra firma*. With advance notice, however, the appropriate cake may be ordered for a birthday or anniversary. Flights are offered year-round. Reservations are required, and a champagne flight for two is priced at $270. Flat shoes and comfortable clothes with long sleeves are recommended.

The less adventurous among you should consider the more traditional flight options offered by **Sundance Aviation.** Telephone (804) 798-6500.

Theme parks are fun, too. On your way out of town, check out a great one located a few miles north, just off Interstate 95 at Exit 98. **Paramount's Kings Dominion** is a 400-acre family park made up of eight different theme areas. New attractions open yearly, with the 1995 offerings including Nickelodeon, Splat City and Paramount On Ice. Other favorites are the Days of Thunder racing simulator, the Anaconda Roller Coaster with its underwater tunnel, the Walk Around Star Trek, the White Water Canyon raft ride, the Shockwave stand-up roller coaster, Hanna-Barbera Land and Hurricane Reef water park. Those enjoying the electric atmosphere but preferring milder entertainment will like viewing the park from the 330-foot replica of the Eiffel Tower. You may also chat with wandering cartoon characters, browse in the many shops, and sample food from one or more of the restaurants. Alternatively, you can sit back and relax at one of the shows offered at various times throughout the day. The park is open on weekends only between April 1 and Memorial Day; every day from Memorial Day through the week after Labor Day weekend; and again on weekends only from that date through the first weekend in October. Call (804) 876-5000 or fax (804) 876-5864 for further information.

Scottsville
This Sleepy River Town
is a Dream Come True

*L*et your imagination roam freely. Where do you want to take the love of your life for a peaceful and undisturbed romantic break?

How about an early 19th-century house that was once left to ruin, but has now been lovingly and painstakingly restored? Each of the rooms has been individually furnished with a tasteful combination of antiques and fabrics. The proprietor is an accomplished chef capable of whipping up distinctive European and Mediterranean cuisine. It has its own vineyards yielding delicious wines. Located on 50 acres dotted with gazebos, ponds and forests, it is high on a hill above the James River. It boasts both spectacular views to the distant Blue Ridge Mountains and proximity to a 250-year-old town of considerable historical interest.

High Meadows Vineyard & Mountain Sunset Inn is all of this – and more.

Towards the end of his 30-year service in the navy, Peter Sushka and his partner Mary Jae Abbitt were stationed in London, where he was the U.S./U.K. liaison naval officer. During this period they became interested in country inns and "auberges"; so much so, that they decided to open a similar place in the U.S. after his retirement. Planning ahead, they accumulated antiques and other unique pieces of furniture while still in Europe. During visits back home, they started searching for a suitable property. Finally, in 1984, they discovered and fell in love with High Meadows. The original Federalist-style building dated from 1832 and a Victorian addition was made in 1882. By 1984, it was merely an empty shell. But this did not discourage Peter and Mary Jae. They purchased the property in 1985 and began the arduous task of restoration. First came extensive hours of research and documentation. They wanted to capture the original character as authentically as possible, while adding the modern facilities expected by discriminating guests. A 1.25-acre vineyard was installed, and High Meadows' high quality Pinot Noir grapes now produce over 180,000 bottles of wine annually.

The inn was officially opened on July 4, 1986. Also in that year, High Meadows was nominated to the National Register of Historic Places; this led to its later designation as a Virginia Landmark. Work continued on the original house until two suites, five bedrooms and the public rooms were completed. Elsewhere on the grounds, a modern two-bedroom cedar carriage house was constructed.

In December 1991, Peter and Mary Jae purchased a 1908 Queen Ann house adjacent to – and historically linked with – the original High Meadows Vineyard Inn. Named High Meadows Mountain Sunset for its marvelous views west to the Blue Ridge mountains, this features one suite and three rooms.

Meticulous care has been taken to furnish each of the rooms with period-perfect antiques, original art and fine ceramics, as well as choice fabrics and Oriental rugs. All rooms have a private bath and some come with a two-person whirlpool or hot tub. As an extra welcoming touch, there is a decanter of port or sherry in each room. But don't expect to find a TV. The public rooms are equally beautiful and elegant. On Thursday, Friday and Sunday, a set menu of French bistro cuisine with complimentary wine is served in the restaurant for $40 to $60 per couple. European Evening Supper Baskets, complete with Virginia wine and priced at $50 per couple, are available Monday through Wednesday. For those guests staying through Saturday evenings, a six-course candlelight dinner is included in the tariff.

In High Meadows Vineyard and Mountain Sunset, Peter and Mary Jae have created a very special escape from the pressures of everyday life. In fact, this place is so charming and romantic that some couples will find it a struggle just to leave their room. For an interlude, indulge in coffee and a game of either chess or checkers in the parlor. Alternatively, take tea in the tea house and rose garden. Or play croquet and horseshoes, followed by a stroll around the delightful grounds. Don't forget to stop for a kiss in one of the gazebos. Whatever your inclinations, be sure to return by 6:45 p.m. for the most charming of customs – a platter of hors d'oeuvres accompanied by the tasting of three or four wines.

Rates here range from $95 (for the Eastmont Room during the week) to $235 (for the luxurious Cabernet n' Creme Suite over the weekend). The minimum stay is two nights during the spring and fall, on weekends and all holidays. Smoking is not allowed (although children and pets are) and there is one room with handicapped access.

The inn's address is Route 4, Box 6, Scottsville, Virginia 24590. To get there from Charlottesville, take exit 121 South on I-64 in Charlottesville. Proceed on Route 20 South for 17 miles. After crossing James River Road (Route 726), take a left turn onto High Meadows Lane. Reservations are recommended; call (804) 786-2218 or (800) 232-1832.

Should you desire a change of scene, the surrounding area has plenty of interest. Just down the hill on the northern bank of the James River's Horseshoe Bend is the historic town of **Scottsville**. In 1744, Albemarle County – then much larger than it is today – was formed from Goochland County. Because of its strategic position as a river port, Scottsville became the county seat. As the importance of river transportation declined, so did the fortunes of Scottsville – so much so, that today it is just a quiet backwater town. However, its history and former wealth are reflected in its numerous beautiful homes. The town is now recognized as an historic district and the local authorities have produced "A Walking Tour Guide" that is well worth following. To complement your tour, the **Scottsville Museum** is also open to visitors on weekend afternoons.

The town has a more modern connection as well. The area is the actual setting for the popular television series *The Waltons*. In his scripts, the series' creator Earl Hamner referred to a place called the "Dew Drop Inn." The original inn was located at 17 Valley Street and is now known as the **Pig N' Steak**. Besides being a tourist spot in its own right – attracting visitors from around the world – this inn serves the most delicious food. The house specialty is barbecue, but try an order of French fries as well. You will be amazed by both the quantity and quality. After lunch, *Waltons* fans may enjoy a visit to the **Walton Mountain Museum**, telephone (804) 831- 2000.

Just upriver, but by a rather roundabout route – 20 North to 726 West and then 625 South – is the small hamlet of Hatton. Here there are two attractions of note. **The Hatton Free Ferry** is the oldest of the two surviving ferries of its type in the continental U.S.A. However, it is only open between 8 a.m. and 5 p.m. on Fridays, Saturdays and Sundays during the summer months. The more energetic among you can take to the James for canoeing and rafting, between March and October; or tube trips, between May and September. These trips can only be taken if the combined air and water temperature is above 150 degrees. They are operated by **James River Runners Inc.**, which is open between 8 a.m. and 6 p.m. For information or booking call (804) 286 2338. Add a dash of romance to any of these adventures by asking the innkeepers to prepare you a picnic hamper – with champagne, of course – to enjoy at a secluded spot along the river banks.

For those wishing to venture a little farther afield, Thomas Jefferson's **Monticello** is just 20 miles away in Charlottesville. Also nearby is **Ash Lawn-Highland**, the home of Jefferson's contemporary, President James Madison. In addition, Charlottesville is home to the **University of Virginia**, with its many fine examples of Jeffersonian architecture.

During the year there are many attractive local events. The most notable of these are the **Albemarle County Fair**, in August; the **Autumnal Spectacular**, from mid-September to early November; **Easter** and **Historic Virginia Garden Week,** in April**; the Foxfield Races**, in both April and September; **High Meadows Inn's Anniversary** and **Scottsville's July 4th** celebration; the **High Meadows Vineyard Harvest**, in late August; the **Montpelier Hunt Races**, in early November; **Romantic Victorian Valentine's Day** and **ski-ing**,in January and February; and **Thanksgiving, Christmas and New Year's Galas**.

Charlottesville
It's Cavalier to Love... Jefferson Style

There are many cities surrounded by beautiful coun-tryside; still others have important historical connec-tions. Some even have both. But few of these have been touched by the hands and mind of a genius. Charlottesville is most fortunate indeed; it's been blessed by nature, steeped in tradition and touched by Thomas Jefferson.

The county of Albemarle was named in 1745 for William Anne Keppel, the second Earl of Albemarle. By 1762, Char-lottesville – which derived its name from King George III's wife, Princess Charlotte of Mecklenburg-Strelitz – was already well-established as the county seat. The court house was built the same year. It briefly housed the Vir-ginia State Legislature when it was forced by advancing British troops to flee from Richmond during the Revolu-tion. The advent of the railroad in the mid-19th century led to an increase in population and the town's subsequent charter in 1851. By 1888, it had grown sufficiently to warrant its incorporation as a city.

Today, Charlottesville is recognized as a major cultural and intellectual center. The credit for this goes to one man – Thomas Jefferson. His enduring legacy attracts people from every corner of the world. There seems to have been nothing that was beyond his intellect and ability. As a politician, he was instrumental in the Revolution, penning the Declaration of Independence and serving as governor of Virginia. He was also the first United States minister plenipotentiary to foreign governments, acted as secretary of state, was elected vice president and – between 1801 and 1809 – led the country as its third president. These repre-sent just a portion of his achievements. But it is his activities as an educator and architect that have left the biggest mark on Charlottesville.

 High in the surrounding hills is Jefferson's beloved home, **Monticello.** You may think you've never seen it before. But you probably have a picture of it in your wallet or pocket, imprinted on the back of every nickel. This house, built and remodeled over a 40-year period, has been described as one of the country's foremost architectural masterpieces. Touring through it certainly gives insight into Jefferson's ingenious mind. He also took a keen interest in garden design, both ornamental and practical. Indeed, he was an avid horticulturist, testing over 250 varieties of vegetables and herbs – including many strains of English pea – in his 1,000-foot vegetable garden. During his tenure as U. S. Minister to the Court of Louis XVI of France, he was introduced to the finer points of wine. Not surprisingly, he was the first to bring European varieties of grape to America. In this area, as with many others, he was a visionary. Today, there are 10 licensed farm wineries producing internationally recognized vintages in this area. As a result, Charlottesville is now known as the "Wine Capital of Virginia." To reach Monticello, (540) 984-9822, take either Exit 121A or Exit 121, when traveling from the east and west, respectively, on Interstate 64. Then simply follow the signs. Plan to visit between 8 a.m. and 5 p.m., from March through October; or between 9 a.m. and 4:30 p.m., from November to February. Admission is $8.

As you exit from the interstate, you will see signs directing you to **The Charlottesville-Albemarle Convention & Visitors' Bureau**, (540) 977-1783, open from 9 a.m. to 5.30 p.m. daily. This should be your first stop. While there, ask for a copy of the "Charlottesville Virginia" brochure. It provides colorful and helpful maps of both the downtown and surrounding areas. This complex also doubles as **The Monticello Visitors' Center.** In addition to numerous exhibits and artifacts, the center shows an award-winning film entitled *Thomas Jefferson: The Pursuit of Liberty,* twice daily. You might also consider purchasing the President's Pass. This is a combination ticket for entrance to Monticello, Ash

Lawn-Highland and Historic Michie Tavern that, at a cost of $17, saves you a little money if all three are on your itinerary.

A half-mile before Monticello you will pass **Historic Michie Tavern**, (540) 977-1234. Here you may partake of a traditional Southern buffet lunch. This is served between 11:30 a.m. and 3:30 p.m. in The Ordinary, by hostesses in period dress. You may also tour the Meadow Run Grist Mill, which dates from 1797 and was relocated piece-by-piece from nearby Laurel Hill. Here you will find well-preserved 18th-century milling operations, as well as a general store that represents a distinct departure from modern supermarkets. Choose a treat for yourselves from among the unique gift items, specialty foods and Virginia wines. The complex is open between 9 a.m. and 5 p.m. daily, at a cost of $5. If you want lunch, it's an extra $9.50.

Just two and a half miles past Monticello on Route 795 is the home of the fifth president, James Monroe. Interestingly enough, he came to live at **Ash Lawn-Highland** in November 1799 as a direct consequence of his close friendship with Thomas Jefferson. The atmosphere on this 535-acre estate recalls that of an early 19th-century plantation. Many of Monroe's possessions are on display in the house and peacocks roam freely in the formal gardens, which are an ideal place for a picnic. On a clear day you may even catch a glimpse of Monticello. Ash Lawn-Highland is open from 9 a.m. to 6 p.m. between March and October, and from 10 a.m. to 5 p.m. during the remainder of the year. The entrance fee is $6. Every summer Ash Lawn-Highland plays host to the **Summer Festival of Opera and Musical Theater**. In addition to opera, the **Music at Twilight** series features classical, jazz, folk and contemporary music; and **Summer Saturdays** offer puppet shows, traditional theater, music and dance. Call (540) 293-9539 for specific details.

Back in Charlottesville, you will find another of Jefferson's legacies – this one with a particularly lasting impact. Given his lifelong interest in education, Jefferson had developed very definite ideas on the subject. In 1817, he served as a member of a state-appointed board entrusted with the task of planning a new central college. The cornerstone of the first building was laid on October 6, 1817. In 1818, the Virginia senate established a commission to recommend a site for a state university. Naturally, Jefferson proposed that this be incorporated into the site of the central college. On January 25, 1819, the Virginia legislature approved the charter for the **University of Virginia**. Uncomfortable with the concept of a single-building school, Jefferson designed what he termed an "Academical Village." He believed that this arrangement would be more conducive to productive study. On either side of a rectangular lawn, he constructed two parallel rows of five houses, or "Pavilions." These were connected by low, colonnaded walkways and interspersed by student rooms. Behind each of the Pavilions is a small individually landscaped formal garden. The focal point was the Rotunda. Designed after – but in smaller proportions than – the Pantheon in Rome, this was placed in a position of prominence at the north end of The Lawn. The Pavilions are all of the Federal style, yet no two are alike. Forever comprehensive in his approach to a task, Jefferson didn't overlook the law of perspective either. The number of student rooms between the Pavilions increases as they progress away from the Rotunda. As a result, the Pavilions appear to be evenly spaced when viewed from that most important vantage point. The upper floors of the Pavilions were originally living quarters for the professors, with the ground-level floors housing classrooms and offices. Today, faculty members reside in the Pavilions, while a select group of fourth-year students – chosen on the basis of their academic record and service to the University community – occupy the Lawn rooms. Though short on modern conveniences, assignment to a Lawn room is considered a great honor indeed.

Thomas Jefferson began work on this architectural ideal in 1817. Only a small part of the Rotunda remained unfinished when he died on July 4, 1826 (50 years to the day after the signing of the Declaration of Independence). A fire in October 1895 destroyed much of the Rotunda, and it was rebuilt in 1898 using a different style. It remained so until 1973, when the decision was made to restore it to Jefferson's original design. This work was finally completed on April 13, 1976, the date of the U. S. Bicentennial and the 233rd anniversary of Jefferson's birth. Today, visitors marvel at how three oval rooms can fit into the ground floor of the Rotunda. Also in 1976, the American Institute of Architects proclaimed the "Academical Village" the most significant architectural achievement of the nation's first 200 years. Later, in 1987, the United Nations Educational, Scientific and Cultural Organization (UNESCO) placed UVA on the World Heritage List in recognition of its universal cultural value, which transcends political or geographic boundaries. This is a distinction shared by fewer than 400 sites around the world! Begin your visit at the Rotunda, which is open daily except during the winter break (from mid-December to mid-January). Explore on your own or join one of the student guides. The latter conduct informative tours of both the Rotunda and The Lawn starting at 10 a.m., 11 a.m., 2 p.m., 3 p.m., and 4 p.m. Pavilion VIII on the East Lawn is open to visitors during the academic year (but please don't disturb the classes). As for the other Pavilions, they're open to visitors only one day each year (during Garden Week in April). The following brochures, available at the Rotunda, will help you to understand the many facets of this "complex" complex: "University of Virginia," "Thomas Jefferson's Academical Village," "Pavilion Gardens" and "The Rotunda, Information for Visitors."

One of Jefferson's more enlightened concepts was the assembly of students and faculty in a defined – but not confined – space that was intellectually stimulating. He believed this would produce a spark that would burn in the hearts and minds of Virginia's leaders for years to come. As with most projects he undertook, he certainly succeeded. Today the University of Virginia is a prestigious institution that has produced more Rhodes Scholars than any other state university. Entry standards are extremely competitive and, although enrollment has grown to over 18,000, there may be as many as 19,000 applicants vying for just 3,000 first-year and transfer openings. The faculty has also increased from the eight professors appointed by Jefferson to include over 1,700 today.

Needless to say, the University of Virginia has a tremendous influence on the city of Charlottesville. The area is economically rich, and the surrounding countryside is peppered with large estates. The town itself boasts a surprisingly cosmopolitan mix for what is still a somewhat provincial city. This is most apparent on the **Downtown Mall** where, if you didn't know differently, you might swear you were in Europe. No sterile shopping malls here. Instead, you'll find a delightful pedestrian area comprised of a half-dozen or so blocks' worth of small shops, restaurants and cafés. Many of these boast outdoor dining spaces delightfully centered around splashing water fountains. There is even a kiosk with a variety of newspapers and magazines. When you add avantgarde students, trendy faculty members, and conservative visiting parents, this tree-shaded mall takes on a character that is intriguing in its complexity and charm.

If you want to learn more about Charlottesville's past, the **Walking Tours of Historic Downtown Charlottesville** are a good place to start. They leave from the McIntire Building at 200 Second Street NE at 10 a.m. every Saturday from May through October. The guides are Historical Society volunteers who, for a suggested $3 donation, will lead you on a one-hour tour. You will walk the entire length of the original (1762) town, visiting the court house in which Thomas Jefferson, James Madison and James Monroe conducted their business. In inclement weather, call the society at (540) 296-1492 to see if the walk is still scheduled.

With all of the activity here, there is quite a demand for accommodation. And the supply more than meets that demand. Though we've been selective, we've still included more places here than in a typical chapter. As you will see, these have been chosen to suit a wide range of tastes and budgets.

It is difficult to know where to start. Let's first consider the imposing **Keswick Hall**, located just five miles from the center of town. When traveling from Charlottesville, go east on the Route 250 bypass. Turn east again onto Route 22, then onto Route 744, continuing until you reach the sign. From Richmond, take Interstate 64 west to the Keswick/Boyds Tavern exit. Turn right onto Route 616. After a third of a mile, you'll come to the entrance on the left. Whichever way you go, you can't miss this entrance. (It's a gatehouse flanked by two electronically-operated wrought iron gates.) As soon as your reservation has been confirmed, the right one opens, allowing you access to the estate. Once inside, turn immediately to your left and proceed slowly up the drive to a mansion that would not look out of place in the Tuscan or Andalucian countryside. Set on a pinnacle of land, it overlooks 600 acres of rolling hills and woodlands cossetted by the emerald green grass of an 18-hole golf course designed by Arnold Palmer.

The site was not always like this. Until the late 19th century, a pre-Civil War mansion named Broad Oak stood there. In 1912 a private residence called the Villa Crawford was erected. In 1939, it became a clubhouse for the newly formed Keswick Country Club. Enter Sir Bernard Ashley, a man who has very definite ideas of what a hotel should be. He saw an opportunity to fulfill his dream: to create a hotel like a fine estate, drawing on the best traditions of English country life. Today, the Villa Crawford mansion – with its heart pine floors, ornate ceiling moldings and grand staircase – forms the north wing of an extended Keswick Hall. It houses many charming public rooms and is an absolutely delightful place to take afternoon tea the way it really should be done – with scones, cream and strawberry jam. Later, partake of vintage malt whiskey or port over a game of snooker. If the port doesn't warm the cockles of your heart, the fire surely will. Seventeen of the hall's 48 bedrooms are also located in this wing. As with the others in the complex, each of these is spacious and furnished according to its own particular theme. Included are all the possessions of a family residence – from charming porcelain and old prints to books and family photographs. The rooms have a sense of a warmth that is both comforting and relaxing. In fact, this same warmth permeates the entire hall, even the more modern parts. The service – often rendered by maids in Victorian black and white – is both formal and exemplary.

Keswick also features a restaurant of sufficient renown to justify a separate visit. Its chefs use quality ingredients in combination with classic European recipes and modern techniques to create some masterful dishes. These are complemented by an intriguing collection of wines from both the old and new worlds. Drinks and canapes in the Grand Hall beforehand are, of course, *de rigueur*.

Another highlight of Keswick Hall is the Keswick Club. Housed in a separate building to the side of the main hall, the clubhouse pavilion offers an indoor/outdoor pool, spa, fitness equipment, and retail shop. Personal services such as massages, facials and manicures are also offered, along with superb dining facilities. In addition, there is access to the 18-hole Arnold Palmer signature golf course and tennis complex, with a full range of professional instruction and other services on hand.

If you like, simply relax on the terrace and drink in the scene before you: golfers putting away, horses going through their paces, and the distant mountains, beautiful at any time of the year. Keswick Hall combines the best of two worlds. It offers the outstanding European service found in a British Edwardian household, combined with Virginia's renowned hospitality. As you no doubt will have guessed, none of this comes without a price. A regular state room ranges from $345 to $395; a studio junior suite is from $445 to $495; and a full master suite rents from $545 to $645 per night.

Not cheap, especially given its distance from any major city. However, that is part of Keswick Hall's charm. Also endearing is the Hall's attention to detail – right down to the crystal glasses on the tables. This is an atmosphere of absolute luxury. So, if you **really** want to pamper your loved one, this is the place to go. There are numerous special promotions throughout the year, so telephone (540) 979-3440 or (800) ASHLEY 1, or fax (540) 977-4171 to see what's available.

Equally impressive – but with a different style and ambience – is nearby **Clifton, The Country Inn**. Coming from Charlottesville, begin as if you are going to Keswick but don't turn left onto Route 22; rather, continue a short distance and make a right onto Route 729. After a few hundred yards, follow the signs to your left up the driveway. The circa 1790 manor house, constructed in a combination of Federal and Colonial styles, is not only a Virginia Historic Landmark, but is recognized on the National Register of Historic Places. It is situated on a cliff-top property that was part of a 1735 land grant to William Randolph. However, the most impressive historical connection is to Thomas Mann Randolph. The grandson of William, he served as governor of Virginia, a member of the Virginia House of Delegates, and a member of the U.S. Congress. Through marriage to his third cousin Martha, he was also Thomas Jefferson's son-in-law. The original five-room structure was built at the time of his marriage for use as his North Milton office. The back of the inn was then the front, and this was terraced in seven levels down to the Rivanna River. Some additions were made to the original building between 1833 and 1846. A second story was added and the southern wing enlarged during the Colonial Revival renovations of the 1920s. Finally, the front side's impressive five-bay porch and box columns date from sometime after 1930. Inside, the same wide plank pine floors, paneled walls and fireplaces that warmed Randolph family get-togethers have been preserved in the house's older sections. Indeed, great care has been taken to ensure consistency of style, even in the more recent additions.

There are 14 rooms and suites between the manor house, the carriage house, the livery and Randolph's law office; each has a private bath, fireplace (with fresh firewood) and down comforters warming its antique or canopy bed. Interestingly, the styles vary from the more formal and traditional air of the manor, to the more rustic wood paneling and loft bedroom of the carriage house. Prices run from $165 to $225 per night, but include either early morning Continental breakfast or Clifton's "Plantation Breakfast," as well as afternoon tea. One thing is certain: you won't be disappointed with your evening meal. Co-owner Craig Hartman is an executive chef who attracted national attention by being selected as a spokesman for the DuPont No-Sticks Country Inn Chefs Advisory Panel. Each night you may savor his delightful creations in the intimate ambiance of the dining room. Afterwards, guests are encouraged to wander into the kitchen and help themselves from a jar of freshly-baked chocolate chunk cookies. The set price for the meal is $48 per person.

Among Clifton's many attractions are its grounds — 48 acres of gently rolling countryside shaded by magnificent trees. Here you may choose to participate in a game of tennis, croquet, volley ball or badminton. If it's hot, you may head to the secluded lake for some fishing, swimming, or tubing. You might even take a dunk in Clifton's cleverly constructed pool, which uses water recycled by waterfall. While there, share a dip in the hot tub, which is open year-round. Also in this recreational area is a large outdoor barbecue, a perfect spot for evening parties.

You may want to consider ringing in the New Year during the inn's three-day celebration. This is characterized by culinary treats, live entertainment and lively company. Both chef Craig Hartman and Clifton, The Country Inn have garnered numerous awards. In the February 1993 issue of *Country Inns* magazine, Clifton was designated one of the top 12 such establishments in the country. *International Living* magazine also rated it one of the world's top three or four historic hotels. It is a place you'll want to experience, so call (540) 971-1800 or fax (540) 971-7098 and make reservations for a truly unforgettable visit.

All of this might weave a magical spell on you; you may want to get married right on the spot. However, be careful what you say and do; Craig Hartman is also a justice of the peace, and the pagoda is a most romantic place for a wedding ceremony.

Just eight miles north of the center of Charlottesville is another enchanting country venue. Follow Route 29 to Route 1520 and turn right at 3001 Hollymead Drive to reach the **Silver Thatch Inn**, (540) 978-4686. Don't be confused or put off by the fact that it is surrounded by a modern housing complex. The oldest part of this structure is a two-story log cabin built in 1780 by Hessian soldiers captured during the Revolution at the Battle of Saratoga (New York) and marched south to Charlottesville. The inn's center section dates from 1812 and has served, among other things, as a boys' school, tobacco plantation and melon farm. The newest wing was added in 1937 by B.F.D. Runk, a former dean of the University of Virginia. The cottage was built as recently as 1984.

Together, these white clapboard buildings present a charming image that is further enhanced by the gracious interior. An old-world pub complements the intimate candlelit dining rooms. Here you'll feast on modern American cuisine. This varies with the season, featuring grilled meat and fish along with unusual seafood and vegetarian dishes. The selection of wines is fine enough to merit the *Wine Spectator* Award of Excellence. The inn has seven rooms, three in the main house and four in the adjacent cottage. All are named after former presidents and feature American country furnishings; three even have fireplaces. Rates range from $110 to $150, including breakfast. Guests also have use, in season and weather permitting, of the community pool and tennis courts next door.

Of all the places in Charlottesville itself, we have selected two. Each is quite different from the other. First, let's talk about **200 South Street – A Virginia Inn,** (540) 979-0200 or (800) 964-7008 and fax (540) 979-4403. Located in a semi-residential neighborhood just two blocks away from the Downtown Mall, this is a small two-house complex with a common private car park. The larger house dates from 1856; it was built by Thomas Jefferson Wertenbaker, the son of Thomas Jefferson's librarian and close friend at the University of Virginia. It served as a residence well into this century but is believed to have functioned, during various periods of its history, as a girls' finishing school, a brothel (with no known connection to the school!) and a boarding house. The meticulous restoration of both houses, completed in April 1986, has resulted in an intriguing combination of old and new. The resulting 17 rooms and three suites each have a private bath and are furnished with 18th- and 19th-century English and Belgian antiques. Some have canopy beds, fireplaces and/or whirlpool baths. Private sitting rooms are offered as an optional extra. Rates range from $95-$175 a night and include Continental breakfast and afternoon wine or tea, served in the library. An ongoing exhibition of works by Virginia artists hangs in the main gallery; many of the walls are also adorned with historic photographs of Charlottesville from the private Holsinger collection.

Many people who come to Charlottesville are interested in antiques and spend much time foraging through the numerous shops. Sooner or later, they'll chance upon DeLoach Antiques at 1211 West Main Street, a short walk from Jefferson's "Academical Village." They will also notice **The Eighteen Seventeen Historic Bed & Breakfast**, (540) 979-7353 or (800) 730-7443. Yes, they are connected. Both are housed in buildings constructed in 1817 by James Dinsmore. (One of Thomas Jefferson's master craftsman, he was also the principal carpenter for Monticello and the nearby Rotunda.) Both facilities are operated by Candace DeLoach Wilson; and both are antique shops in their own right. In other words, the entire bed and breakfast – including the three bedrooms and two suites, with two more rooms due to open soon – is furnished and embellished with antiques. And all of them are for sale! Just imagine: after a beautifully romantic weekend you can go home with the bed. However, it is nearly impossible to describe the roomsadequately; perhaps "antique with avant-garde" says it best. Each has a private bath, air-conditioning and cable TV. Rates are $89-$195, including a Continental-plus breakfast and refreshments upon arrival. Innkeepers Candace DeLoach and her husband Jon – not to mention manager Hernan Luis y Prado – are attentive and informal. You are likely to get another friendly greeting on your way from the private car park by their friendly black Labrador. One definite advantage is this establishment's proximity to the University of Virginia, as well as numerous specialty shops, restaurants and cafés.

You may notice in some of these places a card from Steven J. Savitt of **Vacation From Stress**, (540) 980-3875. A nationally-certified massage therapist, he is more than qualified to relieve those aching muscles. A massage is a perfect way to unwind – especially when you've been traveling. You can arrange an appointment at either his place or yours.

Due in large part to the presence of the University of Virginia, Charlottesville is endowed with an eclectic array of sophisticated restaurants. Those mentioned in conjunction with the inns and bed and breakfasts are definitely recommended, but there are numerous others in town as well. Many of these are part of, or close to, the Downtown Mall area. They include the following:

The **Metropolitan,** housed at 119 West Main Street when we visited recently, will likely be relocated to a slightly larger venue a block away on Water Street. This move is necessitated by its growing popularity. American chef Tim Burgess and his French cohort Vincent Derquenne assure us that the style and ambience won't change. In the present premises, the kitchen is directly by the front door, and this is where it will be in the new location. As you might expect from this cross-cultural team, the cuisine is an interesting mix of American and Continental styles. But the atmosphere is very much that of a Parisian bistro – just right for an informal yet serious culinary experience.

At 213 Second Street SW – just across from the 200 South Street Inn – is a charming house dating from 1840 and an equally delightful restaurant, **Memory and Company**, (804) 296-3539 or fax (804) 293-2433. If this place feels like home, it's because owner/chef John Paul Corbett does in fact live here. The menu is prix fixe at $30 (excluding tax and gratuities), and changes completely every couple of months. There is not a lot of choice – usually only three appetizers and the same number of entrées – but the selections are all so enticing and unusual that you may still have difficulty making a decision. The dinner hour begins at 6 p.m., Wednesday through Saturday, and brunch is served between 11:30 a.m. and 2 p.m. on Sunday. Reservations are suggested.

Back towards town, at 215 West Water Street, is a restaurant and tapas bar of a decidedly different character. **Brasa**, telephone (804) 296-4343, is large and informally decorated. Besides a huge black papier-mache bull hanging from the ceiling (you'll never see one with *cojones* like that in Spain), it boasts what is known in Spain as a *horno de asar* – an open brick oven. Needless to say, the menu is dominated by Spanish and Tex/Mex dishes. However, they also offer pastas and brick oven-baked pizzas. Peppers and garlic figure prominently in most recipes, but don't hesitate to ask them to spice up your selection even further. If you are exceptionally hungry, try a Brasa Caesar Salad, topped with wood-grilled chicken breast and a tapa. This will satisfy all but the heartiest appetites. Care has obviously been taken to match wines with food; look for bottles from America, France, Italy, Spain and Morocco. In warmer months, you may dine on the outdoor terrace, even though it is a little close to the road.

At 415 East Main Street (on the Downtown Mall itself) is a curiously enchanting café called **The Nook.** Your best bet here is lunch, eaten either inside or out. The building dates from 1876, and the café has been operating here since the 50s, an era which is still recalled in its nostalgic ambiance.

Before you leave town, consider ending your trip on a truly exalted note. Call the **Bear Balloon Company,** (804) 971-1757 or (800) 476-1988, to arrange a sunrise balloon flight over "Jefferson country." Owner Rich Behr has been a commercial balloon pilot since 1974 and has logged over 3,000 hours of experience, opening his business here over 15 years ago. You will share your flight with up to 10 other adventurous souls on one of the largest passenger-carrying balloons in America (it is 11 stories high and holds 240,000 cubic feet of hot air.) Flights are scheduled between 6 a.m. and 7 a.m., from March through October. They depart from the Boar's Head Inn, located on Ivy Road/Route 250 West. The trip lasts about one hour and costs $135 per person. Although every effort is made to accommodate last-minute requests, call as far ahead as possible. The entire experience – including a champagne reception back at the Boar's Head Inn – lasts about three hours. But the memories will last a lifetime.

We have mentioned previously that the surrounding area is famous for its wineries. One of the better ones is **Oakencroft Vineyard & Winery,** (804) 296-4188, just off of Route 664, Barracks Road (which can be accessed from the north-west part of the 20-250 Bypass). The location is delightful, next to a lake full of wild waterfowl and enveloped by the lush rolling hills that are typical of the area. Tours are conducted between 11 a.m. and 5 p.m. during the months of March through December; after the tour, you may head for the tasting room to sample a selection of these medal-winning wines. Their

Virginia Chardonnay was one of the three wines served at President Clinton's first formal state dinner. Once you've chosen a favorite, purchase a few bottles to take home. They'll be a perfect accompaniment for the picnic lunch you will have surely brought with you. Oh, and by the way; share some food with the ducks and geese. It is not wise to get on their bad side.

There is no shortage of special events here; a full calendar of annual happenings may be obtained from the Convention & Visitors Bureau. April is very busy, with the **Annual Dogwood Festival, Thomas Jefferson's Birthday Commemoration**, the **Champagne and Candlelight Tour** of Ash Lawn-Highland, **Historic Garden Week in Charlottesville and Albemarle County**, the **Spring Garden Week Wine Festival** and the **Foxfield Races** (steeplechase racing). The **University of Virginia Commencement Exercises** take place in May. Starting in June, and continuing through August, is the **Summer Festival at Ash Lawn-Highland**, along with festive **Independence Day Celebrations** in July. The end of August sees the start of the **Albemarle County Fair**. September brings with it the **Virginia Blues Festival** and another day of steeplechasing at the **Foxfield Races**. On the Sunday of Thanksgiving weekend there is the **Blessing of the Hounds Service** at Grace Episcopal Church, 10 miles east of Charlottesville. After this you may watch the local hunt club hack off towards that first covert. During the **Thanksgiving Hunt Weekend** at the Boar's Head Inn, visitors may join in the annual Turkey Trot (a 5-km run), the Foot Hunt and the feast. Also during this season, various local wineries hold their **Open Houses**. Throughout the Christmas holidays, celebrations of note are: the **Annual Yuletide Traditions**, held at Ash Lawn-Highland, Historic Michie Tavern and Monticello; the **Merrie Old England Christmas Festival**, held at the Boar's Head Inn over the actual days of Christmas; and **First Night Virginia**, which ushers in the new year with downtown Charlottesville's very own New Year's Eve celebration.

Smith Mountain Lake

If the Fish Aren't Biting, Take a Hike

It all started with a dam. In 1966, the Appalachian Power Company completed construction of a 235-foot-high, $85-million dam across the Roanoke River. As a fringe benefit of power production, one of the premier lakes in the eastern United States was created. Surrounded by beautiful mountains and contained by over 500 miles of shoreline, the 22,000 acres of clear, clean water have become a recreational paradise. Although people own condos or vacation homes there, it remains free from the negative effects of mass tourism. It is not that remote, either – just a half-hour or so from Roanoke and Lynchburg. So, before too many people catch on and commercialization takes hold, visit Smith Mountain Lake for a weekend.

The first thing you'll need to do is decide where to stay. Although there are not too many options, the ones that exist are good. The topography of the lake shore makes it a trifle inconvenient for those coming in from the south, but most facilities are located on the northern side of the lake shore. Therefore, this is the area of choice when it comes to accommodation.

If you want space, luxurious modern furnishings, a shore location with marvelous views and privacy, then head for **Bernard's Landing Resort and Conference Center**. Each of the 16 one-bedroom condominiums has cathedral ceilings with skylights, plush carpeting, fireplace, a deck accessible through sliding glass doors, and a fully equipped kitchen. You'll have to share the chores, as there is no maid service. But each condo does have a dishwasher, washer, and dryer. They are especially attractive and rent for $120 a night if you stay for two or more nights. If they are all reserved, ask for a two-bedroom or larger version.

As wonderful as they are, these rooms aren't the only attraction. An authentic antebellum plantation home serves as the clubhouse. Here you may relax in comfortable surroundings, swim in the Olympic-sized pool, soak in the jacuzzi spa or compete on the tennis, racquetball, volleyball, or basketball courts. There is a lovely white sand beach for sunbathing, and marinas where you may dock or rent a boat.

If you don't feel like cooking and want to eat nearby, take a leisurely walk over to The Landing for an exquisite gourmet meal. Afterwards, drop by Castaways Bar and Grill overlooking the marina for either cocktails or a brew from one of the widest selections of bottled beers on the lake. Sip slowly and discuss the day's events while watching the dying sun paint the shimmering lake with fiery colors. With just 90 minutes' notice, the Castaway's kitchen will fix you a picnic for tomorrow's day on the lake.

Bernard's Landing is located at Route 3, Box 462, Moneta, 24121. In Virginia, call (800) 572-2048; out-of-state call (540) 721-8870 or (800) 368-3142. It's not too difficult to find. Turn off from Route 122 just south of the lake (and at the only stoplight in the area) onto Route 616. Bear left onto Route 940 and you'll find Bernard's Landing at the end of the lane.

If the lake shore is not close enough to the water, we can recommend something closer. How about romancing your mate on a houseboat? You will be pleasantly surprised at the boats for rent at **Boats at Smith Mountain Lake Inc.**, Route 5, Box 113 (Route 122), Moneta, 24121, (540) 721-5363 or (800) 488-4516. Don't be confused by the address; simply head towards the visitors' center at the Bridgewater Plaza Shopping Center, on the south side of the Hales Ford Bridge. Boats at Smith Mountain Lake will be right across from you. Now to the pleasant surprise – the houseboats themselves. Two sizes are offered: a 45-footer that sleeps six to 10, or a 37-foot version sleeping four to six (with the latter most appropriate for a couple). On board you will find a range, a full-sized refrigerator, and a gas grill for cookouts. There is a hot-and-cold-water shower fed by a 120-gallon fresh water tank, and a stereo with cassette to provide a little mood music. All this is powered by an 85-horsepower outboard motor with a 48-gallon fuel tank. Spacious outside decks and a rooftop sun deck complete the alluring amenities in your floating hotel room. Best of all, you may navigate this craft wherever you want. During a day cruise around the lake, you may stop to swim or fish; perhaps you'll happen upon one of the many small, deserted islands which offer a perfect haven for a private picnic. At night, choose an isolated spot to weigh anchor. Then you may begin your romantic evening by sharing a wonderful meal and watching the glowing embers of the retreating sun. In season, the rent for a houseboat from Friday to Sunday is $500, with the out-of-season price dropping to $350. Although the idea may take some time to "sink in," you will definitely have fun.

Bed and breakfast lovers have a delightful option here as well. Five minutes away from Smith Mountain Lake, south on Route 122, is a magnificent 120-acre estate called **The Manor at Taylor's Store**. This elegant dwelling was originally built in the early 1800s as the manor house for a prosperous plantation. Skelton Taylor, a member of Virginia's Bedford Militia, opened the store here in 1799 (it was a general merchandise trading post that served locals and settlers headed west.) Later, this became an "ordinary" or public house and, in 1818, a U.S. Post Office.

The rooms are all delightful. There are six suites, each with a different theme. All are furnished in a luxuriously classical style, and most have beautiful views. Particularly charming is the three-bedroom Christmas Cottage, also located on the grounds. The public rooms are also really exceptional. You'll enjoy relaxing in the formal parlor with its grand piano, or in the sunroom with its lovely views. A huge area downstairs features a room with a fireplace, wide screen TV and movies, a billiard room, a fully equipped exercise room, and a guests' kitchen for staving off the late-night munchies. Before turning in, be sure to take a soak in the large hot tub.

This is set in a semi-enclosed porch, with lattice work and windows for star-gazing.

Guests of The Manor will enjoy hiking, fishing, canoeing, or swimming in one of the six private spring-fed ponds. After your morning activities, take a picnic to the gazebo for a quiet, romantic lunch – but don't disturb the resident geese! Prices include a tasty breakfast and range from $80 up to $125 for the Castle Suite, also known as the "honeymoon suite."

In the afternoon, try something more adventurous. As an option to their bed and breakfast package, innkeepers Lee and Mary Lynn Tucker have arranged for Denny Laughlin of Blue Ridge Balloons, (540) 721-6092, to whisk you away on a sunrise or sunset ride. You and your loved one will float high above the countryside, marveling at the panoramic views of both mountains and lake. Upon landing, you'll be treated to the balloonist's tradition, a "mini picnic" of champagne and hors d'oeuvres. It's a fitting end to an unforgettable trip, and costs $150 per person.

Having made your reservations, you will now want to plan your leisure time activities. Not surprisingly, most choices here revolve around the lake. **Bridgewater Marina Boat Rentals**, conveniently located behind the visitors' center at 8 Bridgewater Plaza, Moneta, telephone (540) 721-1639 or (800) 729-1639, can meet your every aquatic need. One of the more popular ways of getting around is the 24-foot pontoon boat equipped with a 40-horse power engine. Stock your cooler with a picnic lunch, and off you go. Do a little fishing, a little swimming, a little sunbathing – or perhaps enact your own private episode of "Fantasy Island" on one of the many deserted shores. Rates are $75 for a half-day, $95 for a full day, and $135 for a 24-hour day. A less expensive choice is the 14-foot fiberglass fishing boat with a 5-h.p. motor. This goes for $35, $50 and $65 respectively for the time spans listed above. If you prefer speed, then try the Fish-N-Ski (75 h.p.), or Run-A-Bout (100 h.p.), renting for between $80 and $240. They also have Wave Runners, which may be rented for a third of a day, a half of a day, or full day at from $75 to $160. A half-day is defined as either 7 a.m. to 12:30 p.m. or 1 p.m. to 6:30 p.m. A full day is from 7 a.m. to 6:30 p.m. These prices do not include fuel, oil, or damage deposit. Between mid-September and mid-May there are hefty discounts on everything except the Wave Runners.

If you can't decide between ballooning or boating, visit **Bridgewater Para-Sail.** For $38 you can take flight on a scenic aerial ride at 500 feet over the water. Unlike some of the other water sports, this requires no skill tests or age limits. This company also has a convenient agreement with Bernard's Landing that allows you to rent boats at either location.

Maybe you fancy a spot of serious fishing. If so, there is no finer place than Smith Mountain Lake. It is stocked regularly with game fish such as striped bass, largemouth bass, smallmouth bass and muskellunge. As a result, it enjoys a reputation as one of the best all-around fishing spots in the eastern United States. In fact, it is rated the number one lake for trophy stripers in Virginia. So don't just dream about it – go out and try to beat the state record of nearly 46 pounds! Captain Dave Sines will be happy to share his expertise with you. He operates **My Time Striper Guide Service**, 111 Long Island Drive, Moneta, telephone (540) 721-5007 or (800) 817-5007. Climb aboard his fully insured, U.S. Coast Guard-licensed, 22-foot TRI-Toon deck boat. Here you'll take advantage of his knowledge and state-of-the-art equipment to find stripers galore. Throw a little luck into the equation and you'll feel the thrill and excitement of catching a fighting striper. Half-day trips take four to five hours, and full days eight to nine hours. For two people, the cost is $160 and $250, respectively. Equipment is provided, and Polaroid pictures are taken of the day's catch. In addition, the fish are filleted and coolers made available for your food and beverages. Should you catch something you'd be proud to put on your wall, take it to **Ed's Taxidermy**, Route 4, Box 825, Rocky Mount, 24151, (540) 483-0051. For $4.50 an inch he will preserve the memory for you. However, be prepared to wait for two or three months, and to pay shipping charges. Ed is one of the best around and he is always busy, especially in the fall.

Perhaps fighting a striper is too strenuous an activity. You'd rather kick back and enjoy yourselves while others do the work for you. Well, that's an option as well. **Paddle Wheel Cruises**, located at the end of State Route 853, telephone (540) 297-7100 or (800) 721-DARE (3273), offers two choices. The luxuriously appointed *Virginia Dare,* a 19th-century side wheeler with enclosed decks and panoramic windows, offers lunch, dinner and Sunday brunch cruises with regular entertainment between March and December. In addition, there are Cocktail and Moonlight cruises when other commitments allow. They also have *The Blue Moon,* a 51-foot motor yacht. If you really want to spoil yourselves and get a taste of "the good life," charter the latter for a private cruise. This will cost $370 for a minimum of two hours. You must take your own champagne, but they provide the ambience.

As for off-the-water activities, options are limited. You may discover more about the lake's origin at the **Appalachian Power's Visitors' Center,** located next to the dam. Various exhibits demonstrate how power is produced and a ramp gives access to an overlook area with fantastic views of the dam and gorge. You may even have lunch in a picnic area near the base of the dam itself. The visitors' center is open from 10 a.m. to 6 p.m. daily and may be reached by returning off Route 40 onto either branch of Route 751 and then following the road to the dam. The 1506-acre **Smith Mountain Lake State Park** on the eastern side of the lake offers four short but lovely trails, as well as a swimming beach. Further information may be obtained by calling the visitors' center at (540) 297-6066. Does the thought of a trail ride entice you? To arrange this, call **Mallard Cove Stables**, (540) 721-6333 at the stable or (540) 721-8902 at home. To get there, take Route 122 to the intersection with 616, follow 616 for a mile and take a left onto Route 949. The stables are 1.7 miles ahead on the right.

History lovers may be interested to know that the **Booker T. Washington National Monument** is located not far from the Manor at Taylor's Store, (540) 721-2094. Here – where this controversial black educator, orator and public figure was born a slave – the National Park Service has recreated the environment of 19th-century slavery in Piedmont Virginia. Visit between 9 a.m. and 4:30 p.m., year-round.

On a lighter and more refreshing note, how about visiting the local winery? This one is unique, but hard to find. The address of **Tomahawk Mill Winery** is Route 3, Box 204, Chatham, 24531, telephone (804) 432-1063. But to get there, turn south onto 626 off of Route 40, travel 8.2 miles, and turn left onto Route 649. The winery will be on your right. What is special is the fact that it is housed in a well-preserved mill. Built in 1888 by James Anderson, this water-powered grist mill operated almost without interruption on Tomahawk Creek for 100 years. It ceased operations in 1988. Today, the steep surrounding hills are planted with vines and the wine tastings are conducted on the inside of the mill, a fascinating place in its own right. Although it's a little out of the way, that is part of its charm.

Along Route 40, you will notice intriguing little log cabins. These were used to store tobacco before it was sent to market, most probably at Danville.

To see the region in full scope, take to the air in a slow-flying, high-wing Wilga aircraft. These are perfect for sight-seeing. Call **Virginia Air Services,** (540) 297-4500. The cost is $25 per person.

We have already mentioned two places for dining – The Landing at Bernard's Landing and the *Virginia Dare.* There is no shortage of restaurants in the area, but there is one more we would strongly recommend. **The Anchor House**, located at Bridgewater Plaza, (540) 721-6540, is easily reached by either road or boat. You may eat in the restaurant, in the café, or outdoors on the patio overlooking the marina. The lunch menu is innovative, trendy and casual, while the dinner menu offers traditional seafood and steak options.

Shopping at Smith Mountain Lake is both pleasantly relaxed and unusual. Scattered around are dozens of quaint little craft and antique shops. There are no supermarkets, however. Look instead for the traditional country stores of a gentler age. These are surprisingly well-stocked and each has its own distinctive character.

We knew little about Smith Mountain Lake before researching this chapter. But it didn't take long to realize that it more than lives up to its nickname, "The Jewel of the Blue Ridge." In short, Smith Mountain Lake is a wonderful place for a romantic break. For more information, don't hesitate to pop in or call the friendly folk at the **Visitors' Center**, 2 Bridgewater Plaza, (540) 297-1001, (540) 21-1203, or (800) 676-8203.

Charles City County
Plantation-Hopping in the
Land of Tobacco

Everyone knows about the grandeur of the South's once-great plantation houses. Not many realize, however, that in one small corner of Virginia, you can not only visit a half-dozen such houses, but you can also stay in two. And the area has more to offer. Follow Route 5 – which runs between Richmond and Williamsburg – along the banks of the river that hosted the first American settlers.

The men who arrived here early in the 17th century were adventurers and loyal to their homeland; hence the names given to the river (the James) and the area (Virginia, for the virgin queen). Life here was not easy. The ravages of disease and the threat from indigenous Indians delayed the establishment of a permanent colony. Once tobacco was discovered to be a profitable crop, plantations were established. These boasted beautiful homes staffed by slaves. Many of these survive today, offering an intriguing glimpse into America's past.

Almost halfway between Richmond and Williamsburg you will find one of the most unusual and delightful bed and breakfasts anywhere. **Edgewood Plantation**, (804) 829-

2962 or (800) 296-3343, is located at 4800 John Tyler Memorial Highway (Route 5). The Gothic-style home was built in 1849 for Spencer Rowland, who had recently moved here from New Jersey. It was actually constructed on land that was originally part of Berkeley Plantation, just across the road. Much of the area's folklore centers around Edgewood's role in the Civil War. The third floor was used as a Confederate lookout; here, rebels spied on Union troops that were stationed at Berkeley. The ancient gristmill ground corn for both armies. Legend has it that "Jeb" Stuart once stopped here for a coffee break en route to Richmond; he carried information for Robert E. Lee regarding the strength of the Union forces. There is a sad story associated with Edgewood, too. Rowland's daughter Lizzie died of a broken heart when her lover failed to return from the war. Her name is inscribed on one of the bedroom windows, but you may see a more ephemeral presence. Don't worry; by all reports, she is a friendly ghost!

First glances often speak volumes about a place. This is certainly the case with Edgewood — especially if you arrive after dark, when its lights emit a reassuringly warm glow. This is especially true during the Christmas season, when lavishly adorned trees are visible through every window, hinting of the 17 or more trees throughout the house. Once across the threshold, you're in for a surprise. Most period inns feature antique furniture, and Edgewood is no exception. Most also display collectibles and memorabilia; Edgewood has these as well. But this place elevates these attributes to an art form.

Virginians take pride in their individuality, and quintessential Virginian Dot Boulware has lovingly created an atmosphere here that is reflective of her character. Even the tiniest space is filled with some antique or unusual decoration and, believe it or not, she knows where each piece belongs. Don't be surprised to see her rag dolls hanging over the magnificent three-story free-standing staircase. On the third floor, you might even stop to chat with a family of oversized rabbits taking afternoon tea around a table.

There are six bedrooms in the main building. Each is graced by elegant furniture, often including an antique canopy bed and, sometimes, a working fireplace. All of the appointments unite to reinforce the room's unique theme. You will feel as if you have stepped into a "living museum" where the inhabitants have simply evaporated, leaving their surroundings totally intact. Behind the main house are the old slave quarters. These have been transformed to house additional rooms of a similar style, each with an outside entrance. The cost for this memorable experience ranges between $110 and $178 a night, depending upon the season and the size of room.

Once you've settled in, a glass of wine and enchanting tales of Lizzie await in the parlor. Ask Dot to give you a preview of the beautiful room where you will partake of a full country breakfast the next morning. Also take a peak in the kitchen. Definitely ready for work, it is nonetheless enchanting.

If you are really fortunate, your visit will coincide with one of Dot's High Victorian Tea Parties, complete with the traditional scones, clotted cream, tasty sandwiches and delicious pastries. Although such customs are largely a thing of the past, Edgewood seems an appropriate place in which to recreate them. On a practical note, Edgewood makes a handy base from which to explore other area plantations. When you are ready for a respite, come back for a swim in the outdoor pool, or enjoy the lovely gardens while relaxing in the gingerbread-style gazebo.

If there can be any criticism of Edgewood, it is simply that there is not enough of it to satisfy the demand. This problem is exacerbated by the fact that there are no cities (or even large communities) in this distinctly agricultural county. The center of the community is still the 18th-century Charles City Courthouse, which serves as a 250-year-old link between past and present. Accommodation and restaurants are few and far between, but what choices there are prove interesting.

North Bend Plantation Bed & Breakfast, (804) 829-5186, located just a mile south of Route 5, may be reached by taking Highway 619 (Wyanoke Road) two miles east of the courthouse. The clear lines of this Greek Revival house, built in 1819 and now designated a Virginia Historic Landmark, are visible for some distance. The inside is no less impressive, as is the heritage of the owners. The house has been in the possession of the Copland family for five generations and the present owner is the great-grandson of Edmund Ruffin, the Southerner who fired the first shot of the Civil War. It was originally built for Sarah Harrison, a sister of the ninth U. S. president, William Henry Harrison. General Sheridan made North Bend his headquarters when he occupied the area in 1864. In fact, one of the house's many treasures is a desk used by the general. Its pigeon holes still bear labels showing the names of the different companies to which his papers and orders pertained.

Four large bedrooms – each with a private bath – are decorated in keeping with the house's character. Of particular interest to romantics is **The Sheridan Room.** This features a magnificent queen tester four-poster bed, which was built circa 1810-1840 and is complemented perfectly by both General Sheridan's desk and an inviting chaise longue. It rents for $125 nightly. **The Rose Room** – which features a gas log fireplace – goes for $135, while the two remaining rooms are a bit less at $115. For your entertainment, there is a billiard room, as well as opportunities to play backgammon, croquet, horseshoes, and volleyball. Other attributes include a pool and, of course, the gracious hospitality of one of Virginia's oldest families.

As you drive along Route 5, you will come across a group of farm buildings on the northern side of the road. Don't be fooled, however. Set in the middle of this working farm is a turn-of-the-century farmhouse, which has been tastefully converted into one of the area's most applauded restaurants. This, the **Indian Fields Tavern**, (804) 829-5004, is located at 9220 John Tyler Highway, just two miles west of Charles City Courthouse. No ornate decor here; the tavern is not that kind of place. Rather, the attention is on good food. Chesapeake Bay seafood, locally produced Virginia hams and aged western beef are skillfully and innovatively mixed to produce American and classic Southern dishes the likes of which you'll seldom encounter elsewhere. If it's excellent food and not frills that you prize, then this restaurant is for you. Its AAA Three-Diamond rating is fully deserved, and reservations for dinner are strongly recommended.

After a good night's sleep, it is time to visit the plantations. Of these, **Shirley** – situated a few miles to the west of Edgewood on Route 5 – is our favorite. Founded in 1613, it's the oldest in Virginia. Construction of the mansion and other outbuildings was begun in 1723 by Edward Hill III for his daughter, Elizabeth, and her husband, John Carter. Today, the house is occupied by the 10th and 11th generations of the Hill-Carter family. Its world-famous flying staircase – whose design is credited to Christopher Wren – has no visible means of support and is the only one of its kind in America. Another family tradition is visible on the window panes. Here, on their wedding mornings, the Carter women inscribe their initials with the diamond of their engagement ring. It is also interesting to note the designer's frequent use of the pineapple motif, a traditional symbol of hospitality. Of these, the 3½-foot finial on the peak of the roof is the most obvious. You will learn much more about the history of Shirley Plantation by taking one of the informative tours offered between 9 a.m. and 4:30 p.m. daily. It doesn't close until 5 p.m., so before leaving take time to visit the gift shop and stroll the lovely grounds. The latter boast huge ancient trees and delicate gardens on a lawn rolling right down to the river.

Back along Route 5, and right across from Edgewood, is **Berkeley**, (804) 829-6018. Of all Virginia's plantations, this is the most historically important. A land grant was accorded the Berkeley Company in 1619 by King James and designated the "Town of Berkeley Hundred and Plantation." ("Hundred" was the term used to designate a tract of land that was supposed to provide support for 100 fighting men of the King's Army.) When the first colonists landed here on December 4, 1619 – a year before the Pilgrims reached Plymouth Rock – they announced that "the day of our ships' arrival... shall be yearly and perpetually kept as a day of thanksgiving." This was the very first Thanksgiving Day. These first settlements did not fare too well. It wasn't until more than a century later, after its acquisition by the Harrison family, that Berkeley Plantation began to thrive. Those first settlers did leave one lasting heritage: America's first bourbon whiskey was distilled at Berkeley in 1621-22.

In 1726, Benjamin Harrison IV and his wife Anne constructed a Georgian-style mansion on a hill overlooking the James. This was done using bricks fired on the plantation. Surrounded by 10 acres of formal terraced boxwood gardens, this is said to be the earliest three-story brick house in Virginia. The initials of Benjamin and his wife appear on a datestone over a side door.

The son of the builder – also named Benjamin Harrison – inherited the property. In addition to signing the Declaration of Independence, this Harrison served as governor of Virginia for three terms. George Washington and each of the following nine presidents (one of whom was the owner's third son and the ninth president, William Henry Harrison) were all received here. His grandson, yet another Benjamin Harrison, went on to become the 23rd president. In 1862, during the Civil War, President Lincoln visited Berkeley to review General McClellan's 140,000-strong army. In that same year the haunting military melody "Taps" was composed there. This history, combined with the allure of a house filled with magnificent 18th-century antiques, makes for a fascinating visit. Stop by any time between 8 a.m. and 5 p.m. daily.

You will find one more pleasant surprise at Berkeley. The **Coach House Tavern**, (804) 829-6003, one of the Richmond area's top 10 restaurants and recipient of the AAA Three-Diamond award, is housed in a restored outbuilding just a stone's throw from the main house.

You won't have to travel far to find the next two plantations. In fact, they are adjacent to each other. The first of these was originally a part of the 1619 land grant made in the name of Westover Plantation.

Evelynton Plantation, (804) 827-5075, was named after William Byrd II's daughter Evelyn. Since 1847, it has been home to the Ruffin family, whose patriarch, Edmund Ruffin, fired the first shot in the Civil War at Fort

Sumter, South Carolina. Whether through retribution or
fate, the original house was destroyed later in that same
war. The current residence was not built until two generations later, in 1937, by Edmund's great grandson, John
Augustine Ruffin, Jr. and his wife Mary Ball Saunders.
This Georgian Revival manor house is listed on the National Register of Historic Places and is open between 9
a.m. and 5 p.m. daily for guided tours. In addition to his
other achievements, Edmund Ruffin made significant agricultural contributions and published the *Farmer's Register*, which earned him the sobriquet, "father of American
agronomy." Even today, the 2,500-acre farm is family-
owned and operated.

The second plantation is **Westover**, (804) 827-2882. This
was built around 1730 by William Byrd II, the founder of
both Richmond and Petersburg. The house has lovely proportions and boasts one of the country's finest early 18th-
century gates. The grounds and gardens, which overlook
the James River, are open daily between 9 a.m. and 6 p.m.
The house itself is open for five days only during Historic
Garden Week.

A few miles away – on the other side of Charles City
Courthouse – is **Sherwood Forest Plantation**, (804)
829-5377. It has its origins in a 1616 land grant known as
Smith's Hundred. Among its prestigious owners have been
two U. S. presidents: William Henry Harrison, who inherited the plantation in the late 18th century and became the
ninth president; and John Tyler, the first vice president to
ascend to the presidency in 1841. The 300-foot house,
constructed around 1730 in the Virginia Tidewater tradition, is the longest frame house in America. President
Tyler was responsible for the expansion that earned it that
distinction when, in 1845, he added a ballroom designed
specifically for the Virginia Reel. Since that time it has
been owned by his direct descendants. In the mid-1970s, it
was restored by the current owner, his grandson. The
house is open daily.

By this time you are less than 30 minutes' drive from
Williamsburg. Because of its proximity and the limited
number of nearby choices, you may want to refer to the
options detailed in the chapter on Williamsburg. Note

particularly the **Liberty Rose** and another restaurant, **The Dining Room at Ford's Colony**. The **Williamsburg Winery** and **Historic Air Tours** would also be convenient from the plantation area.

While in the area, be sure to visit the Hopewell City Marina, home of the *Pocahontas II* cruise boat. Just a few miles from Shirley Plantation, it is reached by crossing the James River via the Benjamin Harrison Bridge. A cruise will give you a delightful view of these marvelous plantations from the river. If you like, you may even have brunch, lunch or dinner on board. Certainly a romantic memory to savor. Call (804) 541-2616 for reservations or more information.

Virginia's Eastern Shore

Chincoteague
A Natural Choice for a Great Break

Have you every fantasized about stepping from your doorstep onto a stretch of totally unspoiled Atlantic Ocean beach? Well, this is one fantasy that can come true. Such a place exists. It is only 170 miles from Washington, D.C., and here you will find not only Atlantic beaches, but fantastic woodlands, marshes, back bays and a wide array of diverse wildlife. This dream spot is located on two islands in the northeastern part of the Eastern Shore of Virginia, just south of Maryland. The larger of these is a barrier island that stretches past the Maryland state line all the way up to Ocean City. The smaller one is tucked between the larger one and the mainland.

It was in 1671 that the first white settlers claimed this fascinating island, then known to the local Indians as "Gingoteague" or "Beautiful Land Across the Water." Although a patent was issued to a rich Maryland landowner, further ownership disputes arose soon afterwards. Eventually, the land was divided in half between the states of Maryland and Virginia. During this period, it was used primarily as a livestock range. There is no question that early life was quite harsh on Chincoteague (pronounced shin-co-teague); the 1800 census showed a population of only 60 living on this island, which is just seven miles long and 1½ miles wide. Following the further division of the land into smaller parcels, the number of inhabitants increased. People began taking advantage of the surrounding waters to earn their livelihood. As far back as 1830, the oysters for which the island is famous were being cultivated for sale. Then, as today, they were tended in much the same way as a gardener would tend a vegetable garden. These early islanders were not only industrious, they were very progressive. In 1845, after the Virginia State Assembly enacted a law allowing the creation of public schools, Chincoteague was one of the first communities to support a free school. A superintendent was promptly hired to oversee the project at a princely salary of $50 a year. Chincoteague is protected on its eastern coast from the Atlantic Ocean by the larger, elongated Assateague Island, whose treacherous shores necessitated installation of a lighthouse as early as 1833. It was not until 1857, however, that the 145-foot brick tower that still stands as one of the island's most recognizable landmarks was constructed. This structure played an interesting role in the ensuing Civil War. Although the rest of Virginia's Eastern Shore voted in 1861 to join the Confederacy, Chincoteague's allegiance remained with the Union forces. The Assateague light – one of only a handful operating during the war – helped maintain sea trade with the north.

In an effort to preserve this natural wonderland, Assateague Island has been divided into three major protected public areas. In the north are the 680 acres which make up **Assateague State Park**. These are administered by Maryland's Department of Natural Resources. The portion that lies within Virginia's boundaries comprises the **Assateague Island National Seashore**, which is managed by the National Parks Service; and the **Chincoteague National Wildlife Refuge**, which is operated by the U. S. Fish and Wildlife Service. Strict regulations ensure the preservation of this area; consequently, there is limited commercial activity. To find accommodation and resort activities, you will have to return to the small island of Chincoteague.

When traveling from the mainland to Chincoteague, take Route 175 to Route 13, which links Maryland and Virginia. Don't hurry, as you may want to make a stop on the way. Halfway between the turnoff and your destination – before you cross the main body of the bay – you'll pass the **Goddard Space Flight Center**, (804) 824-1344. Operated by NASA, this is a special complex for suborbital aeronautical and space research. There is a visitors' center with a small museum and gift shop. Here you can literally "have a blast." One of their specialties is rocket launches. At 1 p.m on the first Saturday of each month (and the third Saturday of June, July and August, weather permitting), they arrange model rocket launches. Model rocketeers are invited to bring their own flight-ready ships. While there, keep your eyes open for another aerial activity. The runway across the road is used by pilots conducting training exercises in Air Force 1, the president's personal plane.

As you leave Wallops and the mainland, continue over the Chincoteague Bay and across two much smaller islands before the final bridge span deposits you at Main Street, on the western side of Chincoteague. You will immediately feel a change in the atmosphere, and it won't take you long to absorb this area's laid-back, nautical flavor. Given the island's small size, there is a disproportionately large number of hotels, motels, inns, bed and breakfasts, and rental agencies. But remember that, due to the seasonal nature of the resort, some may be closed in the winter.

Turn onto Maddox Boulevard, the major east/west thoroughfare, and drive away from town to the island's east side. Just past the strange traffic circle that is home to the Chamber of Commerce Tourist Office (and before the bridge to Assateague Island) is an establishment that is worth your consideration, no matter the season. Open year-round, **The Refuge Motor Inn**, 7058 Maddox Boulevard, (804) 336-5511 or (800) 544-8469, offers a wide range of romantic rooms and a variety of recreational facilities. Two luxury suites offer private decks, the Veranda Suite has a romantic spiral staircase, and many deluxe rooms feature king or queen-sized beds. Five specialty rooms have been innovatively decorated in keeping with country, nautical, Victorian, traditional and English country themes. The Refuge has a complicated seasonal structure with rates ranging between $135 and $205, ($65 to $110 for the deluxe rooms). There is an unusually high five-day minimum during the wild pony round-up (more on this later). Other facilities are an indoor/outdoor pool, jacuzzi, sauna, exercise room, and a picnic area with tables and hibachis. Perhaps you can use the latter to cook the day's catch.

Back on the western side of the island (not far from the shopping center) is a hotel beautifully situated on the Chincoteague Bay, with numerous well-appointed rooms. The main wing of the **Island Motor Inn** sports four queen-sized petite suites. The new annex – which boasts an indoor pool overlooking the bay – has 12 non-smoking rooms with king-sized beds. Prices are between $125 and $160, with a four-day minimum during the pony penning. You may keep an eye on things from the spacious observation deck, steal a kiss in the gazebo overlooking the bay or work up a sweat in the fitness center (open to guests only). End your session with a soak in the oversized hot tub, which is surrounded by large picture windows.

Those craving a more homey atmosphere should head for 4141 Main Street. Here, in a grand old Victorian house dating from 1886, is **Miss Molly's Inn.** A charming bed and breakfast establishment overlooking Chincoteague Bay, it was built by Mr. J. T. Rowley, "The Clam King of the World." His daughter "Miss Molly" lived there until she was 84 – hence its name. The house has been fully restored, with many modern conveniences (notably air-conditioning) added. Seven bedrooms of varying size are available, five of them with private baths. The hostess, Barbara Wiedenheft, hails from Yorkshire, England. She is renowned for her full breakfast and traditional English afternoon tea. Good conversation (in your choice of French, Dutch, German or English), a decor warmed by comfortably interesting antiques, and evenings on the porch enjoying the breeze make for a truly relaxing stay. An interesting cultural note: Marguerite Henry stayed here while writing her famous children's book *Misty of Chincoteague.* So who knows what great works of art – or works of the heart – your stay will inspire? Barbara and her husband David have recently taken over the equally charming "Channel Bass" Inn; you can be sure they will be leaving their mark on that, as well. For information or reservations, call (804) 336-6686 or (800) 221-5620.

While touring the island, you will see some beautiful private properties. In the off-season (usually between Labor Day and Memorial Day weekend) these are available for rent. Often detached properties situated on their own secluded plots, they offer much more privacy for couples than the usual choice of accommodation. True, they are a little more expensive than regular hotels, and the rules are different, but they have their own advantages. Most notably, they are usually rented for a minimum of three nights. (The check-out time in most hotels can be as early as 11 a.m., which can severely disrupt your last day.) Renting a property for an extra night doesn't mean you have to use it, but it does give you a lot more flexibility. **Island Property Enterprises**, (800) FINALLY, has many of these on its books and will be happy to arrange your stay.

Most people will have heard the name Chincoteague in connection with **The Pony Round Up**. The following is the story of how wooden houses, the island's isolation, wild ponies, and Volunteer Firemen contributed to create this, the island's most popular event. The island's narrow and congested streets, which are lined with wooden houses, were always a fire hazard. It took one such conflagration for the island's residents to realize the problems posed by their isolation from the mainland's fire department. The issue arose at a community meeting in 1905, after which money was collected to purchase a hand pump and a small gasoline engine. These were not maintained properly, however; when they were needed on September 5, 1920, one wouldn't function and the other was just too small. As a consequence, that fire destroyed 12 properties on the east side of the island. On February 25, 1924, a similar disaster struck the west side, and many of those buildings were destroyed. Determined not to relive those disasters, the Chincoteague Volunteer Fire Company was formed a short time later. One of their first decisions was to purchase an American La France pumper. But there was one major problem: finance. To raise the money for the initial payments on the equipment, they organized a carnival that included a "Pony Penning Day."

There is some questions as to how the shaggy, pint-sized wild ponies arrived on Assateague Island. One legend has it that horses being transported in a Spanish galleon swam to shore when the vessel wrecked off the coast. Another has it that 17th-century mainland farmers grazed their livestock on the island to evade paying livestock taxes. Over the years, these wild animals have been regularly rounded up and forced to swim over to Chincoteague, in an effort to contain the damage they inflict on Assateague's crops. Seeing an opportunity to raise revenue, the firemen took over this task, selling the foals at auction before returning the remainder to freedom. The custom continues to this day, attracting visitors from all over. The pony swim and auction take place on the last Wednesday and Thursday of July, but earlier in the week the firemen herd the ponies to a corral on the south end of Assateague, about a mile from the Assateague Lighthouse. There they are allowed to rest before swimming the channel to Chincoteague under the watchful eyes of the firemen and thousands of tourists. Following another rest, they are driven along Main Street to the carnival grounds, where they are penned in anticipation of Thursday's auction. In the early days, the going price for a foal was about $20, but now it has risen to $900. Most are sold as pets for children who have always wanted a real Chincoteague Pony. Their popularity was enhanced by the 1947 publication of Marguerite Henry's *Misty of Chincoteague*. This book was subsequently turned into a major Hollywood movie, using local people as extras. As the firemen benefit from the revenues, they are the ones responsible for the upkeep and health of the herd (each member of which bears the firemen's brand). In 1943, when the Chincoteague National Wildlife Refuge was established in the Virginia section of Assateague Island, special attention was given to these ponies, the only wild herds still grazing east of the Rocky Mountains.

Later in the year, on Columbus Day weekend, there is another event that will appeal to many peoples' tastes. The annual **Chincoteague Oyster Festival** is held at the Maddox Family Campground to promote the area's seafood industry and to mark the arrival of the oyster season. As might be expected, oysters are served in nearly every manner imaginable as residents echo the old Chincoteague saying, "Eat fish – live longer; eat oysters – love longer; eat clams – last longer." Oysters are accompanied by crabs, clams and all the other foods that comprise a great cookout. Then they are followed by something extra special. The Oyster and Maritime Museum sponsors a dessert booth, with the proceeds going to the museum. If you plan to go, be aware that the event is always a sellout. Admission is limited to 2,000, and entry is by advance ticket only. These may be purchased, beginning April 1st, from the **Chincoteague Chamber of Commerce**, P.O. Box 258, Chincoteague, Virginia 23336. Call (804) 336-6161 for more information on this or any other local event or attraction.

It is virtually impossible to visit the Eastern Shore and not notice the many decoys. These come in all shapes and colors, and are for sale throughout the area. Demand for decoys has advanced far beyond that created by their original, practical use. They are now an art form in their own right and make prized souvenirs. Not surprisingly, Chincoteague is home to some of the finest artists and most talented carvers. One of the highlights of Easter weekend is the **Easter Decoy Festival,** which has earned a reputation as the most important wildlife art and decoy show on Virginia's Eastern Shore. Exhibitors come from all over the country. This allows visitors an inside look at how the artists and carvers perfect their craft, as well as an opportunity to purchase unique gifts. While browsing, don't miss the food tent; local restaurants host a variety of concession stands offering an authentic taste of Chincoteague. If you can't visit during the festival, stop by the **Island Florist & Country Gifts** shop, located at 3705 Willow Street, telephone (804) 336-6102. Featured are a wide range of decoys and other specialty collectible items. Betty Daisy, the owner, will also be pleased to have roses – or any other flower – delivered ahead to your room.

There is much in the way of water and nature activities to occupy your time on thse islands – especially during the warmer seasons. Seeing all this water inspires most visitors to get out on boats, either to relax or to study the amazing array of birds and wildlife. There is no shortage of opportunities in this vein. A small motor vessel called *The Osprey* sails daily between Memorial Day and October on a professionally guided nature tour of the Chincoteague and Assateague area. The sailing time is one and a half hours, the cost is $10, and tickets and information are available from The Refuge Motor Inn, (804) 336-5593. Morning excursions, moonlight cruises and special occasion parties are also offered. But why not treat your loved one to a special occasion all your own? Charter *The Osprey* for a private moonlight cruise, complete with champagne, picnic basket, and a dozen red roses. The cost is only $200 for an hour and a half of pure romance. Alternatively, try **Captain Barry's Back Bay Cruises**, dock phone (804) 336-6508 or boat phone (804) 824-8471. This company offers a wide range of nautical adventures. Because "girls just want to have fun," Captain Barry has designed a special **Fun Cruise.** This half-day trip takes you around the Back Bay as the crew spins tales of pirates and smugglers. Next you'll drop off crab pots and take in a little fishing. Finally, you'll disembark on a very private island for shelling, clamming, swimming, or whatever. All this for just $30. Other options are a **Fishing Trip**, **Bird Watching Expedition**, an **Up-The-Bay Moonlight Excursion** and a **Champagne Sunset Cruise**. As with the Osprey, a private cruise for two may also be arranged.

The more adventurous among you may want to try **Sport Fishing,** and the 44-foot ocean sport yacht *Mar-Shell* offers the opportunity to do just that. If you've dreamed about coming back with a huge tuna, marlin or mahi mahi, this is your chance. But it isn't cheap. A half-day – approximately six hours – costs $495 and a full day (eight hours) will set you back $695. The *Mar-Shell* is docked at the Chincoteague Inn on South Main Street and reservations can be made by calling (804) 336-1939.

Perhaps you'd like to find a secluded beach for that special tryst. A 16-foot motor boat from **Snug Harbor** boat rentals, (804) 336-6176, will certainly get you there. But you are responsible for packing the picnic – and the wine. If you want to speed things along, take one of their jet skis for a half-hour spin beforehand.

"Land lovers" have options too. The Chincoteague National Wildlife Refuge offers a **Wildlife Tour** between April 1 and November 20. Besides getting "up close and personal" with the plentiful wildlife of Assateague's back trails, you will learn about the past, present and future of the island on this informative 14½-mile trip. For information and reservations, call the Chincoteague Wildlife Refuge Visitor Center at (804) 336-6155, or the Island Motor Inn, (804) 336-3141. Perhaps you would like to take some of the wildlife home as trophies. If so, call Andy Linton at (804) 336-1253 and make arrangements for him to take you **Waterfowl Hunting**.

No matter what the season, a visit to Chincoteague's wonderfully wild barrier island neighbor is an absolute must. Formed by sand that the waves have brought up from the ocean floor, Assateague is perpetually changing. The violent storms that hurl waves onto the beaches are continually altering the shape of the shoreline. Resources here are closely protected and every effort is made to maintain the island's original state. For instance, private cars are only allowed access to a very small part of the island and are prohibited along the Atlantic Ocean beach. An exception to this rule is made for overland vehicles which, at certain times and with prior permission, are allowed on the south end. The **Wildlife Refuge** was purchased by the government in 1943 as a wintering area for migratory fowl, using revenues from the sales of Duck Stamps. Today, it is home to over 300 species of birds, and one of the highlights of the area is the fall migration. Both the Assateague Island National Seashore and the Chincoteague National Wildlife Refuge offer activities ranging from guided walks and evening campfires to presentations in the auditorium. Information on these is available at either the **Refuge Visitor Center** or **Tom's Cove Visitor Center**. Behind the dunes, the island's forests and marshes are home to whitetail deer, the small Sika deer, and even Oriental elk. Not to be forgotten are the wild ponies. And they **are** wild. Appearances can be deceptive! Observe them strictly from a distance as they are prone to unpredictable behaviour, and do not feed or pet them under any circumstances.

By now, you might be ready for an afternoon on the beach. And what a beach it is: 10 miles and totally unspoiled. However, the wildest and emptiest areas are only accessible by foot.

Outdoor activity and fresh sea air normally leave you with a ravenous appetite. Luckily, there is no shortage of restaurants in Chincoteague. None, however, is more romantic than **a j's... on the creek**, located at 6585 Maddox Boulevard, (804) 336-5888. Here you may reserve one special table tucked in a secluded corner of the dining room. A lace curtain hangs over the front and may be drawn for extra privacy. If you desire, owner April Stillson will decorate the table with hearts and cupids, a special cake, a favorite floral bouquet, or whatever else you specify. The menu is romantic, too; plenty of fish, oysters and clams (remember that old Chincoteague saying!) In summertime, this restaurant offers a special "Potpourri Salad," featuring home-grown herbs and edible flowers. Your romance should certainly bloom here!

Chincoteague and Assateague host numerous special events throughout the year. The aforementioned **Decoy and Art Festival** and **Spring Craft Show are both held at Easter. The Chincoteague Island Shrimp & Beef Fest** is in early June. July is perhaps the busiest month, with the **Annual Chapter of Deborah Craft Festival**, the **Old Fashioned Fireworks Display** on July 4th, and the **Annual Chincoteague Firemen's Carnival** running throughout the entire month and culminating with the Pony Penning. The **Annual Chincoteague Oyster Festival** comes in October and November, welcoming both **Assateague Island Waterfowl Week** and the **Annual Chapter of Deborah Waterfowl Show**. Finally, for the child in everyone, an **Old Fashioned Christmas Parade** is held on the first Saturday evening in December.

Northern Virginia

Fredericksburg
Where the Battles are Civil & Surrender is Sweet

*T*wenty-five years ago this town was the last place one would have considered for a romantic weekend. Although we came with low expectations, what we discovered was a delightful surprise. Sitting just to the east of Interstate 95 — almost halfway between Washington D.C. and Richmond — Fredericksburg has capitalized on its history, encouraging the spread of antique and theme shops, restaurants and cafés, bed and breakfasts and inns. In the process, it has acquired a charming, low-key atmosphere.

There are a number of noteworthy hotels in and around Fredericksburg. Flexibility may be necessary, however, as most have a limited number of rooms. We would recommend one of the following:

In the very center of town, at 711 Caroline Street opposite the visitors' center, is an imposing brick building that fronts directly on the sidewalk. **The Richard Johnston Inn** was constructed towards the end of the 18th century and became home to Fredericksburg's mayor from March 1809 to March 1810. Susan Thrush is the proprietor. She has ensured that the seven bedrooms, two suites and public rooms — each decorated with antiques and reproductions — retain the character of the age while providing all of the modern amenities. Each morning, guests are lured to the large Federal-style dining room by the appetizing aroma of freshly baked breads and muffins. These are served on tables laid with fine period china, silver and linens. Since the inn is actually a bed and breakfast, no other meals are available. Prices range from $90 to $130, according to the room. Included in the tariff is the convenience of off-street parking, but neither pets nor smoking are permitted. Reservations may be made by calling (540) 899-7606.

A half-mile or so away, Alice Rawlings owns and operates the more modern **Kenmore Inn.** Located at 1200 Princess Anne Street, telephone (540) 371-7622 or (800) 437-7622 and fax (540) 371-5480, this is a lovely, warm building whose owner prides herself on maximizing her guests' enjoyment during any season. There is an inviting porch and garden for relaxing during the warmer months and hot mulled cider to enjoy before a crackling fire when winter winds are howling. Inside there is a dining room with meals prepared by a master chef. There is also a pub named "Redcoats and Bluenotes," where jazz and blues are performed on the weekends. Four rooms in the old section of the building feature working fireplaces and are available at $125 per night. The charge for the eight other rooms is $95. All of the rooms are exceptionally well-appointed and feature a welcoming decanter of sherry. While staying either here or at the Richard Johnson, you can leave your car at home and travel by train; the Amtrak station is just two blocks from the visitors' center.

There are two other establishments worth mentioning – one to the north and one to the south. Both are only a short drive from town.

To the north is **The Renaissance Manor Bed & Breakfast Country Inn and Art Gallery.** Located at 2247 Courthouse Road in Stafford, this may be reached by taking Exit 140 off I-95 at Stafford and travelling four miles due east on Courthouse Road/Route 630. Though in a rural spot, it's impossible to miss. If the white fence and windmill aren't obvious enough, the house will be. It is designed and decorated to resemble George Washington's Mount Vernon, itself located just 20 miles north. Although recently constructed, its high ceilings, oak floors and fireplaces recall an age of gracious southern hospitality. It even features a rear portico and formal gardens with a gazebo. The reference to the Renaissance is there for a reason. Viewing the founding of America as the crowning achievement of the Renaissance, innkeepers Deneen Bernard and JoAnn Houser have made their establishment a cultural retreat. In fact, the home's centerpiece is a gathering place featuring a library of classical literature and music. Each guest room is furnished with exquisite period pieces and interesting collectibles. The rooms bear the names of such figures such as William Shakespeare, Wolfgang Mozart, Thomas Paine, and George and Martha Washington. The display of original works by local artists provides an ever-changing decor throughout the inn. It also affords guests the opportunity to begin – or add to – their own private collections. For $45 per hour, with advance notice, you can have a masseur/masseuse come to your room for a relaxing hour-long massage. Prices range from $65 for a room with a double bed and private bath to $125 for a room with a king-sized four-poster bed and private jacuzzi. The tariff includes breakfast and afternoon tea, either of which you may take in the garden. For reservations, call or fax (540) 720-3785, or (800) 720-3784.

Almost the same distance (14 miles) from Fredericksburg – but this time to the south – is one of the most unusual places we have ever seen. **Roxbury Mill Bed & Breakfast** is rather difficult to find, but don't let that put you off. Take the Thornburg exit off I-95 (the second one south of Fredericksburg), and turn right onto Route 606. Travel a quarter-mile to the light at the junction with Route 1, and take another right. Immediately turn right again onto Route 632 (Roxbury Mill Road) and continue one mile to the bridge. The mill is at number 6908 on the left. Make sure you reserve well in advance by calling Joyce Ackerman at (540) 582-6611. There is only one room, but what a room!

Roxbury Mill was built as a working mill for Roxbury Plantation in the beginning of the 18th century. It was surrounded by 2,000 acres of land running from the Po to the Ni Rivers, originally granted to Beverly Standard by the King of England. The Standard family was prominent in the area and played an important part in its early history. Many historic relics discovered on the property are on display in the mill, which was in operation as recently as the late 1950s. The building itself is quaint, but the location is spectacular. There is no better vantage point from which to appreciate this than the 900-square-foot master suite with its wide pine floors, exposed beams and 18th-century walnut bed. A picture window overlooks the river, but it is the private deck – extending directly over the dam and millpond – that is the centerpiece. What could be more romantic than sharing a glass of champagne while watching the herons waiting for their next meal and the turtles sunning themselves on the dam? (You'll also be serenaded by an orchestra of frogs, cicadas, crickets and song birds.) At night, fall asleep to the lullaby of the rushing water cascading over the millrace. Also included is a champagne and hors d'oeuvres reception, snacks, and a rose on your pillow. Plus breakfast – or brunch if you prefer – featuring traditional Colonial fare prepared from the original family's recipes. The total cost: $150 a night.

Where you eat on the first night depends on where you choose to stay, and the time of your arrival. As related earlier, the Richard Johnston doesn't offer dinner service, but if you check in too late to take advantage of the many fine local restaurants – or if you are just in the mood for a private evening in your room – Susan will arrange to have a food basket and wine waiting for you. The Kenmore's dining room serves until 9:30 p.m., while hot plates are available in the pub until 10:30 p.m. Those staying at the Renaissance should take into account its more remote location. Either eat prior to arrival or pack a basket of favorite treats, tucking in a pair of candlesticks and linens for a romantic picnic. If you're a guest at the Mill, don't even consider eating anywhere else. With advance notice, Joyce will delight your palates with a delicious meal served in your choice of location: the dining room, the patio, or your own private deck. She also packs a delightful "gourmet" picnic basket.

Before exploring Fredericksburg, make a stop at the visitors' center, 706 Caroline Street, telephone (540)

373-1776 or (800) 678-4748. Hours are 9 a.m. to 5 p.m. daily, with the closing extended until 7 p.m. between June 15 and Labor Day. In addition to the helpful staff with their maps, brochures and hints, there is a 12-minute slide presentation, which gives an overview of its history and orients the visitor to the 29-point historic tour.

You will learn that Fredericksburg was founded in 1728 as a tobacco trading post. It achieved prominence because of its location just below the fall line of the Rappahannock, the furthest point upriver that ocean-going vessels could then travel. It quickly became a major trading center and, by 1835, boasted five churches, 14 schools, four taverns and 97 stores. This legacy is evident today in the 40-block National Historic District, which has more than 350 houses and buildings dating prior to the 1870s.

The city was the boyhood home of George Washington and the homes of his family members are still standing, despite the ravages of the Civil War. At 1200 Charles Street is the **Mary Washington House**, which Washington built for his mother in 1772, and to which he returned for his mother's blessing prior to his 1789 inauguration. **The Rising Sun Tavern**, located at 1306 Caroline Street, was built by his brother around 1760 and offers visitors an insight into tavern life of the day. The most spectacular example of period architecture with Washingtonian connections is found at 1201 Washington Avenue, however. Shortly before the American Revolution, Colonel Fielding Lewis began construction of **Kenmore** for his wife Betty, the only sister of George Washington. The latter was a frequent visitor at this magnificent house. Tradition has it that he helped design the elaborate plaster decorations in what are considered three of the most beautiful rooms of the Colonial period. During the Civil War Battle of Fredericksburg, Kenmore was caught between the front lines of the Union and Confederate armies, and was blasted by cannon fire from both. During this and the later Battle of Chancellorsville, it was used as a hospital. In recent years, an unexploded cannonball was discovered wedged between its floors. In 1922 Kenmore became one of the first of the national preservation efforts. Today the mansion houses a modern gallery with rotating exhibits. Visitors are served tea and gingerbread in the kitchen, a tradition which began when Mary Washington was visited by the Marquis de Lafayette.

Because of its strategic location between the capitals of the Union (Washington, D.C.) and the Confederacy (Richmond), Fredericksburg saw intense fighting during the Civil War. No fewer than four major battles were fought locally. Nearly 6,000 acres of land in the Fredericksburg and Spotsylvania National Military Park commemorate these battles, with visitors' centers offering exhibits and audio-visual presentations.

An ideal way to see the town is to take the 75-minute **Trolley Tour**. This departs conveniently from the visitors' center at 9:30 a.m., 11:30 a.m. and 2 p.m. on Saturdays; and 1:30 p.m. and 3:30 p.m. on Sundays. It offers an informative commentary on 35 points of interest. Alternatively, join one of the Living History Company's actor historians and step back in time on a **Living History Walking Tour**. Jane Houlson Beale and her friends make the passing traffic disappear as they bring to life the city's rich past. The tours last approximately 90 minutes and leave the visitors' center at 10 a.m., 1 p.m., 4 p.m. and 7 p.m., Monday through Saturday. Those wishing to take the tour on Sunday may arrange a convenient time by contacting Helen O'Donnell at (540) 899-1776.

Visitors preferring to explore on their own may find one or more of the five walking tour brochures helpful. These focus on the social history, architecture and archaeology of several notable neighborhoods in Fredericksburg. Before setting out, it would be wise to check the ticket pass options from the visitors' center. They offer up to 30% off of individual admission prices. The Hospitality Pass is $16 and covers admission to the seven major historic sites. The Pick Four – no, not a lottery variation – allows you to visit any four of the participating sites for just $11.50.

Although visitors to Fredericksburg cannot escape history, this city has much to offer in other areas as well. A number of antique shops cater to all tastes and budgets. Book shops and an amazingly eclectic array of specialty stores line Caroline Street. The **Made in Virginia Store**, at 807, carries a wide range of uniquely Virginian gifts, including wines, which they will ship to the recipient of your choice. Just up the street at 815 is a gift shop for cat lovers called **The Cats Closet**, and **Irish Eyes**, at 725, sells nothing but Irish memorabilia. The Irish theme is one that's reflected throughout town; it's largely a legacy of the Irish brigades who fought for both sides during the Civil War. If you get tired, there are plenty of interesting cafés and restaurants just waiting to revive you.

In the afternoon, try a change of pace. Cross the river and head to **Ferry Farm**, on Route 3 East at Ferry Road in Falmouth. George Washington called this home from ages six to 20, and it was here that he received his formal education. It was here also, as legend has it, that he chopped down his father's cherry tree and threw a coin across the Rappahannock River to the Fredericksburg shore. This site was later an important artillery base and river crossing point for Federal forces during the Battle of Fredericksburg.

A short drive away (take 17 north to Route 612/Hartwood Road) is the **Hartwood Winery**, which offers tours and tastings.

Although there are many fine restaurants in Fredericksburg, each having its own merits, one in particular has captured our attention time and time again. The **La LaFayette** is located at 623 Caroline Street, telephone (540) 373 6895. It's actually part of The Chimneys, which is generally regarded as one of the town's finest examples of Georgian architecture. Erected around 1769, it remained a private home until 1967, when the Historic Fredericksburg Foundation acquired it to house their headquarters. It was recently purchased, restored and converted into a restaurant by a local businessman. The building's exterior has undergone numerous changes over the years but the interior retains much of its original character. The elegant drawing room – lavishly trimmed in the ornate late Georgian style – remains virtually unaltered. Original wide plank flooring may be seen here in both the main hall and the bar. The latter, which was the original dining room, features a cage-style bar with an exposed portion of interior wall that reveals heavy beam construction and unusual brickwork.

The emphasis is French, with recipes enhanced by the freshest Virginia ingredients. Plan to have a late dinner and, before eating, treat your partner to a real surprise. Call Helen O'Donnell in advance at (540) 899-1776 to arrange a personal romantic tour of Old Towne Fredericksburg. For $20 per couple, you will be met on the steps of La LaFayette by a guide in period costume who will show you the sights and recount the most romantic stories the town has to offer. The tour ends back at the restaurant, where your reservation will have already been made. Here you will be presented with a tiny pewter pin and a tin heart as a remembrance of your special weekend. You will have signed an "I love you" card beforehand to give during the dinner. But don't stop there. Call ahead to **Jan William's Florals**, (540) 373-8826, and arrange for a dozen red roses to be on the table. For those who prefer an "after dinner" surprise, Jan can arrange to deliver flowers to your hotel room.

Sundays should be days of leisure, especially on a romantic weekend break. So no rushing around! Call Haley James, (540) 752-9379, who will meet you at your hotel at 10:30 a.m. in her **horse-drawn carriage.** What follows is a genteel, narrated 45-minute town tour. During the summer months, disembark at the city dock around 11:30 a.m. in time to board the paddle wheeler, *The City of Fredericksburg.* Here you can enjoy lunch while cruising the Rappahannock River. Reservations must be made in advance through Fredericksburg Cruises by telephoning either (804) 453-BOAT (2628) or (800) 598-BOAT (2628). Dinner cruises, which are offered on Friday and Saturday evenings, are an interesting alternative to in-town dining.

By this time you'll be "walking on air," so try matching your altitude to your attitude. Schedule a session with **Dettinger Aviation**, (540) 371-2563, located at the airport just four miles southeast of town on Route 17. Flights will be tailored to your preferences, with night flights a particularly romantic option. This will give you a chance to see things from a different perspective; it also offers an ideal opportunity to take unusual photographic souvenirs of your weekend.

Speaking of photographs, men can arrange a sitting for their ladies on Saturday afternoon at **Bill Buttram's Studio**, (540) 786-7000. In professional Hollywood style, they will arrange her hair and apply make-up, then take either "head and shoulders" or "boudoir" shots. Ladies, if your man is adventurous, make him an appointment as well.

Alexandria
George Washington Slept Near

There is a town within sight of the nation's capital that most everyone has heard of, yet only a few know about. Though located in the shadow of Washington D.C., Alexandria is certainly not overshadowed by it.

This town gets its name from the Scotsman who purchased this land in 1669 for 6,000 pounds of tobacco. The Virginia Assembly established Alexandria in 1749 and, in July of that year, lots were auctioned off from the town square. The surveying was done by John West, Jr., a descendant of one of the original landowners. Legend has it that he was assisted by a 17-year old George Washington. The streets – many of them named in honor of prominent people – were laid out in a north/south pattern. One, Oronoco, was named for the variety of tobacco transported to the town's first warehouse, located at the bottom of that street.

Alexandria's prime location accounted for its rapid growth into a major commercial center. Trade was mainly in tobacco which, under British rule, was the sole product the colonies were allowed to export to England. By the Revolutionary War, it was one of the main colonial trading centers and ports, as well as an important social meeting place. In 1755, General Braddock made his headquarters here, occupying the Carlyle house while planning his campaigns against the French. George Washington – whose major residence was just nine miles away – maintained a town house here. He also served as a trustee of the town and as Worshipful Master of Masonic Lodge No. 22.

After the hard war years, prosperity not only returned to Alexandria but greatly increased. The new-found freedom brought the opening of trade routes to the West Indies, Spain, Portugal, Holland, Italy, and, of course, England. The ensuing decline in the wheat and tobacco trade was balanced by an increase in the export of fish and slaves. Consequently, the largest slave trading company in the United States made its headquarters within the town's boundaries. Ironically enough, this situation also gave rise to the establishment of several "free black" communities in Alexandria; their citizens were primarily artisans, businessmen, and churchgoers.

In 1810, Revolutionary War general "Light Horse Harry" Lee moved to town. His son, Robert E. Lee – later the commanding general of the Confederate forces during the Civil War – lived here prior to attending West Point. The commercial gains of the previous years were nullified during the Civil War; Alexandria was occupied by the Federal forces and used as a base for their operations in Northern Virginia. Following the war, the town rebounded once again and the 1870s and 1880s saw considerable economic growth, with the emergence of an urbanized town.

Many historic districts benefited from preservation and urban renewal projects begun in the 1960s. Alexandria's most successful efforts are wonderfully reflected in the Old Town Historic District. Antique shops, specialty stores and boutiques abound, and there are an incredible number of restaurants featuring a wide variety of ethnic foods. This mixture makes Alexandria a wonderful place to go for a relaxing romantic break.

There is no shortage of accommodations here. But one hotel is so elegant and unique that discerning visitors will probably flock to it. The **Morrison House** is located at 116 South Alfred Street, half-way between the river and the Amtrak and Metro stations and only two blocks from Washington Street (the main north/south thoroughfare linking Alexandria to D.C. and Interstate 95). At first glance, you will sense that this hotel is special. Guests enter this 18th-century-styled manor house through an ornate wrought iron fence that stands guard over a brick garden and fountain. It is flanked on either side by elegant curving staircases leading to a porticoed semi-circular entrance. Within moments the well-trained staff will unload your belongings, park your car, and escort you to the reception desk. The service is as uncommon in scope and style as the character and understated luxury of the establishment itself. It doesn't take too long to understand how the Morrison House has earned AAA's Four-Diamond and Mobil's Four-Star awards for six consecutive years, In 1990, it was even named "Best Inn of the Year" by travel writers in a national contest.

Though no two of the 45 rooms are exactly alike, they are all enhanced by fine Federal period reproductions. These include a mahogany four-poster bed, brass chandeliers, a decorative fireplace, and an Italian marble bath. The bathroom features a lighted cosmetic mirror and is stocked with imported terry robes and oversized towels. You will also find two telephones, individual climate control, AM/FM radio, and color cable TV with remote control. This mix of old and new is deliberate, but illusory. The Morrison House was convincingly copied from a grand manor of the Federal period (1790-1820), but was in fact built from scratch in 1985.

The public rooms are of the same style – comfortable yet unpretentious. There are 24-hour butler, concierge, room and valet services with health club privileges offered as well. Retire to a neatly turned-down bed with chocolates on your pillow and wake in the morning to find your freshly shined shoes and a newspaper outside your door. Afternoon tea is served from 3 p.m. to 5 p.m. in the parlor. You may dine on-site in the Elysium, a recipient of the AAA's Four-Diamond award. This restaurant features Mediterranean cuisine served in your choice of the casual, club-like Grill and Piano bar, or the elegant dining room, which is ideal for an intimate dinner.

However, truly great hotels are judged by more than their facilities and services; it is an attentive and friendly staff that make the difference, and this is where the Morrison House really shines. They employ people who speak Spanish, French, German, Chinese, Japanese and Farsi. The deluxe rooms normally rent for $240 a night, but be sure to inquire about the special promotions offered throughout the year. Maybe you'll opt for the Romantic Escape Package. For $250 a night, this includes champagne served with luscious chocolate-dipped strawberries, valet parking, and a Continental breakfast served either in the dining room or your bed. As an interesting aside, during the 1994 World Cup the Italian soccer team chose to stay here when playing in Washington. Needless to say, they occupied the entire hotel! They were no doubt attracted by the Morrison House's romantic European feel and its early American charm. Reservations may be obtained by calling (703) 838-8000 or (800) 367-0800, or by faxing (703) 684-6283.

If you really want to surprise your loved one, call **ROSExpress**, (202) 842-1000, and arrange for them to deliver roses to the room prior to your arrival. Some people may think all roses are the same, but those offered by ROSExpress are truly the finest available. No other floral service offers such a wide range of colors — even lavender, black and a variety of two-tones are available by special advance order. You can also appeal to your partner's sweet tooth with chocolate roses. They come in three flavors: milk, dark, and white chocolate. A delightful treat on their own, they're even more unforgettable when mixed with real roses.

Your first stop in Alexandria should be six blocks down King Street at number 221. This is the Ramsay House, which is home to the **Alexandria Convention & Visitors Bureau**, telephone (703) 838-4200 or (800) 388-9119. It is open from 9 a.m. to 5 p.m. daily. Originally built in 1724 by the first Lord Mayor, William Ramsay, it was restored in 1956 and dedicated as a historic site marking the city's oldest house. When choosing from the many brochures available, be sure to ask for "Alexandria, Virginia" and the "Visitor's Guide." You may also want to purchase a block ticket to the Alexandria Historic Museums. If you intend to drive, request a free 24-hour visitor's parking pass, valid in the two-hour metered parking spaces. A word of caution: driving in Alexandria is not much fun and it's almost impossible to find parking spaces on weekends. The good news is that, because of the small size of the area, you won't need wheels. Leave your car in the car park and set out to enjoy the flavor of this unusual town in the best way possible – on foot.

Using the "Alexandria, Virginia" brochure as a guide, wander around the historical area, which is contained in 80 square blocks. Here you will be struck by the imposing array of disparate buildings. If you begin at the Ramsay House, the Carlyle House will be right next door nestled in its own private gardens. This home was completed in 1753 by the Scottish merchant John Carlyle; at that time, the Potomac River nearly reached to the formal garden in the rear. Across Market Square, which was once used as a parade ground for General Braddock's colonial troops, is Gadsby's Tavern. In the late 1700s, this was regarded as one of the finest inns in America. It was frequented by the ubiquitous George Washington, who met with other patriots and danced here at his annual Birthnight Ball. Three blocks west on Cameron Street is Christ Church, where the Washingtons, Lees, and other notables worshipped and where George Washington purchased a pew. The churchyard was used as the town burying ground until 1815. Just north from these are two totally different houses made famous by the Lees. At 607 Oronoco Street is the brick house that "Light Horse Harry" Lee used as his residence beginning in 1812. Robert E. Lee – the only man offered control of both opposing armies in a war – lived here until 1825. The clapboard Lee-Fendall House, located at 614 Oronoco Street, was built in 1785 and was home to 37 Lees from that time until 1903. On the southern side of the historic area, one finds buildings of even more contrasting styles. The Lyceum and The Athenaeum were constructed in 1839 and 1851, respectively. Their Greek Revival architecture is quite elaborate compared with the Old Presbyterian Meeting House located nearby. The latter was constructed in 1744 by Scotch-Irish pioneers with a simplicity of line reflecting the austerity of those who built it. These are just a few of the more important sites, but wherever you go in Alexandria you can't help but be captivated by the differing characteristics of the buildings surrounding you.

Nine blocks west – on King Street and outside of the historic area – is the towering George Washington Masonic National Memorial, telephone (703) 683-2007. This landmark houses important Washingtonian memorabilia including the family Bible and a clock which supposedly stopped at the time of his death.

For an interesting alternative, see this historic district as its contemporaries did – from a carriage. **Olde Towne Horse and Carriage** will pick you up at the Morrison House for a delightful guided tour. Arrange to begin around the dinner hour and have the carriage transport you in style to the restaurant of your choice. Phone Anne at (703) 765-8976 to make a reservation. Otherwise, you can meet the carriage at one of its regular waterfront stops on the corner of King and Strand Streets.

King Street, the dividing line between north and south Alexandria, runs down to the central portion of the waterfront. Meanwhile, Union Street runs parallel to the Potomac. These streets – with their colorful amalgam of shops and restaurants – is the seat of the action. It seems as if every other place is an eatery of some kind. Whatever you fancy, it's there – from Italian, French and Basque, to Lebanese, Oriental, Irish, Creole, and Mexican. There's even Moroccan and Scottish food, as well as any variety of American options, including McDonald's. So where do you eat? Here, more than most places, you can really indulge your mood of the moment. However, we particularly recommend the following:

 At 219 King Street is the **Two-Nineteen Restaurant.** In this splendid Victorian atmosphere, you may choose from a selection of authentic Creole dishes, with Louisiana and Eastern Shore seafood figuring prominently on the menu. The perfect beverage may be found on their award-winning wine list. Entertainment in the form of jazz is provided nightly. A novel touch is the heated outdoor dining space – quite a treat in the winter. Two-Nineteen is open daily for lunch and dinner; their New

Orleans Sunday Brunch is a delight. To reserve a table, call (703) 549-1141.

At 1 Cameron Street is an airy and colorful building over-looking the river. This is home to the **Chart House Res-taurant**, (703) 684-5080, which features a cocktail lounge, fireplace lounge, oyster bar and outdoor patio. A relaxed, tropical atmosphere prevails in everything from the bright, cheerful decor to the waiters and waitresses dressed in aloha patterns. Even the design of the menu follows this theme. The food is great, as well; there is plenty of choice, plenty of quantity, and plenty of quality. All this – com-bined with a glorious view from the picture windows – makes for a highly enjoyable meal. Just don't order too many of the Chart House Signature Drinks. It's hard to stop if you like rum; sometimes there are three varieties in one of their cocktails! Chart House is open for dinner only from 5 p.m., Monday through Saturday. On Sundays, brunch is served between 11 a.m. and 2:30 p.m., with the dinner menu available after 4 p.m.

For a more unusual culinary experience, make your way to the waterfront and step aboard *The Dandy.* Designed in the tradition of the Parisian restaurant-riverboats, this vessel cruises under the bridges of the capital, offering you a different perspective while eating. The interior is sump-tuously decorated, and the menu selective yet wide-rang-ing. The cruises range from two-and-a-half to three hours, featuring three- , five- , and six-course meals. After dining, you may dance to a variety of music while floating lazily past the illuminated Washington skyline. Morning, mid-afternoon, and midnight cruises are occasionally offered. For information on all the cruise choices, call (703) 683-6090; then call (703) 683-6076 for reservations.

While in the waterfront area, you shouldn't miss the **Tor-pedo Factory.** Masterfully converted from its original purpose in the 1970s and 1980s, it has become the city's leading tourist attraction and is open daily. It now houses the studios of nearly 200 artists and craftsmen; the labora-tory and exhibits of one of the nation's largest and oldest urban archaeology programs; and a food court with numer-ous eateries. These include Radio Free Italy, which serves California-style pizzas baked in a wood-burning oven; and the Torpedo Grille, modeled after a World War II submarine.

There is one additional restaurant just 15 minutes away that no seafood lover should miss. Especially if they love seafood cooked in the Spanish Mediterranean style. From Washington Street, head south onto the Washington Memorial Highway; 6.7 miles after you pass the last traffic signal in Alexandria (one mile north of Mount Vernon), you will arrive at the **Cedar Knoll Inn on the Potomac**. Housed in a quaint 18th-century home perched on the banks of the Potomac, this restaurant offers elegant indoor and outdoor terrace dining with an unparalleled view of the river. What it also has is a Malagueno chef – and no Spanish city is more famous for its seafood than Malaga. If your appetite is whetted by thoughts of authentic Spanish tapas, paella Valenciana, roast duck Sevilla, or zarzuela de mariscos (a kind of shellfish casserole), then this is the place for you. This is – in the true Spanish tradition – a meal to linger over. The inn is open for lunch and dinner daily, with a champagne brunch served on Sunday. To avoid disappointment, call Maitre d' John Reynolds to ensure a reservation. As a special treat, travel to and from the Cedar Knoll in luxury by arranging a limousine through the **Dominion Limousine Service**, (703) 281-1217. Another call to ROSExpress, for a single red rose in the limousine or a dozen on the restaurant table, should really set the mood for the evening.

Mount Vernon, the lovely, historic home of George Washington, is so close that you may decide to schedule a visit. It is open 8 a.m. to 5 p.m. from April through August. During the rest of the year, it either opens an hour later or closes an hour earlier, depending on the season. Best to call (703) 780-2000 for exact details. A really delightful time to visit is between December 1 and January 6, when "Holidays at Mount Vernon" are celebrated. You will step back through time into an 18th-century celebration and experience how the Washingtons entertained during this festive season. You may even participate in the gaiety as volunteers in Colonial attire serve traditional cups of hot spiced cider and ginger cookies. George Washington's birthday on February 20 is also a good time to visit.

The views of both Alexandria and Washington are beautiful from the water, so when you return to town, take to the river for a cruise. **The Potomac Riverboat Company**, (703) 548-9000, offers two such choices – a 40-minute narrated "Alexandria By Water Cruise" aboard *The Admiral Tilp*, or a 90-minute "Washington By Water" cruise aboard the *Matthew Hayes*.

There is so much to do and see in Alexandria that you probably won't want to wander into Washington. But if your heart is set on a jaunt to D.C., don't take your car. Travel on the Metro is quick and easy; if you found parking difficult in Alexandria, you should expect much, much worse in the capital.

Alexandria hosts numerous important and interesting events throughout the year. The **Lee Birthday Celebrations** are held the third Sunday in January. During George Washington's Birthday weekend, there are three celebrations: the **George Washington Birthday Banquet and Ball** on Saturday evening, for which reservations are required; the **Revolutionary War Encampment** on Sunday afternoon; and the **George Washington Birthday Parade** on Monday. In March, celebrate **St. Patrick's Day** with the city's annual parade and lively parties in many restaurants. In April, take a **Tour of Homes and Gardens**; on the second weekend in June, enjoy the **Alexandria Red Cross Waterfront Festival**; and on the fourth weekend in July, be either a spectator or a participant in the **Annual Virginia Scottish Games**. On the fourth Saturday of September, there is the **Annual Tour of Homes**. Christmas celebrations include **The Scottish Christmas Walk** on the first Saturday in December, followed on the second weekend by the **Old Town Christmas Candlelight Tour**.

Middleburg

Where the Wine is Fine
& the Hunt is On

*M*iddleburg was named entirely for its location, halfway between Alexandria and Winchester on the 18th-century Ashby Gap trading route (today's Route 50). While Middleburg got its name in a mundane manner, it is anything but.

Located in the very heart of the lush, rolling countryside – with the foothills of the Blue Ridge Mountains slowly rising to the west – this area still retains the aura of the 1700s. Here you will not only feel you've traveled back in time, you'll also think you've been transported to a village in the English countryside. If you time it right, you'll even see fox hunters "riding to hounds." This is "horse country" with a capital 'H.' All around the area, you will notice huge well-kept equestrian estates. You'll also note that many of the village's specialty shops are laden with "horsey" and "hunting" items. And everywhere, the fox motif! Make no mistake, this is an affluent area. However, don't expect people to show it in their dress. In Middleburg, "dressing down" has been elevated to a fine art.

Around 1728, Joseph Chinn – a first cousin to George Washington – built a stone structure and opened in it a tavern called Chinn's Ordinary. He chose for its location a point on the Ashby Gap Road that became known as Chinn's Corner. Much of the surrounding land was a part of Lord Fairfax's huge estates and, in 1747, George Washington passed by on a surveying mission for him. In 1787, Chinn sold 500 acres to Leven Powell, who portioned off 50 acres (including the tavern) and established the town of Middleburg. The Civil War brought fierce fighting around the town, which was frequented by Colonel John Mosby and his famous Rangers. The turn of this century brought with it many affluent northerners in search of sporting venues. Termed "the second Yankee invasion," this migration was responsible for transforming Middleburg into a fox hunting and stee- plechasing center, as well as a hub for thoroughbred blood- stock. These days, the region is considered the nation's "horse and hunt capital," a reputation that attracts a large number of visitors annually.

However, you needn't put foot to stirrup to appreciate the charm of this place. Here – just one hour from downtown Washington, D.C. and 35 minutes from Dulles Interna- tional Airport – you can escape the problems of the late 20th century and savor the atmosphere of a gentler age.

Despite its small size, Middleburg has an interesting range of accomodations. It's appropriate to begin at Chinn's Or- dinary, now known as **The Red Fox Inn** and reputed to be the oldest original inn in America. In 1812 Chinn's Ordinary was enlarged to 35 rooms and was renamed the Beveridge House. During the Civil War, the inn served both as a headquarters and hospital for Confederate troops. It was also a meeting place for General "Jeb" Stuart and Colonel John Mosby and his celebrated Rangers. In fact, the pine service bar in use today, was made from the field operating table of an Army surgeon from General Stuart's cavalry. In 1887, the ordinary became the Middle- burg Inn; it was given its current name in 1937. Over the years, it has remained a popular retreat for Washingtoni- ans escaping the city.

The inn is now spread over three buildings. The Red Fox Inn itself has six rooms, each with either a king or queen- sized canopy bed and private bath. Some of these are two-room suites and some have private fireplaces. All are decorated and furnished in the original style of the period, but with modern amenities such as color TV and direct-dial telephone. Curiously, some have a small bathtub with a hand held shower – and no shower curtain. The tariff ranges between $135 and $150 a night.

The Stray Fox Inn, part of the Red Fox, was built in the early 1800s. It too served as an inn during the 19th cen- tury, its stable boarding change horses for the run to Alexandria. During the Civil War, a badly-aimed cannonball struck its foundation; hence the nickname "Stray Shot." Hand-stenciled floors and walls, along with original fireplaces, give the nine rooms a friendly character. But mind your head, as some of the ceilings are authentically low. The majority of the rooms offer facilities similar to those in the main building. However, two are suites that deserve extra attention. Both have king-sized beds and a lovely view over the gardens. The latter boast an early 18th-century smokehouse that is believed to be one of Middleburg's oldest buildings. One suite has a delightful screened porch, while the other features a piano and separate powder room. Rates for these range from $135 to $225.

Third in the series – and connected to both the Red Fox and Stray Fox by a pergola walkway – is **The McConnell House.** Since this was originally the home of a country doctor, it became known affectionately as the "Pill Box." Extensively renovated in 1985, it now houses five rooms similar to those of its counterparts, with rent varying between $135 and $155 a night.

You won't be short of restaurants here, either; there are seven from which to select. The Red Fox Restaurant offers traditional dishes and a wine list with local vintages. Mosby's Tavern is open daily for lunch and dinner, with brunch on Sunday. The emphasis here is on contemporary American/Mexican dishes in a relaxed environment.

The Red Fox Inn & Mosby's Tavern is the recipient of the AAA Four-Diamond award; the inn is certainly a fascinating place to stay. You may call locally for reservations on (540) 687-6301, from the D.C. area at (540) 478-1808 and outside Virginia on (800) 223-1728. If it is more convenient, fax (540) 687-6187.

If you prefer something a bit smaller and more personal, head down East Washington Street to number 209. This interesting three-story red brick building houses the absolutely charming **Middleburg Country Inn**, (540) 687-6082 or (800) 262-6082 and fax (540) 687-5603. The inn's history traces to Abner Gibson, a lawyer and manufacturer of wagons and wagon wheels who purchased two lots on June 8, 1818 from Burr Powell, son of the town's founder Leven Powell. (The purchase price was $141.52.) It wasn't until 1820 that the west brick portion was constructed. In 1856, John's Parish vestrymen purchased the property to serve as the Episcopal rectory, stipulating that it could only be used "as a place for Public Worship or as a burial place." Perhaps the latter accounts for the "bumps in the night!" Two years later, an east side extension was added to the parsonage. John Parish retained ownership of the structure until 1987. Then it was sold to the present owner, who opened the inn in 1990.

There are just six rooms, some of which have a king or queen-sized bed. Others are bridal suites, featuring jacuzzi tubs. Each of the rooms offers a four-poster canopied bed, a fireplace, cable TV with VCR, private bath and Colonial furnishings. The availability of cordless phones is a nice touch. Enjoy the large outdoor hot tub and complimentary drinks in the parlor. Also included in the $145 – $275 room price is a full country breakfast. You're also entitled to a marvelous five-course dinner served in the Lafayette Dining Room at 7 p.m. When it's time to retire, be warned: authentic to the period, some of the beds are so far above the floor that you must use the wooden steps beside them to climb in. You wouldn't want to forget that in the middle of the night. The Middleburg Country Inn certainly has much to offer and we are sure you will find it a delightful experience.

Those preferring an even more rural environment will find just the place about 12 miles to the west on Route 50. **The 1763 Inn** is located two miles past Trinity Episcopal Church near Upperville. Separating the road from a very large and pretty pond is an old stone house with a rather new wing. Slightly closer to the pond and next to the tennis court is a log cabin. Inside these are 16 rooms finished in a hodgepodge of styles – some German and some French, with a "George Washington" room and even a honeymoon cottage. Canopy beds, fireplaces and whirlpool tubs help to create an atmosphere. The small cocktail lounge is a cozy corner for your favorite tipple; or maybe you'd fancy a drink in the lounge and bar overlooking the 50-acre farm. When you are suitably refreshed, it may be time for a stroll through this tranquil countryside, or possibly some fishing from the small wooden pier. A picnic would be fun, too; but don't share too much of your food with the geese! The building that houses the restaurant was once owned by George Washington and dates from 1763, hence the inn's name. Serving German and American cuisine, it is open from 5 p.m. to 9 p.m Wednesday through Friday; from midday to 9 p.m. on Saturday; and from midday to 8 p.m. on Sunday.

If this entices you, book a room by calling (540) 592-3848 or (800) 669-1763, or fax (540) 592-3114. It will cost between $95 and $175 a night, depending upon which room you choose.

 For details on local events, stop by **The Pink Box** information center in town. They have brochures and fliers on all the happenings and sights in the area. But don't get there early, because it doesn't open until 11 a.m. It's located at 12 North Madison Street, (540) 687-8888, just around the corner from the main entrance to the Red Fox Inn.

Use your extra time to wander behind the Middleburg Country Inn. Here you will find the town cemetery. It is surrounded by an iron railing that follows the undulating contours of the land and stands guard over headstones tracing the history of this intriguing town. Not everyone's cup of tea, admittedly; but it is about the closest in this country to an authentic English churchyard.

Back at the Pink Box, get a copy of the town map. This will give you a good idea of Leven Powell's original layout. Note also the street names, many of which honor his Federalist friends. The brochure entitled "A Walk With History – 1787 to 1987" was published to celebrate the Middleburg Bicentennial and is well worth the $1 price. It certainly lives up to its title, giving a background on the area, a guided tour, an account of the historic buildings, a helpful street plan, and a brief list of nearby attractions. You won't find many of the latter. But that is not the reason one visits Middleburg. If you and your partner prefer a fast-paced lifestyle, this is not the town for you. If, on the other hand, you simply want to relax, enjoy one another's others company and drink in the enchantingly anachronistic ambiance, then put this town at the top of your list.

If you have your heart set on attending the area's many steeplechase and point-to-point races, then spring and fall are the best times to visit. It is during these seasons that Middleburg – as well as nearby towns such as Upperville, The Plains, Leesburg and Warrenton – come into their own. If you would like to learn more about thoroughbred horses, plan to attend the popular **Hunt Country Stable Tour** in May. In June comes the gala **Upperville Colt & Horse Show,** the oldest competition of its kind in America. In December you might enjoy the **Middleburg Hunt Country Christmas Tour**. Should you visit between late May and early fall, take a peek into another totally different lifestyle. **The Middleburg Polo Club** plays in the Virginia Polo League every Sunday at Kent Field (off Route 50 west of town). Here, for just $5, you may join in the fun of tailgate parties and picnics while cheering on a likely team.

There is one place nearby that merits inclusion in your itinerary. Drive east on Route 50 and turn north (left) onto Route 15 at Gilbert's Corner. After a short while, you will see signs for **Oatlands**, (540) 777-3174. This large Greek Revival mansion was built in 1803 by George Carter, the great-grandson of Robert "King" Carter. Soon afterwards, Oatlands became a 3,000-acre working plantation, with its own gristmill, brick manufactory, blacksmith shop, store, school and church. Oatlands' fortunes declined after the Civil War and, in 1897, the Carters were forced to sell the plantation. New owner Stilson Hutchins, a founder of *The Washington Post*, never resided on the property. In 1903, he sold it to Edith Morton and her husband, William Corcoran Eustis, each of whom had come from a philanthropic Washington family. They initiated a comprehensive restoration of Oatlands, decorating the interior with French and English antiques and restoring the four-acre walled garden to its former splendor. At the same time, they indulged in their love for fox hunting and the breeding of champion Old English sheepdogs. During the 1920s and 30s Oatlands became a weekend retreat for their prominent and wealthy friends. Eustis died in 1921; his wife died in 1964. One year later, the couple's daughters gave Oatlands in its entirety – house, furnishings and 261-acre estate – to the National Trust for Historic Preservation. In 1972 it was designated a National Historic Landmark.

You may tour Oatlands between the hours of 10:30 a.m. and 4:30 p.m. Tuesday through Saturday or from 1 p.m. to 4:30 p.m. on Sundays, from April through December only. Throughout this period there are numerous special events here including the Loudoun Hunt Point-to-Point in April, the Sheep Dog Trials in May, the Celtic Festival in June, Civil War reenactments during the summer, Draft Horse and Mule Day in September, and special "Christmas at Oatlands" tours during November and December.

This area is also famed for its wineries, and there are two interesting ones close to town. To the east on Route 50 is the **Swedenburg Estate Vineyard**, (540) 687-5219. Located on the Valley View Farm, this was originally a part of a royal grant which Colonial-era owner Bryan Fairfax leased out for £4 annually. The stipulation was made that the lessee build "a dwelling house 20 feet long and 16 feet wide and other such houses as his ways of husbandry require." That original house is now a part of the main home. This land has supported a working farm for over 200 years. Now these largely treeless rolling hills are home to both premium vinifera grapes and registered Angus cattle. Before a tour of the winery – which will be followed by tastings – ask to see their prize bulls.

Before visiting the other winery, stop in town to pick up your favorite picnic fare. The local Safeway is a special treat. Don't be fooled by its rather run-down appearance; a quick tally of the wine shelves will reveal a selection of vintage ports and fine sherries rivaling that of any specialty store. You might also stop by The Upper Crust – an excellent bakery next to the Safeway – and the Black Walnut gourmet shop a few blocks east.

Beginning at the town's main intersection (the only one with a traffic light), head south down the hill. After two-and-a-half miles, turn right onto Route 628, a dirt road known as Logan's Mill Road. Just when you are convinced you are lost, you will see a sign to **Meredyth Vineyards**, telephone (540) 687-6277. The countryside here is heavily wooded and the winery more rustic than Swedenburg. Select your favorite wine at the tasting, buy a bottle to add to your other goodies. You have your choice of two picnic areas; the larger one is close to the winery, while the other, more secluded one is next to the ruins of a house you probably noticed earlier. You will be set to enjoy a beautiful afternoon with good food, fine wine and tasty company! Don't get too carried away, however. Once, while spraying the vines, owner Archie M. Smith inadvertently soaked a couple who were too preoccupied to hear him coming.

Once you have spent some time driving through the area, you are bound to be curious about the houses at the ends of those long driveways. Hidden from the road, they tease the imagination. There is a way to obtain an unobstructed view – not just of the estates, but of the lovely scenery and the nearby mountains as well. Robert Thomas, the pilot/owner of **Balloons Unlimited**, (540) 281-3000, will whisk you into the clear blue yonder on your choice of morning or evening flights. The rate is a reasonable $125 per person. Follow directions carefully, however, when traveling to the takeoff site. Follow Route 50 west until you see a sign on the right for Purcellville (Route 611, which is also Ford Road). Here you take a right. Continue on for 6.2 miles and, after passing a sign on the right for "Portadown," take the next left onto Route 630, a dirt route known as Unison Road. After another half-mile or so, you'll go around a sharp bend to the left. Take the next driveway to the right, which is across from a mailbox, and look for the sign "Corgi Crossing." Complicated, yes, but well worth the effort.

Other interesting events in this area include: **A Taste of Middleburg Wine Festival** in May, the **Middleburg Garden Tour** in June and the **Hidden Horse Day Townwide Celebration** in July. In October there is **October Wine Month** and the Christmas Season brings forth **Christmas in Middleburg,** the **Middleburg Candlelight House Tour** and the **Annual Christmas Shop**.

Virginia's Shenandoah Valley

Bayse
Alpine Magic is Nearer Than You Think

*W*ay up in the northwest corner of Virginia, nestled up against the West Virginia border, is an area that resembles the foothills of the Alps in either Switzerland or France. Naturally, there is a ski resort here but, regardless of the season, there are activities galore. Even if you just want to relax, you'll find the scenery absolutely enchanting. There are several of these all-season resorts in Virginia. Although this is one of the oldest, it is probably also the least known – perhaps because of its remote location. Whatever the reason, this works in its favor. After all, one of the delights of coming here is getting away from the crowds.

The most direct route to **Bryce Mountain** is Interstate 81 to Exit 273, turning east off the ramp, south on to Route 1, and then west onto Route 263. Soon the road will begin to climb. After 10 miles of picturesque scenery, you will suddenly face a panoramic view looking down into a beautiful valley. This is home to the small town of Bayse, and to the resort still out of sight.

Before leaving this marvelous overlook, make a mental note to come back up here one evening to the very unusual **Alpine View Restaurant at Sky Chalet Country Inn**. Disregarding the chalets, which are somewhat rustic, the restaurant and pub have all the character you would expect if you were actually in the Alps. Charles Blough, a former executive, recognized the potential and has developed a great combination of pub and restaurant. The Super Lick Pub, which opens at 4 p.m. on weekdays and at 1 p.m. on Saturday and Sunday, has the largest selection of draft beers in Shenandoah County. (That's including its own "Alpine Ale.") There are always customers involved in one pub game or another, and entertainment is offered most nights of the week. The restaurant, phone (540) 856-2555, specializes in European cuisine and offers a number of fine European wines. Be sure to time your visit so you can share a glass of wine on the terrace while watching a glorious sunset over the valley! Reservations are recommended.

Continue down to the valley floor and make a sharp right on to Route 836. Press on into this lovely, tight valley. As you pass the front nine holes of the golf course, the **Bryce Resort Lodge** is to your right, at the base of the ski slopes. You will see, too, that there is a much easier way of getting here – if you have your own plane. Just fly it straight in and land at the Sky Bryce Airport. Whatever the season, you'll not be disappointed, nor short of things to keep you busy.

In winter, Bryce is a wonderland. There are six slopes (rated by ability) for both skiers and snowboarders. These cover a total of 25 acres, with the longest being a 3,000-foot, intermediate run. There are also two teaching and beginner areas. Slopes are served by two double chairs and two surface lifts which have a combined uphill capacity of 2,500 skiers per hour. Tickets are sold on a first-come, first-served basis. The usual array of all-day, extended day, half-day, twilight and night sessions are offered and a large supply of high-quality rental equipment is available. If you want instruction, then the Horst Locher Ski School offers your choice of either group or private lessons. Non-skiers, or those needing a break, may spectate from either The Hearthside Restaurant or The Copper Kettle Lounge, located in the lodge.

Perhaps you enjoy ski racing. If so, you'll be interested to know that Bryce has developed a special racing program aimed towards the USSA-sanctioned races. On weekends, the National Standard race offers recreational skiers the chance to test their abilities against the pros in a race handicapped by age and sex. The 1995 season's unusually warm and wet weather brought many ski resorts to a close; but not Bryce. The resort's 25 HKD Tower Snowguns – which stand 30 feet tall and produce up to 10 times the amount of snow nightly as conventional guns – kept the slopes open. For an update on the ski conditions before leaving home, call (800) 821-1444.

At other times of year, there are a myriad of activities from which to choose. For golfers there is a par-71, 18-hole championship course of 6,260 yards. There are also a driving range and putting green, with professional instruction and club and cart rental offered. If you take it easy in the morning, you may save a little on the green fee. This is reduced after 3 p.m. for the twilight session, and includes a mandatory cart. The pool is open between 10 a.m. and 6 p.m. from Memorial Day weekend to Labor Day. Outdoor tennis is available, with three lighted courts; you'll be charged on a per-hour basis. There are various grass skiing packages, with mountain bikes and roller blades also available. Across Route 263 is the 45-acre man-made Lake Laura. This private undertaking has its own sandy beach, but no life guards. If you feel inclined to take to the water, you have your choice of sailboard, canoe, or paddle wheeler. Nearby are the T. Jay Stables, (540) 856-8100, which offer guided trail and pony rides.

Bryce is a resort with all the ingredients to ensure an unforgettable romantic weekend. You can obtain more information and current prices by calling (540) 856-2121, or faxing (540) 856-8567.

There is one way to get a truly incredible view of this stunning area and the surrounding Appalachian Mountains. Mark Nelson runs the **Virginia Balloon Society**, (540) 856-3337, which offers hot air balloon flights from the airport. So relax and climb into the basket. You'll be whisked upwards on an adventure you will never forget. Take your camera!

You won't find many hotels here, but that doesn't mean there isn't first-class accommodation right in the valley itself. **Chalet High at Bryce Resort**, (800) 848-9858, has luxurious two-bedroom, three-story townhouses right by the golf course. These feature queen-sized and twin beds, a kitchen outfitted with every modern convenience, a TV/VCR system with cable, a working fireplace, and a private jacuzzi tub. The two-night minimum rental is extended to three on holiday weekends, with rates varying from $98 to $138 per night, according to season. Included are two passes to the nearby Creekside Fitness Center, which features an indoor pool, strength and conditioning areas, aerobics, sauna, and jacuzzi. Similar townhouses in a similar location – but with full wood-burning stoves – are available at Stony Court at Bryce Resort. These cost just $99 a night, including access to the fitness centre. Telephone Blue Mountain Realty Inc. at (800) 296-0947 for a reservation or more details.

For properties for rent, both on and off Bryce Resort, contact **Benchmark Realty**, (540) 856-2149 or (800) 296-2149, located just off the airport runway. One-bedroom townhomes rent for as little as $75 per night, condominiums from $95 a night, and a variety of private houses, individual in style and often well-appointed, have tariffs ranging from $275 to $600 for two nights. There is an additional $100 fee for three-night minimum periods.

At nearby Mount Jackson, near the junctions of Interstate 81 with Routes 11 and 263, is a delightful bed and breakfast. The **Widow Kip's Country Inn** is situated on seven rural acres with a 32-foot outdoor pool. It centers around a gem of a house that dates from 1830, as well as two restored cottages. To reach the inn, which is located at 355 Orchard Drive, take Interstate 81 to the Mount Jackson Exit (273), and follow Route 11 south for 1.3 miles. Take a right onto Route 263 and then the second left, after the overpass, onto Route 698. The Widow Kip's is the second house on the left.

Each of the main house's five rooms has its own distinctive charms. The first-floor **Sweet William Room** is furnished with an eight-foot-high Lincoln double bed, an Empire dresser, an armoire, an Oriental rug, bookcases, and a large wing chair. It rents for $65 a night. The **Wildflower Room** boasts a four-poster canopied queen-sized bed, a rocker, an armchair, and mountain views. The **Marigold Room** has a southern exposure overlooking the mountains. It features charming 1920s inlay furniture, with a double bed covered by a homey yo-yo quilt and two comfortable chairs. The **Morning Glory Room** has a hand-carved Victorian queen-sized bed, an Empire dresser, armchairs, and a view overlooking the courtyard. The **Hollyhock Room** overlooks the pool and is furnished with a four-poster canopied double bed and armoire. All rooms have a working wood-burning fireplace. The last four are on the second floor and, with the exception of the Hollyhock (at $65), each rents for $70 per night.

The **Silk Purse,** a restored wash house with a quaint sitting porch, is one of the courtyard cottages. Furnished in the style of the 1920s, it has one bedroom with a double bed, a generously sized bathroom, a sitting room that doubles as a second bedroom, and a full kitchenette. It is furnished with white wicker furniture and offers cable TV – all for $85 a night. The other cottage is a restored hen house. It, too, has a porch, double bed, bath, and cable TV, but is furnished with 1930s furniture. Known as the **Sow's Ear**, it rents for $75. All rates include a full country breakfast, but there's a 4% surcharge if you pay with Mastercard or Visa.

Incidentally, Mount Jackson wasn't always so named. On January 28, 1826 an act of the General Assembly of Virginia changed the name from Mount Pleasant to Mount Jackson in honor of General Andrew "Old Hickory" Jackson. That was a full two years before he was elected president.

Now to the most unusual accommodations, perhaps the most unusual in this guide. They are only a few miles from Bayse, in a tiny hamlet sheltered by trees at the foot of the Great North Mountain. Following Route 263 to its end, you'll find a very curious little mountain village that almost defies description. **Orkney Springs** sprang up during the 18th century, when it was one of the most famous mineral spring resorts (spas) in Virginia. People came from near and far to "take the waters" at seven different kinds of springs. Since the 1920s, it has been a respite of a different kind. The Episcopal Diocese of Virginia purchased The Orkney Springs Hotel – along with the surrounding 950 acres – and transformed it into **Shrine Mont**, a popular church conference and retreat center.

Today the town has fewer than 50 inhabitants. All of its buildings are painted green and white and have tin roofs. Without doubt the old hotel, now listed in the National Register of Historic Places, is the centerpiece. The first part of the present structure – the two-story, 50-room Maryland House – was built in 1850. Legend has it that it served as a place of rest and recuperation for Confederate soldiers during the Civil War. The 96,000-square-foot Virginia House is the main part of the hotel. Built later, in 1873, it underwent a recent restoration in 1987. The four-story white clapboard structure has unusually tall windows, as well as an unsupported – and truly grand – 100-by-50-foot ballroom.

Don't expect telephones or TVs, though; at Shrine Mont, people are more important than things. The hotel does, however, have two pools, four tennis courts, well-maintained recreation fields, campfire rings and scenic hiking trails. You will also find home-style cooking in the Southern tradition. A bell rings to announce the meals, which are served either buffet or family-style in two dining rooms. All this for just $50 per person double-occupancy. But bring cash; no credit cards are accepted.

As befits Shrine Mont's primary purpose, there is a lovely open-air cathedral. The Cathedral Shrine of the Transfiguration was consecrated in 1925. Each of the stones with which it was constructed was pulled by horse or rolled by human hands from the nearby mountains. The baptismal font was originally a dug-out stone used by Indians to grind corn.

The hotel is open between April and October but – with the exception of August, which is reserved for outside guests – those attending the conference center have first choice of the rooms. You may inquire about availability by calling (540) 856-2141.

Every summer this incredible place is the setting for the **Shenandoah Valley Music Festival**. On six selected weekends between Memorial Day and Labor Day, you can hear concerts to suit just about any taste – from symphonic or folk to jazz or big band. But there's more to this than just music. The festival is a real "happening," with no equal in the mid-Atlantic region. So call (800) 459-3396 to inquire about the schedule; that way, you can schedule your trip to Bryce to coincide with the concert of your choice.

You'll also enjoy shopping at the arts and crafts shows and savoring the fare at the old-fashioned ice cream socials. These are held next to the outdoor pavilion and serve both ice cream and homemade cakes. Gates open two hours before performance times, allowing concert-goers time to enjoy a picnic on the lawns or try the country-style buffet dinners at the Orkney Springs Hotel. Since this is a popular event, reservations are essential. They may be made by phoning (540) 856-2141 in advance. What could be more romantic?

Roanoke
Star-Struck & Full of Sparkle

There is a mid-size town with unique origins deep in western Virginia and close to the mountains. Many people wouldn't consider it ideal for a romantic weekend, but they'd be wrong.

This town's history traces to the mid-18th century. It revolves around the salt marshes (salt licks) at the convergence of the Indian and natural animal trails. Originally named Gainsborough, this community – the first white settlement in the area – had grown considerably by 1834. Somewhere in this time frame, it became known as Big Lick. Shortly after this the railroad came by, but bypassed Big Lick. Not to miss an opportunity, the town moved to the railroad and in 1874 was chartered as the Town of Big Lick. The original settlement was renamed Old Lick. When the Shenandoah Valley Railroad arrived seven years later, Big Lick was renamed Roanoke, after the county in which it was located and the river nearby. "Roanoke" was derived from the Indian word "Rawrenock," their name for the shell beads both worn and used in trade. In 1882, Roanoke became a crossroads for what was later the Norfolk and Western Railway. The latter company was responsible for construction of the hugely impressive Queen Anne-style Hotel Roanoke. This hotel epitomized the era of economic and physical growth that led to the town's charter as the City of Roanoke in 1884. Also during this period, a farmer's market was organized and became the focal point of the downtown area. Continued growth made Roanoke the largest city in Virginia west of Richmond, with a population nearing 100,000.

As with similar railroad towns, Roanoke's fortunes slowly declined after World War II. However, a revival had begun by the late 1970s. Now you will find a delightfully sophisticated atmosphere centered around the original farmer's market, now one of the oldest in the nation and still the anchor of downtown commercial activity. This area is home to a delightful array of specialty shops, coffee shops and restaurants. But the real gem is an innovatively restored 1914 warehouse called the **Center in the Square.** This houses five independent cultural organizations and museums; it's also home to more than 20 annual events. The resulting combination makes this Virginia's most successful city center. Even more unusual is the freedom you have to enjoy this central area in relative safety, either day or night. The crime rate is amazingly low; there was only one murder in 1994!

Before exploring Roanoke, it is best to arrange your accomodations. Although there are numerous options in the area, I would recommend you consider one of the following.

By the 1970s, the aforementioned **Hotel Roanoke** had fallen into disrepair, its huge Tudor facade the sole reminder of its glory days. Once frequented by the likes of John D. Rockefeller, Amelia Earhart, General Eisenhower and Elvis Presley, it closed in 1981 and was subsequently donated to the Virginia Tech Real Estate Foundation. In 1991 a commission was established to finance and construct an adjacent conference center. A year later, the Renew Roanoke Foundation was founded to raise the money to complete the restoration of the hotel itself. The Hotel Roanoke reopened in 1995 under the management of the Doubletree Hotels Corporation. The facade – still the most impressive in the city – has been retained, and efforts were made to recreate the original atmosphere of the public rooms. Of course, each of the 332 rooms is totally new, redecorated and refurnished. In their words, this hotel and convention center was "inspired by the past but created for the future." Rates run $79-$149 for a room (double occupancy) and $99-$450 for a suite. For futher information, call (540) 985-5900 or fax (540) 345-2890.

In 1925, a smaller yet no less grand hotel opened at 617 Jefferson Street. The 11-story **Patrick Henry** featured a massive lobby with elaborate iron railings, ornate carvings embracing the ceiling and walls, and brilliant chandeliers suspended from a 30-foot ceiling. No expense was spared on the guest rooms, either. Over the years, the Patrick Henry earned a reputation as a favored meeting place and a truly grand hotel. However, like the Hotel Roanoke and the city itself, the Patrick Henry fell into decline. By the late 1970s, it was a parody of its former elegance. Taken over by the Radisson Group, it has been restored to its former splendor. Today, it is the only hotel in Roanoke to be designated a Virginia Historic Landmark and placed on the National Register of Historic Places. (The Hotel Roanoke was in the process of applying at the time of this writing.) The Patrick Henry's 128 rooms are large – over twice the size of a typical hotel room – and range $79-$150 per night. The hotel's "Romantic Getaway Package" includes a suite for one night with a complimentary bottle of champagne, a fruit and cheese tray, and breakfast the next morning. The discerning will opt for the very special Governor's Suite. Deliberately left with all of the original-style furnishings, it boasts one unusual feature – its own private sauna. Just think about the romantic opportunities! This rents for $250 a night. To make a reservation, either call the Radisson worldwide toll free number, (800) 333-3333, or call the hotel directly at (540) 345-8811, or fax (540) 342-9908.

 For something smaller and more personal, the **Mary Bladon House** offers an ideal alternative. A Victorian bed and breakfast inn at 381 Washington Avenue, S.W., telephone (540) 344-5361, it is located just a few minutes from downtown in the **Old Southwest** historic district. This area traces to the late 18th century, when King George III granted 150 acres to James Alexander. Until the decline of the post-World War II era, it was considered the city's premiere neighborhood. In the late 70s and early 80s – during the nationwide trend to revitalize historic areas – the district was rediscovered. With help from the local government and private institutions, people began to relocate there in an effort to restore the area. Their success was recognized in 1985, when "Old Southwest" was officially listed in The Virginia Landmarks Register and The National Register of Historic Places. In this atmosphere, the Mary Bladon House seems right at home.

Bill and Sheri Bestpitch are the innkeepers here. They offer two double rooms, each with a private bath; or a two-room suite with a double bed, a queen bed and a private bath. All rent for the same price of $80 per night. Both these and the public rooms are furnished with Victorian antiques. While there, don't miss the opportunity to cuddle on the old-fashioned swing, which hangs from the wrap-around porch. (There's no better time than while waiting for your hearty breakfast or afternoon refreshments.) Afterwards, walk that off with a stroll around "Old Southwest." Before beginning your explorations, obtain the inn's most informative brochure on the downtown area.

Add a little spice to your trip by calling ahead to **Love Baskets Ltd.**, at (540) 343-3996. Elaine Bond will ensure that roses are waiting in your room and/or on your restaurant table; these say "I love you" as only flowers can. Perhaps you will want a "Romantic Weekend Basket" as well. These are designed with fun in mind. They include a bottle of champagne, a rose "sculpted" from a pair of bikini underwear for her, tiger briefs for the male of the species, and flavored body paint! Elaine can also supply baskets stocked with edible goodies, plus beer and wine (she specializes in the Virginia varieties). If you're headed out to the mountains, be sure to take along her "Blue Ridge Parkway Picnic Basket."

No matter what time you arrive, it will be obvious why Roanoke is called "the Star City." A huge man-made star presides over the city, which is located in the valley that the local Indians called Shenandoah ("daughter of the stars"). Set 1,045 feet up on top of Mill Mountain – one of the parallel ridges of the Allegheny Mountains – the star is 88½ feet high and weighs 10,000 pounds. It's constructed of over 2,000 feet of neon tubing and consumes 17,500 watts of energy. Erected in 1949, it has been illuminated in several different color combinations until midnight every night since. Not surprisingly, it serves as a symbol of Roanoke's progressive spirit.

When your thoughts turn to dinner, there are over 60 different restaurants from which to choose. You should definitely visit **Hunter's Grille, The Prime Steak House**, adjacent to and run in conjunction with the Patrick Henry Hotel. The "prime" in its name is there for a reason. It is the only restaurant in the area that has fresh prime grade aged steaks flown in daily from Wisconsin. These should satisfy even the most discriminating palate. Fish connoisseurs, take note: fresh swordfish is flown in daily as well. You do you pay a price for what you get, but shouldn't you splurge on your special weekend? Telephone (540) 342-7552 to secure your reservation.

In the heart of the market area, at 312 Market Street, is a very different style of restaurant. **Carlos Brazilian International Cuisine**, (540) 345-7661, certainly lives up to its name, specializing in French, Italian and Spanish – as well as Brazilian – food. If you go on Saturdays you are in for a special treat; that's when they serve the traditional

Brazilian dish, feijoada. There are currently 13 restaurants in Virginia owned by Brazilians, many of them in the southwest. Even more surprisingly, they all have their "family roots" in a restaurant called Luigi's, which opened in Roanoke in 1978.

Seafood lovers may want to opt for **Awful Arthur's**, located on the other side of the market at 108 Campbell Avenue, S.E., (540) 344-2997. Designed like its other branches around the state, this is open, airy, and quite informal – perhaps a good spot for lunch. The food is wholesome, hearty, and tasty; a neat touch is the roll of paper towels on a wooden holder at each table.

On Saturday, it's time to experience the previously mentioned **Farmer's Market**, a vibrantly colorful scene awhirl with activity. Besides displays of every kind of seasonal produce, there are bright flowers, numerous gift and antique shops, unique boutiques and country stores. The first licenses were issued to 25 hucksters in 1882. The city's charter had formally authorized a municipally owned market and the first permanent building was completed in 1886. The building that presently houses the market dates from 1922. Nearby is the #1 Fire Station. Built in 1907 and still in operation today, it was modeled after Philadelphia's Independence Hall and is now an historic landmark. Since the **Visitors' Bureau** is just around the corner – at 114 Market Street, (540) 342-6025/(800) 635-5535 or fax (540) 342-7119 – this would be a good time to pop in to ask questions or gather brochures. The "Visitors Guide to Downtown Roanoke" and the "Historic Downtown Walking Tour" are most helpful.

A good place to stop and examine the materials you've just collected is the **Mill Mountain Coffee & Tea Café**, located at 112 Campbell Avenue, S.E. They have more varieties of either beverage than you would ordinarily expect and, if it's a hot day, an equally wide selection of Italian sodas. On top of that, the atmosphere is cheerful and relaxing.

Your next stop should be the **Center in the Square** at 1 Market Square, telephone (540) 342-5700. As mentioned, this is home to five organizations. The dramatic spiral staircase is symbolic of how these have come together to provide both residents and visitors alike with a richer cultural experience. On the center's second level is the **Art Museum of Western Virginia**, (540) 342-5760. This features permanent and visiting exhibits in its galleries of 19th- & 20th-century American art. Also featured are prints, regional and decorative ware, Appalachian folk art, a "sculpture court" and a contemporary gallery. Admission is free, and a museum store sells arts and crafts from the southern mountain region. Art lovers will not want to miss **Art by Night** on the first Friday evening of each month. This is a gallery walk held between 6 p.m. and 9 p.m.; it features 11 galleries, museums and restaurants that extend their hours in a special "open house." Further information may be obtained from **Downtown Roanoke Incorporated**, at (540) 342-2028, or from the visitors' bureau. On the center's third level is the **Roanoke Valley History Museum,** (540) 342-5770. This houses permanent exhibits illustrating the history of southwest Virginia from prehistoric times to today. Additionally, there is an unusual exhibition entitled, "To The Rescue." As its name indicates, this details volunteer rescue and emergency medical services. The $2 admission is reasonable enough, and there is a shop run by the museum on the first level. However, most visitors will be more interested in the center's fourth and fifth levels. Here you will find both the **Science Museum of Western Virginia** and the **Hopkins Planetarium**, (540) 342-5710. The museum itself is an absolute delight. The exhibits – many of them interactive – are so intriguing that the $5 admission fee seems merely nominal. There are also live animal programs; national traveling exhibits; and, among the hands-on exhibits, a Chesapeake Bay Touch Tank. Though many of these may have been designed for children, they appeal to "children" of all ages. I doubt whether there is anyone who won't be fascinated by the **Reflections** exhibit. Using a clever combination of computers, multi-colored lights and mirrors, you can move around in front of a screen and see a surreal reflection of your activities. The more you move, the more interesting the reflection, and once you stand still the reflection carries on for a short while for your closer study. The planetarium has varying shows; they change the rate of admission accordingly.

By this time your appetite for museums may have been satiated. But there is one more you will find especially interesting. Located in the historic Norfolk & Western Freight Station (just a few blocks from the Farmer's Market at 303 Norfolk Avenue) the **Virginia Museum of Transportation** is home to the country's largest collection of steam and diesel locomotives. Virtually everyone is fascinated by the romance of the steam engine era. Here – in the yards and right next to the operational Norfolk & Southern tracks – you may climb aboard one of these authentic iron horses and imagine yourself at the controls. What a sense of power there must be running a steam engine at full speed over the rails! Inside the main building are early autos, freight trucks, fire engines, carriages, and planes, along with other informative exhibits (some of them hands-on).

Now it's time to relax and prepare for the evening's entertainment. By this stage you may be a bit leg-weary, so consider having a professional massage. Tim Rowe, the proprietor of **Bodyworks**, has a studio downtown. But he also offers "room service" at your hotel. Give him a call – preferably in advance – at (540) 344-2189 or (800) 317-7707. Perhaps you can arrange this as a surprise for your partner. After all, can you think of a better way to relax someone?

An evening at the theater is often enjoyable, and there is generally something worthwhile at the **Mill Mountain Theater**, located back at the Circle in the Square. This is a regional, professional, year-round theater group offering dramas, musicals and comedies on either its Main Stage or the smaller, more intimate Theater B. Performances begin at 8 p.m. on Friday and Saturday; phone the box office at (540) 342-5790 to see what's showing. Another option for live entertainment is the **Roanoke Civic Center**, box office number (540) 981-2241. Here you will find anything from the Roanoke Symphony to the Roanoke Express Ice Hockey Team.

You don't want your evening to end in an anticlimax. So consider arranging for a limousine stocked to meet you after the show, complete with a bottle of champagne. Travel in style up to **Mill Mountain,** where you may sip your champagne, admire the view, and kiss next to the Star. **Prestige Limousine Service**, at (540) 342-8049, will be happy to oblige. The cost is $65 per hour.

Sundays are ideal for relaxation – you may need it – and a change of pace. Get out of the city for awhile, and escape into the serenity of the surrounding mountains. Between the months of April and October, you may visit Virginia's interesting new **Explore Park**. Here, 15 minutes from Roanoke – and just a mile off the Blue Ridge Parkway at Milepost 115 – is an authentic 18th- and 19th-century western Virginia settlement in 1,300 acres of unspoiled countryside. Step back a hundred years to experience old-time frontier culture, including a working farm, a one-room school house, a frame church, and the homes of townspeople and crafters. Nor is your experience limited to looking. In Explore Park, you can make furniture, harvest a garden, weave on a loom, sing along with bluegrass musicians, enjoy up-close encounters with the many unusual animals, and wind it all up with a relaxing ride aboard a horse-drawn wagon. There are also environmental education programs and six miles of walking trails for self-guided tours through beautiful Blue Ridge river gorge scenery. Admission is only $4; call (540) 427-1800 for more information.

Twenty miles southeast of Roanoke – take State Route 116 to Burnt Chimney, then turn north on State Route 122 – is another, starkly different example of 19th-century life. The **Booker T. Washington National Monument** – mentioned elsewhere in this guide – is open all year with free admission. It is a tribute to the former slave who rose to prominence, achieving international fame as an educator, speaker and controversial black leader. A tobacco plantation has been reconstructed to simulate Booker's boyhood and, in the summer, uniformed rangers and costumed interpreters narrate the story of his life.

On the way back to town, stop for awhile at the **Mill Mountain Zoo**, located next to "the Star." Here Ruby, a Siberian tigress, is the key attraction.

As we have said before, the Farmer's Market is a really delightful choice for Sunday morning lunch. You may want to pick up a newspaper to catch up on current events. (You won't have any problem getting an out-of-town paper like *The New York Times*.) Then just relax and enjoy the charming, yet surprisingly cosmopolitan, atmosphere.

To cap off your trip, call **Star City Aviation**, operated by Jim and Jenny Delong at (540) 366-9221. Then head out to the airport; a half-hour "City Loop" flight is $39, while a one-hour trip costs $78. The best time is sunset, when the plane circles close to the illuminated star.

Among the more important annual events here are: the **St. Patrick's Day Parade** in March, the **Downtown Anniversary Party** in April, the **Virginia State Championship Chili Cook-Off** and **Festival in the Park,** which begins in May but might stretch into June. August brings the **Virginia Mountain Peach Festival,** while the **Roanoke Railway Festival** is in October, and the **Dickens of a Christmas** celebration is in December.

The Homestead
A First Resort When Romance Springs to Mind

few places in the world develop such wonderful reputations that they become institutions. Virginia is home to one of them. Usually such places are both grand and traditional, exuding an atmosphere of extreme formality. Make no mistake, this one is certainly grand and tradition-laden. After all, the first hotel was built here in 1766! What makes it so different from other places of its type is the atmosphere. This is truly a family-oriented hotel, with no excesses of formality. Impeccable service, definitely; yet you are encouraged to relax in this wonderful place as if it were your own. No unnecessarily restrictive rules apply; just treat it – and the other guests – with respect and courtesy. In return, you'll share in an ambiance that is quintessentially Southern – a curiously easy-going combination of both manners and informality. It's no wonder that guests return here time and time again. In fact, they incorporate it into their own traditions. The location, too, is incredible: 15,000 privately owned acres in the Allegheny Mountains. The name derives from the resort's proximity to natural hot water springs, just a few miles from the border with West Virginia.

For the most direct route, take Interstate 64 to Covington and turn north onto Route 220. No further directions are necessary; it would be impossible for you to miss **The Homestead**. Indeed, it will take your breath away. No photographs will prepare you for your first sight of this huge brick Georgian-style building with its trademark central tower, nestled snugly in a narrow valley and literally within the mountains' shadow.

The resort potential at Hot Springs (formerly Little Warm Springs) was first recognized by Thomas Bullit, who built the first hotel here in 1766. However, it wasn't until 1832, when the land was acquired by Dr. Thomas Goode, that development began in earnest. Improved bathhouses were the first things added and by 1846, he had enlarged the hotel using the original building, cabin and bathhouses as the foundation. This "modern hotel" gained recognition throughout the region and became one of the premier stops on the summer circuit. The doctor died in 1858 and ownership passed through various hands until, in 1891, the Virginia Hot Springs Company – established by the Ingalls family – gained control. They remained at the helm for another 102 years.

Business increased in 1891, when a branch line of the Chesapeake and Ohio Railroad was extended into Hot Springs from Covington. The demand occasioned considerable improvements during the following year. The additions included 10 cottages, the hotel's west wing, tennis courts, the original casino, and a six-hole fairway called The Homestead Course, whose first tee remains the oldest in continuous use in this country.

Disaster struck in 1901, when the entire hotel complex was destroyed by fire. Area citizens were determined not to see a tradition – and their main source of revenue – die an untimely death. Reconstruction began immediately. By 1902, a new Kentucky brick hotel and circular ballroom – the main section of today's Homestead – was completed. The next year saw the opening of the west wing. Reconstruction was finally completed in 1914, when the east wing was connected to the ballroom. But it was not until 1929 that the famous central tower was added. Thirty years later, the Homestead pioneered southern skiing and the ski area and skating rink were opened. The most recent addition, built in a more modern style, is the south wing/conference center. This was added in 1973 with an eye to attracting the convention and business trade. Nine years later, in its 227th year, Virginia Hot Springs Inc. entered into a joint venture with Club Resorts, Inc., the nation's largest privately held golf and conference resort company. According to the terms of this venture, the latter will become full owner of The Homestead in 1999.

This world-class hotel, with its 521 luxurious rooms (including 81 parlor suites), has been the retreat of European monarchs and U.S. presidents, as well as such prominent businessmen as Henry Ford and John D. Rockefeller. Today you, too, can savor its unmatched old-world elegance, style, and grandeur. But there's more to The Homestead than that. Indeed, it is a self-contained entity offering visitors virtually everything they could ever want. In addition, The Homestead is continually adapting to meet new demands. If ever there was a resort for all seasons, this is it.

First, let us consider the various options. The more convenient choices are packages based on the Modified American Plan (MAP), which includes accommodation, breakfast and dinner. Several are offered, but two in particular will appeal to readers of this guide. The **Social Package** covers three days and two nights and costs $228-$328 per person, depending upon both the room and the season. The **Honeymoon and Anniversary Package** is ideal for those who want to savor this extraordinary atmosphere a bit longer. This covers four days and three nights. Besides breakfast and dinner daily, it includes champagne on arrival, one very romantic carriage ride along mountain trails, a photograph of the two of you as a memento of your visit and a day of recreation for two. The latter features your choice of one round of golf, two hours of tennis, one hour of horseback riding, one round of sporting clays, a combination of mineral bath and massage in the spa, or (during the winter) lift tickets and ski rentals for one day. Again, the rates depend upon the season and type of room. At the time of publication, these ranged from $912 to $1,218 per couple. You should also be aware that 15% of your room and board rate is automatically added to your account daily to cover services provided by the doormen, bellmen, food service personnel and housekeeping staff.

From the moment the bellmen meet you at the porticoed main entrance, you will realize that service is taken very seriously here. Yet it's never obsequious; rather, it's like being greeted by old friends. You will be escorted into The Great Hall, the imposing heart of the hotel, which is 22 feet 6 inches in height, 211 feet in length, and 42 feet wide. Whatever you do, be sure to return here daily between 4 p.m. and 5 p.m. to enjoy the traditional afternoon tea. You'll find the fresh-baked pastries and tea sandwiches, coffee, hot chocolate and freshly brewed tea as tasteful as the surroundings. Don't be surprised if you see people with swimsuits walking in from the pool; there is no pretentiousness here.

In order to feel "at one" with the graceful ambience, be sure to request a room in either the hotel's main section or its east wing. If you really want to "splash out," spend the extra amount for a charming suite with a private balcony. While each of the rooms is decorated and furnished to a high standard, those in the south wing are more modern and a bit blander.

Having settled into your room, what do you do next? This may not be an easy decision, for here there is an overabundance of choices. If you've arrived late in the evening, take the time to acclimatize yourself before the next day's activities. The complex is so immense that it's easy to get lost.

At the end of the Great Hall – in a hallway that connects to the main dining room – is **The Palm Beach Corridor**, a row of exclusive shops featuring distinctive clothing, linens, jewelry, pewter, and other specialty items. Here you will also find a variety of "Homestead souvenirs." You can even buy a piece of china in the exclusive Homestead Pattern as a reminder of your stay.

If you fancy a breath of fresh mountain air, take the courtesy bus up to the **Ski Lodge Restaurant**, which is open until 10 p.m. between mid-December and March. The main slope ascends before you, an Olympic-size skating rink is to your left and, if you get too cold on the outside deck, go inside and warm up in front of the huge circular fireplace. The choice of ski burgers, soups, sandwiches, and salads will quell your appetite, while a hot toddy will wet your whistle.

If you are visiting outside of ski season or prefer a short walk, head across the road to a turn-of-the-century building that once housed the Bath County National Bank. There, in **Sam Snead's Tavern**, you may order from the light menu up until midnight; the bar is open until 1 a.m.

If you opt to stay inside, you may want to have a cocktail in the **View Lounge**, which features vistas over the golf course and the Allegheny Mountains. A collection of limited edition silk screen prints by Frederick Nichols adorns the bar. Perhaps **The Sports Bar** is the place for you. Here, a big-screen TV shows the evening's most important contests. Darts and billiards are also on offer – as is a light menu. Be forewarned that after 10 p.m. on Friday and Saturday evenings in season, the Sports Bar becomes a dance club – which can also be fun.

If you prefer to conserve energy, you might fancy watching a first- run movie in the privacy of your own room. Each room is furnished with a combination television and video player unit. Video-tape dispensing machines are located throughout the hotel, with a variety of videos available. These are open 24 hours a day and accept Visa, MasterCard, and American Express cards.

When you wake in the morning, get dressed and make a bee-line for the breakfast buffet. This is held in **The Homestead Dining Room** between 7:30 a.m. and 10 a.m. Though this is actually the formal dining room, informality is definitely in order now. Linger here, enjoying the music of the grand piano, the bubbly atmosphere, and the mouth-watering array of foods while planning the rest of your day.

Begin by joining the one-hour **Interior Tour** of The Homestead. This begins at 10 a.m., just as the buffet is closing down. Not only will this familiarize you with the hotel's history, it will help you find your way around. What you do after that depends on both your interests and your mood. **The Tower News** – the hotel's daily news sheet – lists each day's special events. But that is only the tip of the iceberg.

There are over 100 miles of **hiking and walking trails**, graded at all levels of difficulty. Three of these start from outside the hotel and are clearly marked with different color markers. There's also a 1¾-mile trail that begins at Cascades Gorge, traveling up an 800-foot incline and passing no fewer than 12 waterfalls.

Fly fishing is available at one of Virginia's finest trout streams, also located in the Cascades Gorge. The shuttle service offers transport there and back. Lessons, equipment and licenses are available at the outpost in Cottage Row.

The Homestead maintains its own livery stable; **horse-back riding** is available for all skill levels, in either English or Western tack. If you've never ridden, this is your chance. The Homestead has a riding school as well.

Shooting enthusiasts will have a field day here, too. **The Homestead Shooting Club** offers some of the most challenging and scenic shooting anywhere in the United States. There is five-strand sporting, trap, and skeet shooting, along with a .22 calibre rifle range.

Golfers will think they're in paradise with three championship courses at their disposal. **The Cascades Course**, a 6,566-yard par-70 opened in 1924, is ranked among the top courses in the nation and considered by some to be the country's finest mountain course. **The Lower Cascades Course**, designed by the noted golf architect Robert Trent Jones, was opened in 1963. It features a 6,633-yard par-72 layout. But what golfer could resist playing on the original **Homestead Course?** As mentioned previously, this is the nation's oldest tee still in continuous use. It was built in 1892 and expanded to 18 holes by 1913. Designed by Donald Ross, it is 6,077 yards long and plays as a par-72. A driving range is available for working on those long shots and, for those determined to lower their handicap, there is the Homestead Golf Advantage School staffed by PGA teaching professionals.

If you like **tennis,** then try your (back)hand on any one of the 15 Har-Tru or all-weather courts. This is about the only game where you want to avoid "love." To help you do just that, The Homestead offers a "stroke of the day" clinic in-season. Those looking for more gentle outdoor sport may take part in **lawn bowling**, **croquet**, **boccie ball**, or **horseshoes**.

Many come to The Homestead for the **winter sports** facilities alone. In this they will definitely not be disappointed. Nine slopes and trails cover 45 acres, with 34% beginner, 33% intermediate, 23% advanced, and 10% expert. There's a 3,200-foot elevation and the longest run is 4,200 feet. Best of all, everything is open for both day and night sessions. Additional attractions include a snowboard park (with a "half pipe" chute jump), as well as an Olympic-sized skating rink. There are complete snowmaking facilities, a double chairlift and T-bar, full-service rental and equipment sales, and a staff of professional European ski and skate instructors for either individual or group clinics.

There are plenty of indoor activities, too. You may shape up in the **Fitness Center** with its electronic treadmills, step machines, rowers, Universal weight machines, and complimentary aerobic classes. For a nominal fee, you can indulge in **ten pin bowling** on eight lanes equipped with automatic pin-setters and scoring equipment. **Swimmers** will enjoy The Homestead's indoor pool, located at the lower level of the spa building. It is fed by the naturally warmed waters of the original spa. An Olympic-sized outdoor pool sits adjacent to this, while another outdoor pool is near the south terrace.

Those seeking the complete Homestead experience won't want to leave without indulging in one of the **spa's** exotic treatments. Built as a part of the 1892 expansion, this is thought to have been the first European-type spa established in America. The **sauna** and **steam for men** are complimentary for hotel guests, but there is a charge for all other services. Take a **mineral bath,** soaking in an individual tub of soothing hot water drawn from the Boiler Spring and heated to an average temperature of 104°F. **Dr. Good's Mineral Spout Bath**, a technique developed over 100 years ago, begins with a mineral bath and is followed by a single high-pressure stream of mineral water directed for specific muscle therapy. The **combination bath** is both relaxing and invigorating; first you'll soak in a mineral bath, then get a "salt glow" as wet salt is rubbed over the body to exfoliate dead skin cells. It is washed off by a Swiss shower, which utilizes multiple shower heads that douse you from head to toe. You are finished off with a "Scotch spray," which is a type of water massage. If you like, you may vary the baths with the addition of aromatherapy oils. If that sounds just a little too involved, opt for either a **loofah scrub** or a relaxing and detoxifying **herbal wrap**. For the latter, you must first visit the sauna to open your pores. After this, you're wrapped in a warm muslin sheet soaked in the essential oils of yarrow flowers, linden flowers, blue malva, burdock root, strawberry leaves, chamomile, and lavender. This is then covered with both a rubber sheet and a wool blanket; you remain in this state for approximately 20 minutes. Finally, choose between a **Swedish massage** – as gentle or firm as you desire – or an **aromatherapy massage**. Be sure to make your appointment in advance, and be advised that a 12-hour cancellation policy is observed.

With so much activity, will you have time for shopping? Charming **Cottage Row** offers a leisurely and unique shopping experience. The 10 former guest cottages, constructed in 1892, now operate as boutiques. These feature sportswear, antiques, shoes, quilts, toys, and souvenirs, as well as high-quality art and other specialty items. In addition, there are two other stores that offer services of particular interest to couples. Certainly you will want a photographic reminder of your trip here. As this is no ordinary experience, why settle for an ordinary snapshot? Call ahead and arrange to have the resort photographer take a professional portrait of the two of you. Failing that, how about a dozen long-stemmed roses, or a corsage or boutonniere for your special evening together? The Homestead's own florist will be happy to oblige.

Cottage Row is also an ideal place for a gourmet lunch. The cottage that houses **Café Albert** – named for the Executive Chef, Albert Schnarwler – served as a summer home for V.I.P.s until 1984. Now it is a delightful café, with indoor and outdoor tables set for lunch or a snack.

On the subject of food, dinner may well be the highlight of your visit. First, let's turn to more practical matters. Ladies will want to look their best for such occasions, so a trip to the **hair salon** may be in order. Don't worry, guys, this is your chance to sneak out and do something interesting.

Right next to the dining room is The Homestead's new **wine room.** (You'll recognize it right away by its elaborate stained glass window.) Inside, you'll find a quarry tile floor, an 11-foot ceiling, redwood walls, and heart of redwood racks designed to hold more than 4,000 bottles. About half of these are stored in the 45° white wine area, while fine reds are kept in a 55-57° section. Small private tours are available on request and intimate tastings are sometimes held for groups of no more than 10 people. Think how impressed your partner will be when you confidently order an obscure vintage at dinner!

On The Homestead's meal plan, you actually have a choice of three restaurants. We have already detailed **Sam Snead's Tavern** and **The Grille**, overlooking The Homestead Golf Course, is certainly very nice. But you wouldn't want to miss eating in **The Homestead Dining Room** on a Saturday night. No one else will either, so be sure to make your reservation very early indeed, and press for a table as close as possible to the dance floor. This is the largest dining room in the state, seating over 550 guests. Though the dress code calls for jacket and tie, you may wear these with blue jeans. Dinner jackets and diamonds aren't out of place, either.

As with all other aspects of this resort, the service here is absolutely impeccable. The staff endeavors to make this a dining experience to be savored; no matter how long it takes you to choose from the menu, no one will get frazzled or try to hurry you. And when you see the extensive wine list, you'll be glad you visited the Wine Room.

Once the formalities have been settled, it is time to sit back and soak in this delightfully unusual atmosphere. You may be particularly surprised to see so many children. When the band strikes up a tune, expect to find young children dancing with their parents, their older siblings, and each other. Many of them are literally treading in the footsteps of their family's history. As with everything offered here, your meal will be nothing short of excellent.

Once you have been here, you will never forget it – and you will always look forward to your next visit. Perhaps you will make it an annual romantic getaway, or a new family tradition. For up-to-date information and to make a reservation, call (540) 839-1766, (800) 336-5771, or fax (540) 839-7656.

Although you need never leave the grounds, the immediate area has a few attractions of its own. After all, you might fancy a change of scene for an hour or so. The pleasant little village of **Hot Springs** is within easy walking distance, but it is dominated by The Homestead. The short drive to **Warm Springs** will probably please you more. Along the way you can't help but notice the steam rising from the streams. In the winter – when the ground is snow-covered – this looks downright eerie. To convince yourself that the water really is warm, you should get out and put your hands in it. Here and there, you will see small wooden bathhouses, but at Warm Springs there are two larger ones. The men's pool was opened in 1761 and is thought to have been designed by Thomas Jefferson. The ladies' is more recent, dating from 1836. These are open daily between mid-April and October and, if you wish, The Homestead shuttle will take you there and back.

 While at Warm Springs you may enjoy stopping by the **Inn at Gristmill Square**, (540) 839-2231. The Simon Kenton Pub, named after the 18th-century frontiersman and friend of Daniel Boone, would not be out of place in a traditional English village. It's certainly a wonderful place for a quiet drink. **The Waterwheel Restaurant** is a very pleasant spot for an intimate lunch. It boasts a real waterwheel is on the outside wall, as well as a wooden floor and exposed beams inside. Upon request, you can visit the cellar to select a vintage wine.

In fact, this whole complex of five original 19th-century buildings houses 17 cozy and distinctive rooms. It also offers an outdoor pool, three tennis courts, and a sauna. It is attractive in its own way, and in stark contrast to the The Homestead's high style. If you are looking for total peace and quiet, you might even consider staying here. By special arrangement, their guests may use most of the larger hotel's facilities; "extra activities" are charged at the same rate as for Homestead guests.

When driving in this area, you may miss something you normally take for granted. In the whole of Bath County there is not one traffic light!

Virginia's Southwest Blue Ridge Highlands

Abingdon
Where Country Meets Culture

In the southwest corner of Virginia, surrounded by majestic mountains, is a very special town. The oldest settlement west of the Blue Ridge Mountains, it is rich in tradition. But it's also a cultural center.

Back in 1749-1750, King George II granted Dr. Thomas Walker over 6,000 acres of land in what is now southwest Virginia. He eventually sold some of this land to Joseph Black, who built a small fort known as "Black's Fort." In 1760, on his first trip to Kentucky, Daniel Boone pitched camp at the base of a hill here. During the night his dogs were attacked by wolves that emerged from a nearby cave. Thereafter, the spot was known as Wolf Hill.

The area originally enjoyed a period of peace between the Indians and the settlers. But in 1776, a Cherokee uprising sent many to the fort, which was subsequently enlarged. Later that year the Virginia Assembly created Washington County; Black's Fort was designated the meeting place of the first county court. Dr. Walker, Joseph Black, and a certain Samuel Briggs then donated 120 acres to establish a town. In 1778, the Virginia Assembly passed an act that made the new town, Abingdon, the first English-speaking settlement incorporated in the Mississippi watershed. Although the first structures were built of logs, frame buildings with rock foundations sprouted up within a few years, with the first brick house appearing in 1803. Abingdon grew to be the most important town in western Virginia; it was a staging point for mail as well as supplies for those settlers opening up the wilderness to the west. Although major fires in 1812, 1856, and 1864 destroyed many of the buildings, enough original structures remain for the town to be designated a Virginia Historic Landmark.

Driving into Abingdon and along Main Street, you will be pleasantly surprised by the town's charm and beauty. You will also notice one building at 150 West Main Street that is more imposing than the others. Constructed in 1832 by General Francis Preston as a home for his wife and nine children, the original brick residence still serves as the basis for the **Martha Washington Inn**. Preston had attended William and Mary College, served in Congress, was a member of the Virginia Assembly until 1797, fought in the War of 1812, and was appointed general in 1820. He spent over $15,000 creating this home, which he filled with priceless antiques and used to entertain many of Virginia's most famous and powerful families. Amazingly, much of the original detail has been preserved and the grand stairway and parlors are much as they were in those days. The original living room now serves as the inn's main lobby.

The general died in 1835, but his wife resided in this house until her death in 1858. At that time it was purchased for $21,000 for use as a women's college. This was named Martha Washington College. One of the student traditions called for the girls to inscribe their names in the glass windows. Some of these signatures can still be seen today. The coming of the Civil War soon disrupted normal life and had a dramatic effect on the college. The grounds became a training barracks for the Washington Mounted Rifles. There were also frequent skirmishes around town; and the college was transformed into a makeshift hospital, with the girls caring for the injured of both armies. This period generated many interesting stories explained in the brochure, "A History of the Martha Washington." Although the college survived the war, it failed to survive the Great Depression and an outbreak of typhoid fever. In 1932, declining enrollment forced its closure.

After standing idle for a short period, it was used to house aspiring actors appearing at what is now the famous **Barter Theater**, located just across Main Street. Many who have since gone on to thespian fame still return to visit the place where they got their start – and the Martha Washington.

Around 1935 the building was opened as a proper hotel and many illustrious visitors have since graced it. Although numerous renovations have been performed over the years, these have altered neither the building's historic charm nor its architectural detail. Fortunately, the antique furnishings were retained as well. Even so, the inn's future was never certain until 1984, when the United Company – representing a group of dedicated businessmen – purchased it. They initiated an $8,000,000 renovation designed to preserve and enhance the building's ambiance and architectural integrity, while incorporating all the modern amenities. Without doubt they have succeeded. Since 1986 it has been a AAA Four-Diamond and Mobil Four-Star Award winner. It was also ranked the 37th most successful hotel in America by *Lodging Magazine* in 1993, and has been rated by Mobil in the top 2% of all food and lodging properties in the U.S.

The 61 guest rooms feature striking traditional decor and antique furnishings. They're divided into three categories: standard rooms, deluxe rooms, and suites. These range in price from $115 for a standard up to $275 for the Governor's or Johnson Suites. All of the rooms are of the highest standard and some even have fireplaces. But some have more modern facilities than others; whirlpools and steam showers come to mind. Our personal favorites are in the mansion wing, the oldest part of the house. Here you will find irregularly shaped rooms, marvelously imposing beds, fine antiques and, in some cases, girls' names etched in the windows. And don't be surprised if you come across Beth. Tradition has it that a Yankee officer, Captain John

Stoves, was captured close to the inn. Badly wounded, he was carried to the third floor, where he was tenderly ministered by a Martha girl known only as Beth. Just before he died, she played him a sweet Southern melody on the violin. Shortly afterwards, she died of typhoid fever and was reunited with the officer in the Green Springs Cemetery. They say that on full moon nights, Beth's haunting violin melodies may be heard on the third floor.

The Martha Washington has two restaurants with a wide variety of Continental and traditional Southern dishes, as well as fine wines and cocktails. The main dining room boasts an original hand-stamped tin ceiling as well as the ultimate conversation piece, a 16-foot-long silver table discovered during basement renovations. The latter is in the Art Deco style, with a carved glass top resting on internally illuminated silver pedestals. The Presidents' Club offers its members both privacy and the best in entertainment, dining, and cocktails. The Grand Ballroom – originally added to the main building as the college's chapel – is often used for popular events and private functions.

Browse in the gift shop for quality souvenirs. Relax in the house's elegant parlors and lounges or in its gazebo on the back lawn. Enjoy complimentary afternoon tea, which includes pastries made fresh daily in the bake shop. Tea is served on the inn's trademark front porch. Finish your evening with a nightcap in the basement pub. Whatever you choose to do, friendly and hospitable staff members are always ready to regale you with color-ful stories of the inn's past. The Martha Washington Inn is very special indeed. For information or reservations, telephone (540) 628-3161, (800) 533-1014, or fax (540) 628-8885.

There are, of course, alternatives. If you're unable to secure a reservation at the Martha Washington, or if you prefer something less grand, there are several bed and breakfasts in town. Our top recommendation is the **Summerfield Inn**, (540) 628-5905, located just behind the Barter Theater at 101 West Valley Street. Don and Champe Hyatt own this delightful Victorian property;

they work diligently to provide the ambiance of a private home with the comfort of a fine hotel. The four large guest rooms (with king, double or twin beds) each have a private bath, telephone, and a unique mix of decor. There is also a large public living room, a sun room, and a wrap-around porch. Other nice touches are a guest pantry and a refrigerator stocked with complimentary sodas. A deluxe Continental breakfast is served between 7 a.m. and 9 a.m.

Construction of an extension is currently in progress and should be completed by the time of publication. One of the extension's rooms will be designed for romance and will feature a jacuzzi. Although the Summerfield Inn's regular season is April 1 through October 31, its rooms are frequently available during the off-season by advance arrangement. The price structure is reasonable as well. Double rates are $65 or $75 for the first night, with a $10 discount for subsequent nights. A two-night minimum reservation may be required on special weekends.

Fifteen minutes away from Abingdon – nestled in the foothills of the Clinch Mountains and on the bank of the Holston River – is an unusual bed and breakfast that deserves mention. However, it is a bit difficult to find. Travel on Route 19 North for seven miles and turn right onto Route 611 (North Fork River Road). After following the river for 2.4 miles you'll arrive at the **River Garden Bed & Breakfast**, (540) 676-0335 or (800) 952-4296. There you'll find an unusual house situated literally a few feet above the river and with steps leading down to its bank.

Each of the four rooms is uniquely designed around a particular theme. They can all be accessed through either an inside entrance or a private outside entrance. The "Memories" room is furnished with a 1920s bedroom set, featuring a king-sized bed and mementos of the period. It rents for $65 a night. The "Toymaker" room is decorated with a playful mix of old and modern toys, including handmade Appalachian pieces and furniture from the '40s. The "Homespun" room also has 1940's furnishings and is adorned with needlework, macramé and photography. The "Family" room is outfitted with early 20th-century furniture and filled with pictures of the hosts' ancestors. These last three rooms have queen-sized beds and rent for $60 a night. All four rooms feature a private bath as well as individually controlled heating and air conditioning.

Start each morning with a full breakfast, taken in either the dining room, your bedroom, or on the deck. The living room, dining room, den, and recreation room are all open to guests. The latter features a ping-pong table as well as various table games and a few pieces of exercise equipment. In addition, guests are encouraged to try their hand at weaving on the antique loom. One of the main attractions here is the river. For those interested in water sports, fishing equipment and inner tubes are available. You can also take their canoe out if you fancy a little "canoodling." Keep in mind this is one of those rare places where you can go down to the shore, open a bottle of champagne, and watch the sun set while being lulled by the sounds of the river.

Before setting the dates for your visit, there's one thing to check. Telephone the aforementioned **Barter Theater**, (540) 628-3991 or (800) 368-3240, to ensure that your visit will coincide with a production. Even allowing for all the other available activities, missing a show here would be a shame. The building that houses the theater is located at 133 West Main Street. Constructed in 1835 as the Sinking Springs Presbyterian Church, it later served as a temperance hall and the Town Hall of Abingdon. It is the second oldest structure in the U.S. where theater is performed (predated only by Philadelphia's Walnut Street Theater).

The Barter's name befits its origins as a theater. During the middle of the Depression, an enterprising actor named Robert Porterfield returned to his native southwest Virginia with an extraordinary idea. Cash being scarce, he proposed that people barter produce from their farms and gardens for entrance to a play. When he opened the Barter Theater on June 10, 1933 – with a company of professional actors – admission was set at 40¢, or the equivalent in produce. At the end of the Barter's first season, it was apparent that food was more plentiful than money. The company had grossed $4.35 in cash, two barrels of jelly, and a collective weight gain of over 300 pounds.

Cash did become the standard after World War II, and the Barter's reputation in the national theater community grew to such an extent that it was the first such operation to be designated a State Theater. It was also a founding member of the League of Resident Theaters, the association which negotiates contracts with the actors' union. Numerous actors and actresses of national and international fame got their start here. In addition, many playwrights have had their reputations enhanced when their works were performed at the Barter. Much of the Barter's reputation is due to the theater's refusal to content itself with the ordinary. From its very beginnings, the Barter has been an innovative leader in the staging of new plays and English-language productions of foreign works. Now, after 61 years, it is the nation's longest-running professional equity theater.

Back in Abingdon you may procure information about the area from the **Abingdon Convention and Visitors' Bureau**, located in the Fields-Penn House at 208 West Main Street. Visit between 9 a.m. and 5 p.m. seven days a week, or call (540) 676-2282 or (800) 435-3440. Here you will learn that there is much to do and see, both in Abingdon and the surrounding area. We will begin with the things that you should not miss. Be advised that it is necessary to pre-book many of these before arriving; otherwise you may be disappointed.

Get your trip off to a flying start! Rise early and take to the air for a romantic balloon flight. You will not only get a bird's eye view of the town, but a wonderful perspective of the marvelous surrounding countryside and its spectacular mountains, the highest in Virginia. **Balloon Virginia**, (540) 628-6353 or (800) VA-ALOFT, offers 60-75 minutes air time (weather permitting) followed by a post-flight ceremony where you will be presented with a "First Flight Certificate" and a souvenir balloon pin. Your bravery will also be toasted with champagne. This company specializes in trips for couples at a rate of $300. Be sure to book as far in advance as possible.

Back on *terra firma,* get a feel for the town as you explore the area using the "Historic Abingdon, Virginia, A Walking Tour of Main Street" brochure as a guide. Allow about an hour for the tour itself – that is, if you can resist exploring the tempting array of specialty and antique stores that you will encounter. If not, you may double (or even triple) that time.

You might also want to take time to browse through two art institutions with contrasting styles. First, climb up Academy Drive and head for the magnificent house that is home to the **William King Regional Arts Center**, (540) 628-5005. It is open from 10 a.m. until 3 p.m. on Saturdays and from 1 p.m. and 5 p.m. on Sundays. This historic landmark – the site of one of the first schools in the region – is named for an Irish immigrant who settled here in the 1700s and made his fortune in salt manufacturing. Today it functions as a non-collecting art gallery presenting a diverse schedule of rotating exhibits from other museums around the country. In addition, it showcases works by regional artists, and hosts an annual juried art show of works by local residents. It also offers one continuing nature exhibit – a magnificent view of the surrounding peaks.

Back in town, and next to the railroad in Depot Square, is the **The Arts Depot,** (540) 628-9091. Built in 1890 by the Virginia and Tennessee Railroad, the freight station had been idle for many years when, in 1990, the town of Abingdon leased the structure to The Depot Artists Association. Through their efforts and renovations it was transformed into a center housing a rich cultural mix of studio artists, exhibit and sales galleries, and performing and literary arts programs. Whether you're admiring the consignment gallery's diverse displays or watching the artists carefully create new works, you may be tempted to make a purchase. Or you may have some specific ideas of your own. Don't be afraid to speak with the artists and perhaps commission a work.

North of town on Route 11, at 27323 Lee Highway, you will come to **Cumberland Textiles, Inc.** (540) 628-4862. Bob Harman's family began its tradition of weaving back in England in 1812; they have been weaving in

Virginia since around 1884. Bob – who was taught by his grandfather – fashions his pieces using only natural fibers and following patterns collected from the Southern Appalachian Highlands of Virginia, West Virginia, Tennessee, and Kentucky. One overriding family ambition had always been to found a weaving museum. So, joining forces with established weaver Jeanne Elrod, they have opened the **Cumberland Textiles Museum.** (The name derives from the small water wheel-powered mill used by the family prior to 1890.) Museum tours are scheduled at 10 a.m., noon, 2 p.m., and 4 p.m. on Saturdays only. Meanwhile, the tempting gift shop is open from 9 a.m. to 5 p.m. On the other side of town, but still on Route 11, is the famous **Dixie Pottery.** This establishment's wide selections of porcelain, glassware, homemade candles, pottery, brass, straw, cane, wicker, and bamboo attract visitors from all over the country.

The surrounding countryside is simply spectacular and merits further exploration. There are many options from which to choose; these depend upon your tastes and the amount of time and energy you wish to expend.

The **Virginia Creeper Trail** runs from Abingdon to the Virginia/North Carolina border – a distance of 34 miles – and passes through some of the most beautiful scenery in southwest Virginia. It follows the route of a major Indian trail, which ran from North Carolina all the way to the Ohio River. Near Abingdon, it crossed another trail that passed through the Great Valley of Virginia and Tennessee. Use of these paths wasn't confined to the Indians, either; frontiersmen used them as well. Records mention no fewer than four campsites along the trail used by Daniel Boone. The junction of these two paths was, in fact, the site of "Black's Fort."

In the late 19th century, the Virginia-Carolina (V-C) Railroad laid track along the path. Though intended for the transportation of iron, this ended up carrying a more profitable cargo – timber. When the Norfolk and Western purchased it in 1918, the track reached as far as Elkland, North Carolina – some 75 miles from Abingdon. The Depression and inclement weather resulted in cutbacks but, even as late as 1976, a train ran at least once weekly and was an important local source of transportation. The initials V-C led to the nickname Virginia Creeper, a reference both to the speed of the train and the vine which grew alongside the tracks. In the 1980s the railroad sold its right-of-way to the towns of Abingdon and Damascus, as well as to the National Forest Service. Their combined efforts transformed the old Indian footpath into a haven for walkers, joggers, bikers, horsemen, and even cross-country skiers. Don't worry, though. You won't have to walk all the way if you don't want to. Contact **Blue Blaze Shuttle Service and Bike Rental** at (540) 475-5095 (daytime) or (540) 388-3875 (evenings). Not only do they rent bicycles and helmets, for $5 they offer their rental customers transportation to and from Abingdon and Damascus. Rates are $25 for a full eight-hour day, $15 for four hours, or $5 per hour with a two-hour minimum. As this is a seasonal service, you may want to take note of an alternative rental company. The **Highlands Ski & Outdoor Center**, (540) 628-1329, located next to the Burger King in Abingdon, offers comparable equipment and tariffs. For those with less energy, there is convenient access by road and as well as ample parking. Using the helpful brochure, "Abingdon-Virginia, A Guide To The Virginia Creeper Trail," drive to the spots that appeal most and walk just that leg of the trail.

The **Mount Rogers National Recreation Area**, located to the east of Abingdon, covers over 115,000 acres in Washington and its neighboring counties. Located within the boundaries of this unspoiled recreational paradise are the two highest mountains in Virginia, Mount Rogers (5,729 feet) and Whitetop Mountain (5,540 feet). If you do nothing else on this trip, pack a blanket, a picnic, and a bottle of champagne and drive to the **summit of Whitetop Mountain** just before sundown. The lowering sun seems to set fire to the mountaintops, which roll away into North Carolina and Tennessee. Meanwhile, the fresh clear air allows the most incredible hues to paint the valleys. It's a sight you will carry with you forever.

Hiking enthusiasts will certainly want to spend time in this same area. With over 300 miles of trails winding up to the mountain ridges and peaks, down along the streams and gorges, or through the forests, there is a route suitable for every age and fitness level. Some trails are well marked, while others – seldom used and sometimes overgrown – are more difficult to find. The *Mount Rogers NRA Sportsman's Map* covers the entire NRA and is available for $2 from the USDA Forest Service, Mount Rogers NRA, Headquarters, Route 1, Box 303, Marion,Virginia 24354; or call (540) 783-5196. You might ask for the *Circuit Hikes* brochure as well; this provides details on five medium-distance trails.

For those with a pioneering spirit, the following might well appeal. If you have daydreamed about riding in a covered wagon or blazing through the wilderness on horseback, here's a chance to turn your dreams into reality.

Mount Rogers High Country Outdoor Center, at P. O. Box 151, Troutdale, Virginia, 24378-0151, telephone (540) 677-3900, gives you a variety of options. One-hour wagon rides are offered, but they are not recommended; you barely have time to get into the spirit (or even to Troutdale and back). A full day, taking you high up into wild pony country, is a better choice. This will cost $45 per person, including lunch. Ideally, you should go one better and enjoy nature to its fullest by staying out all night. You can do this on the **Overnight Covered Wagon Trek**. This takes a full two days and one night, costs $200 per person, and includes all meals and equipment (except a sleeping bag, which may be rented for $10 a trip). If you fancy riding a horse the entire trip, plan on an additional $20 per day.

Horse lovers have other options as well. **Wilderness Day Rides** guide you through tall forests and high mountain trails, cost $75 per person, and include lunch served from a chuck wagon. Alternatively, you might settle on an **Overnight Horse Trip with Pack Mules** at a cost of $125 per person per day. These trips are seasonal – May through October – and originate at the Livery Base Camp located on State Road 603 in Troutdale. Allow a little extra travel time as this is not the easiest place to find. Take either Interstate 81, which runs north of the NRA, or Route 58, which runs south. Then turn onto 603 at Troutdale.

If you have decided on one of these overnight trips, you might want to make it the centerpiece of your weekend break. If so, you'd probably prefer a closer base than Abingdon. As luck would have it, there is a convenient and unique bed and breakfast located in Troutdale. The **Fox Hill Inn**, Route 2, Box 1-A-1, 24378, telephone (540) 677-3313 or (800) 874-3313, is not easy to find. In addition, it has a tortuous gravel driveway that climbs up a steep hill. These drawbacks, however, pale in light of the inn's atttributes. Glorious panoramic views and 70 secluded acres teeming with abundant and varied wildlife combine to create a wonderfully relaxing ambiance with privacy aplenty. The building itself is rather modern, and the six bedrooms a little plain, but the large entry hall beckons you into a cozy, traditional country home. The living room's oversized fireplace is welcoming and the dining room opens onto a delightful terrace with uninterrupted views of the mountains. Rates are $75 per night and include a bountiful breakfast.

Llamas are gentle, intelligent and curious animals that make wonderful traveling companions. **Treasure Mountain Farm Llama Trekking**, at 10436 Echo Lane, Glade Spring, 24340, (540) 944-4674 or (540) 628-4710, offers a combination of one-day or overnight hikes in the NRA between April and October. The llamas carry all necessary supplies and equipment in saddlebag packs, leaving you free to enjoy either the relatively easy trails that rise and fall in elevation between 3,200 and 3,600 feet, or the challenge of a high-country adventure hike. Speaking of feet, llamas are choice animals for use in the mountains as their hooves do not damage the sensitive trails. The rate is $60 per person for a day trip that includes a homemade picnic lunch, or $125 per person for an overnight trip with everything included – even a tent and sleeping bag. Having made your reservation, all you need do is dress for hiking (taking into consideration the changeable mountain weather) and be on time.

Fly fishing enthusiasts will want to contact **Virginia Creeper Fly Fishing, Inc.**, at (540) 628-3826, the U.S. Forest Service-authorized fly fishing guide and outfitter for Mount Rogers NRA and Jefferson National Forest.

On the Watauga and South Holston Tailwaters you may
fish for brown and rainbow trout, while smallmouth bass
are found in the New and James Rivers. A walk-in or
mountain bike trip costs $50 for a half-day or $100 for a full
day, including one meal. If you prefer to go by Hyde drift
boat (McKenzie), prices for a minimum of two people are
$150 for a half-day and $225 for a full day, again including
a meal. Fly fishing equipment and a sampler of seasonal
fly patterns are provided, but the license fee is not. Waders
are available for rent. If you find yourself craving fried
trout, you're in for a disappointment, since these trips
operate on a catch and release system. However, photos of
your fly fishing experience are provided as part of the fee.

To the north of both Abingdon and Mount Rogers NRA,
there is a very curious little town with a somewhat strange
history. Its name, **Saltville**, is derived from the rich salt
deposits left by the shallow sea that covered the area over
300 million years ago. The salt has always been an attraction for both animals and humans. Many prehistoric artifacts and fossils, including the most complete musk ox
skeleton discovered to date on the U.S. mainland, have
been unearthed nearby. Not surprisingly, numerous uni-
versities are currently conducting geological, archaeological, and paleontological research projects in the area. The
town, which prided itself on its reputation as "The Salt
Capital of the Confederacy," was the South's principal
supplier of salt, a commodity vital in that era for the
preservation of meat – so vital, in fact, that on October 2,
1864, the North and South fought a battle here for control
of the area's deposits.

If you are more interested in antiques than the great
outdoors, there is one place you should definitely investigate. Take Interstate 81 (or Route 11) south, and in less
than 30 minutes you'll arrive in **Bristol**. Somewhat run-
down in appearance, this is a town that has definitely seen
better days. But it does have one interesting and unique
feature. On the north side of State Street, you are in
Virginia. But walk over to the southern side, and you are
in Tennessee. Just past the old train station a huge arch
reminds you of this fact.

Once back in Abingdon, you may find yourself in need of some relaxation. If so, a massage might be just the ticket. The **Abingdon Center for Therapeutic Massage** at 301 West Main Street, Suite 1, telephone (540) 628-5451, has therapists that are trained to ease all your aching muscles. So call and arrange a session as a treat for you, your loved one, or both.

We've talked about the restaurants at the Martha Washington Inn, the grand **First Lady's Table** and gourmet **Epicurean Room**, and you certainly don't want to miss dining at one of those. However, there are at least two other restaurants that are totally different in style, but equally appealing.

The **Starving Artists Café**, at 134 Wall Street, (540) 628-8445, can be found right across from the Arts Depot – a logical choice of location since it doubles as an art gallery as well. It is called a café, the decor inside resembles a café, and the atmosphere is informal; but the food is of the quality you expect from a fine restaurant. Due to its relatively small size, it is generally crowded, even though during the summer you may eat outdoors. So be sure to make a reservation.

The other restaurant we recommend is at 222 East Main Street, in Abingdon's oldest building. (Constructed in 1779, it is, in fact, one of the oldest buildings west of the Blue Ridge Mountains.) As its name would indicate, **The Tavern**, (540) 628-1118, was originally used as an ordinary, or overnight inn, for stagecoach travellers. Though things have now come full circle, The Tavern served many purposes in the intervening years. The first post office on the western slopes of the Blue Ridge once occupied the east wing; in fact, the original mail slot is still in place and visible from the street. The Tavern has also been an antique store, bank, bakery, barber shop, cabinet shop, general store, private residence, restaurant and even, during the Civil War, a hospital for wounded Confederate and Union soldiers.

The Harris family, who had held title to the building for over 100 years, sold it to the wife of the Barter Theater's founder in 1965. Not until 1984 was it restored to its original state, and then by a local attorney. Ten years later it was re-opened as a restaurant by Max and Kathy Hermann, who had moved to Abingdon in the prior year after having completed 20 years of service in the Air Force. He is from Germany and she from nearby Damascus, Virginia, and their aim is to bring an intercontinental touch to The Tavern. This is clearly evident from the eclectic choices on the menu, as well as the European-style patio and garden. A visiting couple was so taken by the garden's charming setting, they insisted on getting married there – the next day! Before you eat, spend some time soaking up the atmosphere, along with a refreshing drink, in the parlor.

Wherever you choose to dine, set the mood for an enchanting evening by calling the **Abingdon Carriage Company**, (540) 669-6522. Have them meet you with an horse drawn carriage and take you on a genteel tour of the town, ending at the door of your chosen restaurant.

Tourist-wise, Abingdon is still in some ways a frontier town. A line drawn north to the Kentucky border forms a triangle which encloses the southwest corner of Virginia. Within that area is a kaleidoscopic mix of scenery, heavy industry, farmland, and a few places of genuine interest; but there is one thing that you definitely will not find. That is a pleasant place to stay. One day we traveled 300 miles exploring this triangle, and failed to find one place of the standard necessary to be recommended in this guide. (Well, there was one exception – four cottages at Breaks Interstate Park, detailed in another chapter.) This represents a real problem, as many of this area's attractions are out of reach for those staying in Abingdon.

The coal mining industry, wherever it is found,always seems beset by poverty and untidiness. Despite its natural beauty, this area is no exception. While a trip through Dante, Norton or Appalachia may not be pretty, it certainly is enlightening. It is obvious that the surrounding hills and the people that live in them hold much poignancy, and no little tragedy.

If you visit Big Stone Gap between mid-June and Labor Day, a viewing of the longest-running outdoor musical drama in Virginia will teach you more about these proud mountain people. At 8:15 p.m. on Thursday, Friday and Saturday, the curtain goes up at the June Tolliver Playhouse for **The Trail of the Lonesome Pine**. This is the fascinating love story of a beautiful Virginia mountain girl, June Tolliver, who falls in love with Jack Hale, a young mining engineer from the East. The drama, interwoven with beautiful and haunting folk music, depicts how the great boom in southwest Virginia – triggered by the discovery of coal and iron ore – forced these proud and independent people to make major changes in their way of life. Stark tragedy, suspense and violence, combined with the natural wit and humor of these folk, are all elements which bring about the ultimate acceptance of their destiny – and make for a happy ending. To ensure a reservation, call (540) 523-1235 or (800) TRAIL LP.

There are many special events scheduled throughout the year. A full list may be obtained from the Convention & Visitors Bureau. In March the annual **Maple Syrup Festival** is held on Whitetop Mountain, which also plays host to the annual **Ramp Festival** in May. Also in May, **Appalachian Trail Days**, which features a "trout rodeo," take place in Damascus. By far the largest and most important celebration begins at the end of July and carries on through the middle of August. The **Virginia Highlands Festival** attracts over 200,000 people and is considered one of the top 100 tourist events in North America. A much newer and more unusual event, the **Pig Pickin' On The Mountain**, was initiated in August 1992 at Grayson Highlands State Park, and is destined to become an annual event. **The Saltville Labor Day Celebration** is a three-day music festival which has as its grand finale an outdoor concert on Labor Day. Many well known performers, among them Garth Brooks, have played there. Other fall events are the **Washington County Fair & Burley Tobacco Festival**, the annual **Damascus Fall Festival,** held in September; and the annual **Whitetop Mountain Molasses Festival** in October. December is a very special time in Abingdon. It heralds a month-long series of special events including, most notably, the **Community Christmas Tree Lighting, Abingdon Traditions: Sharing the Holidays,** and **Candlelight Christmas in Historic Abingdon.**

The Blue Ridge Parkway

A Breathtaking Place to Make Mountains of Memories

You could not hope to find a more scenic road anywhere in the U.S., regardless of the season. The Blue Ridge Parkway runs from Virginia's Shenandoah National Park to the Great Smoky Mountains National Park in North Carolina and Tennessee. With highlands averaging 3-4,000 feet, it offers 470 miles of unparalleled natural beauty. The parkway is administered by the National Park Service, whose goal is to keep it that way. Your views won't be contaminated by the usual roadside advertising, there are no tolls to pay, and the speed limit is set at a steady 45 m.p.h. There is much to see and do, especially along the section we'll be describing between Roanoke and the Virginia/North Carolina border. But pay attention to the mileposts, as these are the sole locators for some attractions.

First of all, let's consider accommodation. There are several bed and breakfasts to choose from. We will focus on two particular establishments which will appeal to different tastes. Besides these, there are two other incredible options that should be considered. They are, in my opinion, the finest places to stay along, or even near, this section of the parkway.

At milepost 189, nestled in the scenic majesty of Groundhog Mountain, you will find the **Doe Run Lodge**, telephone (540) 398-2212 or fax (540) 398-2833. This is a spacious complex, spread over the mountainside, with gorgeous views towards North Carolina. There are chalets and villas, a clubhouse, lighted tennis courts, swimming pool, stocked fish pond, brook trout fishing and the nearby Olde Mill Golf Course. Here, wildlife abounds. You may expect to see deer, red fox, groundhog, raccoons, hawks and eagles (just to name a few) on your walks around the grounds.

You'll surely work up a "country" appetite in the fresh air, and you can dine well here, too. The **High Country Restaurant** is widely respected and reasonably priced, featuring a seafood buffet on Friday night, a prime rib buffet on Saturday night, and a delightful brunch on Sunday. To enhance your enjoyment of the restaurant's magnificent views, live entertainment is offered on Friday and Saturday evening; and outdoor festivals are held during the summer months. Set the mood for the rest of the evening by visiting the observation deck where, bathed in gentle moonlight, you will find yet more unforgettably beautiful scenery.

The beauty of the accommodations rivals that of the scenery. There are more than 40 chalets, built of natural stone and wooden beams with floor-to-ceiling thermopane glass picture windows. All boast two bedrooms (with a flexible mixture of king, queen and double beds), two full baths, a living/dining area, a fireplace, a porch, and lovely furnishings. The listed price for these, during the season (May 1 to November 4) in 1995, was an amazingly low $129 on Friday and Saturday nights, including a full breakfast. Also available are three large two-story villas, with similar features for an additional $10 per night.

These are in themselves enough to recommend Doe Run Lodge, but the owners have gone a step further and created three detached specialty suites of a quality, style, and decor rarely found elsewhere. Down by the spring-fed lagoon you will find a reproduction of an old grist mill, complete with a working water wheel, appropriately named **Millpond Hideaway**. Inside, it is thoroughly modern, with no convenience lacking. It was obviously designed with couples, romance, and privacy in mind. Features include a king-sized bed; a marble bath with double whirlpool, double shower and steam cabinet for two; a raised fireplace; a full suite stereo and television; a kitchenette; a private balcony; and even an enclosed garage. Prices are $199 per night on Friday and Saturday during the season.

Just across the way, you will see "super suite number two," the **Log Cabin**. Yes, it's a real log cabin, dating from 1865 and relocated to Doe Run from Delps Beach, a well known swimming hole of yore. Again, though, don't be fooled by the exterior. Though somewhat smaller than the Millpond Hideaway, the interior is decorated in a rustic style but incorporates amenities that are very much late 20th century. These include a queen-sized bed, natural stone fireplace, and whirlpool bath.

Our favorite of the three suites is farther back up the hill, and much more contemporary in style than even the Millpond Hideaway. The **Executive Suite** is circular in shape, with picture windows affording breathtaking views and a fireplace framing a large open great room with a king-sized bed, cozy sitting area, and double jacuzzi. For entertainment, there is a huge stack of electronic equipment (television, VCR, compact disc player, turntable, etc.) – all with remote control, of course. Behind all of this, there is a kitchen, a dining area, and a full bathroom. If the style is to your taste, this is one of the most romantic combinations of facilities to be found in any suite in this guide. The rental price for either this or the Log Cabin, on Friday or Saturday, is $169 per night.

Whichever of these suites you choose, you will not be disappointed. Few places offer such a variety of high quality choices, at such reasonable prices, in such a beautiful location – all the ingredients necessary for a peaceful and romantic weekend. But there is yet another bonus; if you intend to visit between November 5 and April 30, you can expect a hefty discount, often as much as 25 percent.

The interesting and unusual choices of accommodation don't end here. In nearby Claudville – take Route 58 to Stuart, then Route 8, and finally Route 103 – there is one of the best-kept secrets in the United States: the **Primland Hunting Reserve**, Route 1, Box 265-C. Sprawling over the Eastern slopes and foothills of the Blue Ridge Mountains, at elevations ranging from 1,500 to 3,000 feet, are 14,000 acres of stunningly beautiful land that is home to one of the finest hunting preserves in the Eastern United States.

Whatever your hunting preference, they have it – along with everything you need to bag it, including well trained dogs. There are upland-style bird hunts for pheasant, quail and chukar; European-style driven shoots; duck, deer, and wild turkey hunts; fishing at three trout ponds; and a sporting clay and five stand. Whether you are a novice or experienced, the trained guides ensure that you enjoy yourself in absolute safety. They will even clean and pack your trophies for you.

The reserve is much more than a haven for hunters. Non-shooters come to enjoy hiking, horseback riding, tennis, and photography. You may spend your nights in one of the handful of beautifully-appointed wooden chalets. These vary in character from rustic to modern, and feature magnificent views of the surrounding mountains and lakes. Priced at $125 per night, they cost even less in the summer, out of the hunting season. For information or reservations, phone (540) 251-8012 or fax (540) 251-8244. If you want something different, this is definitely it, whatever your choice of game.

The two bed and breakfasts could not be more different from each other, or from Doe Run Lodge. The first of these, when travelling north to south, is located approximately eight miles off the Parkway. Take Route 8 south to Woolwine, head north on Route 40, and, after a few minutes, you will see to your left a most delightful Victorian house nestled under the mountains and next to Rock Castle Creek. Just when you think you've passed it, you will see a long gravel driveway that takes you back to **Mountain Rose Bed & Breakfast**, (540) 930-1057. Built around 1900, it remained a private home until 1987. It was uninhabited and considerably deteriorated until the deceased owners' children advertised for innkeepers to turn it into a B&B.

The successful applicants, Maarten and Hermien Ankersmit, both of whom are Dutch, zealously set about the task of revitalizing and renovating the old house. The results are impressive indeed. There are five spacious bedrooms, each with a private bath, porch, and fireplace. Both these and the public rooms are delightfully decorated in a manner reflecting the character of the house. Outdoors, there is a spring-fed swimming pool, a trout-stocked stream, and miles of hiking trails across the 100 acres of forested hills. As attractive as all of this is on its own, one more subtle force is at work here: the famous Dutch sense of hospitality. The prices are reasonable, too; $65 per night includes a huge country breakfast.

Much farther south, between mileposts 194 and 195 at Fancy Gap, you will see on a hill to the west an imposing wooden building with porches on both the lower and upper levels. Take Route 691 (Orchard Gap Road) north and follow it on up to the **Inn at Orchard Gap**, (540) 398-3206. You will be surprised that the building is not as old as it looked from a distance. In fact, it is a relatively new prefabricated building, purchased as separate units and fitted together on-site. In the words of innkeepers Barbara and John DeRemer, it is "a new bed and breakfast in the tradition of a classic Virginia inn." This offers some obvious advantages. Though furnished with antique and reproduction furniture and embellished with family heirlooms, each of the spacious rooms has its own outside entrance and private bath. Some even have a fireplace. After your romantic interlude, you may opt to bring your family here on a vacation. No problem; there is also a cottage with kitchenette. The building is handicapped-accessible, with rates from $60 to $85 a night.

Having established the existence of delightful accommodations, let's turn our attention to the many local sights. The main attraction is the Blue Ridge Parkway itself, and the panorama of beautiful scenery through which it winds. You will find this visit with Mother Nature absolutely enthralling, no matter the season. Fall is the most popular time of year here, and the colors have to be seen to be believed. Spring provides a palette of a softer hue. It is as though a different shade of green is being added to the rainbow of fresh colors every minute. After a summer storm, the lush, dripping foliage resembles a rain forest. In winter, the parkway is at its most stark, with unforgettable walls of ice in the most unusual shapes sparkling in the weak sunshine. Be warned, though, ice forms on the road and sometimes closes the Parkway. If this happens, don't panic. Take Route 221 – which runs roughly parallel to the Parkway – and then cut back on the connecting roads to the Parkway, a few miles east.

If you fancy a leisurely stroll, the Parkway offers trails for hikers of all skill levels, conveniently categorized as "easy," "moderate" or "strenuous." Some are as short as half a mile, while others, such as the 10.8-mile Rock Castle Gorge Trail, are much longer. For a free Blue Ridge Parkway "Info Pak," as well as additional information, write to: BRPA, P. O. Box 453 BRD, Asheville, NC, 28802-0453.

As this section of the Blue Ridge Parkway covers a considerable distance, it is perhaps easiest to describe the ancillary attractions as you drive past them, north to south. Many of the more interesting attractions reflect the traditions of the area. The first one is no exception.

Just six miles north of the Parkway (on Route 8, at milepost 165.2), is the rather nondescript town of Floyd. So small is Floyd, that it has only one stop light. A quarter of a mile before that light, on your left, is **Cockram's General Store**, (540) 745-4563. Located on South Locust Street, it is a veritable Virginia institution that has been in operation for over 75 years.

In the old days, the "general" part of the term "general store" meant just that. As in other small towns, these stores catered to every need. Besides supplies and food, they were central gathering places that offered plenty of companionship. Folks would meet there to discuss business, swap tales and, when the mood took them, relax by playing music for each other. In other towns, these traditions have more or less died a natural death. But not in Floyd. Cockram's remains an old-fashioned general store in every sense of the word. Though space is limited, there is not much you can't find here. Do you fancy "potted possum"? Well, if not, the "fix 'em yourself" hot dogs have a pretty good reputation.

But it's the music that lures people from all over the country. With its **Friday Nite Jamboree**, starting at about 7 p.m., Cockram's General Store keeps a toe tappin' tradition alive. Musicians are the honored guests, so if you play, just turn up. It doesn't matter what you play, whether it's guitar, banjo, fiddle or kazoo; or what style you play, be it old-time, bluegrass, or country; your talents will be appreciated here. And if you don't play, well, turn up anyway to savor the unique atmosphere and listen to locals and strangers sharing, if not a common heritage, then a common language – music.

Floyd is also famed for the crafts people living in the surrounding area. Many of these come to sell their goods in the first weekend of October at the annual **Arts and Crafts Festival**. The old-fashioned July 4th celebrations are also worth a visit.

A little farther south is a place no one should miss, although it is very easy to do so. As you come to milepost 173, at one of the highest points of the Parkway, look for Route 725. Turn towards the west and then take the first left, onto Winery Road. Now, you should have some clue as to what is coming. Yes, a winery, and one with renowned wines: **Chateau Morrisette**, (540) 593-2865 or fax (540) 593-2868. Between 11 a.m. and 4 p.m. on Saturday and from noon to 4 p.m. on Sunday, you may take a winery tour followed by the best part, wine tastings. Many of these wines are award-winners, and you may wish to take some bottles home with you, along with something special from the Chateau's selection of attractive souvenirs. Additionally, every second Saturday, from June to October, the winery hosts lively outdoor music festivals. And don't miss the views looking out over the valley; they have a special appeal for romantics, being wonderfully intoxicating in themselves.

While at the Chateau, you will find an unexpectedly de-
lightful bonus in **Le Chien Noir**. As with some of the wines, the owner has named this fantastic restaurant in honor of a favorite black dog, whose likeness adorns the walls. To say the menu is varied is an understatement. The combinations of foods are uniquely creative and the wine list naturally well-selected. No visit to this area would be complete without a meal at Le Chien Noir, be it lunch on the terrace or an intimate dinner inside. It is open for lunch

Wednesday through Sunday, but dinner is served, by reservation, between 6 p.m. and 9 p.m. on Friday and Saturday only. One word of warning: be careful about the amount of wine you imbibe. The roads aren't forgiving, and neither are the park police.

 Three miles away, at milepost 176, is **Mabry Mill**, a spot steeped in local history. E. B. Mabry operated this mill from 1910 to 1935. Self-guiding trails take you to his gristmill, sawmill, blacksmith shop, and other old-time mountain history exhibits. While the mill itself is the main attraction, the entire complex is a nice place to stop for a picnic or break. A coffee and craft shop, located on the grounds, is open between May 1 and November 3. Outside these dates, the place is rather deserted and you will be left to your own devices, not a bad option either. In fact, one of the prettiest times to visit Mabry is deep in the winter, when everything is covered in thick ice, truly a sight you won't forget.

Wherever you go, expect an interesting selection of the antique and curio shops so immensely popular in this area. If you're seeking a real browsers' paradise, leave the parkway at Fancy Gap, and take Route 52 north for a couple of minutes. It is impossible to miss **Faye's Country Store**, (540) 728-2852. The huge yard and the front porch are filled with all kinds of curios. Inside the store and many outbuildings, everything from junk to antiques can be found. And you'll most likely find them open seven days a week, from 10 a.m. until they feel like closing. Just be sure you have time and money available; you'll need plenty of both.

The longer you stay in this area, the more you realize what an integral part of the local culture music is. Nowhere is this more evident than in Galax, which calls itself the "World's Capital Of Old-Time Mountain Music." This claim to fame has its roots in the **Old Fiddler's Convention**, held there annually on the second weekend of August. People, contestants, and connoisseurs have been coming from far and wide either to test their skills or to listen, learn, and admire, since the first convention way back in 1935. For more information, write to Old Fiddler's Convention, P. O. Box 655, Galax,

Virginia, 24333, or call (540) 236-8541. There aren't many other reasons to come to Galax. However, it might interest you to know that Galax got its name from the Galax leaf, an evergreen plant native to the southern crest of the Blue Ridge, and prized by florists around the world.

If you do decide to head in this direction, leave the Parkway at Fancy Gap and turn west on Route 58/221. Take a moment to stop when you see the signs for **Harmon's**, (540) 236-4844, at Woodlawn. At first glance, this looks like nothing more than a clothing store. But appearances can be deceptive. While the store does sell clothes, boots and an array of other things, the real treat is in the back of the store. The owner, Mr. Harmon, has spent a lifetime collecting anything that took his fancy and putting it on exhibit in his own "museum." The result is unusual, to say the least; there is even a stuffed calf with two heads! Visit any day, except Sunday, between 9 a.m. and 6 p.m.

This part of Virginia is also famous for its fruit, and it's never fresher than when you pick it yourself. Exit the Parkway at Route 691 by Orchard Gap, between mileposts 193 and 194, and take Orchard Gap Road south for a couple of miles to **Levering Orchard**, Route 3, Box 310, Ararat, (540) 755-3593. This claims to be the largest "pick your own" cherry orchard in the south. The cherries may be picked in June and early July, with apricots, peaches and nectarines ripening later in that month. The latter two fruits are still available in August, when they are joined by plums and pears. From September to Thanksgiving, you can "take your pick" of the apples.

Mountain Lake

Try Dirty Dancing
for Good, Clean Fun

There are only two natural fresh water lakes in the state of Virginia, and they couldn't be more different, either in location or style. One – the one that doesn't concern us here – is Lake Drummond, in the Dismal Swamp near Norfolk. The other is across the state, 3,872 feet above sea level in the Allegheny Mountains. No wonder, then, that it is called Mountain Lake.

This lake is said to be over 2,000 years old, but the first recorded sighting was on May 11, 1751, by the famous surveyor and frontiersman, Christopher Gist. An interesting footnote: before his employment by the Ohio Land Company, for whom he was working at the time of this discovery, Gist undertook missions for the Colony of Virginia. His leader on those occasions was no less a personage than George Washington, whose life he is reputed to have saved on two occasions.

Scientists have determined that Mountain Lake was formed when a rock slide dammed the north end of the valley and collected organic debris which filled in around the rocks to form a watertight seal. It is just under half a mile wide and 0.7 miles long; and although the southern end is shallow, it deepens, gradually, to reach a maximum of 100 feet at the northern end. The water, fed by underground streams, is not warm, and the temperature rarely rises above 72° F. The setting, though, is really stunning. Thousands of trees fill the land surrounding the lake. The latter drops steeply down to the water's edge, the altitude giving the impression that you are standing on top of the world.

The history of the ownership of this spot, known previously as Salt Pond, is complicated by confusion over the two earliest land grants (made in 1789 and 1796 respectively). By the mid-19th century, however, Henley Chapman, the first Commonwealth Attorney of Giles County and a member of the convention that framed the first Virginia Constitution, was the undisputed owner. On March 1, 1856, the Mountain Lake Company was formed. In 1857 came the first mention of a "pleasure resort" on the property; by that time, the description on the tax rolls had changed from "Salt Pond" to "Mountain Lake." After the Civil War, the property was purchased by General Herman Haupt of Pennsylvania, who continued development of the resort. It subsequently passed through several hands until, in the early 1930's, William Lewis Moody of Galveston, Texas, acquired the property and began construction of the present-day resort.

Until that time, the original Haupt Hotel was still standing, as were many of the cabins that pre-dated the turn of the century, but with facilities that were somewhat spartan. Even though the country was in the grip of the Great Depression, Mr. Moody, who was knowledgeable in resort management, began a program of improvements.

Cottages were replaced and refurbished in 1931. After the state of Virginia improved the access roads in 1933/34, he decided to build a new hotel with up-to-date facilities. This large, grand, and unusual building was constructed of field stone cut from the nearby Salt Pond Mountain, and the result is no less impressive today than when it was built and opened in 1937. The contrast of the main structure with the wooden cottages, some of them log cabins located on either side of the hotel or between the hotel and the lake, is one of the more charming aspects of this resort. And its charms haven't gone unnoticed, either. In the fall of 1986, set designers for the Vestron Movie Company moved in to recreate a 1960's ambiance in preparation for the filming of *Dirty Dancing*, starring Patrick Swayze and Jennifer Gray. This brought Mountain Lake increased visibility, something on which the resort has capitalized by holding a number of Dirty Dancing weekends.

These days, Mountain Lake is only open during the summer months, between May 1 and October 31 in 1995. That in itself makes it unusual, considering how many mountain top resorts focus on winter sports. Don't worry, though; it would be difficult to get there in the snow anyway. It's hard enough, even in good weather; the final leg of the journey is particularly arduous. When coming via Interstate 81, take Exit 37 and follow U.S. 460 West to Blacksburg, where it is best to avoid the town by taking the U.S. 460 Bypass (left fork) to Route 700. Travel along Route 700 as it ascends for seven twisting miles, until the hotel, romantic wooden cabins, and lake come into view. After experiencing "love at first sight," you will realize that the long drive has not been in vain.

The range of romantic accommodations is as exciting as the scenery. The cottages may look rustic – and they are, at least on the outside – but many of them have been rebuilt recently to incorporate all of the luxuries.

The **Lake Cottage** is a good example of this. It was opened in 1993 after being rebuilt from the ground up using logs from the original building. It still sits by the water's edge, and still boasts the best view of the lake, but there the resemblance ends. Now the king-sized bedroom opens up into a living room dominated by a grand stone fireplace. The bathroom has a separate shower and jacuzzi tub, each with their own private views over the lake. I wonder what the Victorians would have felt about such innovations? A three-day/two-night package with full breakfast and romantic candlelight dinner, plus complimentary fruit and champagne upon arrival and a horse drawn carriage ride, costs $565. Reasonable when you consider that if you want to book the cottage for just the weekend, you'll pay $225 per night during May, June, and September and $245 in July, August, and October. All rates are based on the Modified American Plan (MAP), and include breakfast and dinner daily. Two other nearby cottages, the **Norfolk** and the **Dorland**, were totally rebuilt in 1994 and offer similar facilities at similar prices.

Chestnut Lodge was originally built in 1944 as a dormitory facility to the main hotel and remodelled in 1983/84. Of interest is the **Chestnut Honeymoon Suite,** which features a king-sized bed, fireplace and private balcony, at $425 for the weekend package or from $155 to $195 per night, depending on the month.

If you prefer to stay in the main building itself, then you will find either the **Parlor Suite** or the **Junior Suite** to your liking. The former is characterized by a king-sized bed and living area with fireplace and jacuzzi, while the latter has merely a king-sized bed and jacuzzi. Prices for these are a bit less than the Lake Cottage, but more than the Chestnut Honeymoon Suite, respectively.

You'll never be lacking for something to do here. Wander through the 2,600 acres of tall trees and gentle hills to view abundant wildlife in natural habitats. Using the "Trail Map and Guide," choose one of 14 trails, with a challenge rating of between 1 (easiest) and 5 (most difficult). Explore to your heart's content, but please remember: take nothing but pictures and leave nothing but footprints. However, if you wish to use your own mountain bikes and helmets, they are welcome, too.

Perhaps you prefer to be on, or in, the water. Go onto the roped-off sandy beach or take a spin around the lake in the canoes, paddle boats, and row boats moored at the Boat Dock. Certainly, don't forget to bring your fishing poles. You may fish from the shore, from one of the boats, or take an organized fishing trip on the pontoon boat. If you wish to learn about fly-fishing, there are weekend and full-day introductory programs. For those already experienced in this sport, Guided Stream Excursions are offered. Harry Slone, author of *Virginia Trout Streams* and *Guide to Fishing the Blue Ridge Watershed*, leads these programs, which command an additional fee.

The **New River Canoe Livery**, just seven miles away, offers canoe rentals for use on the New River. For as little as $20 per person, they will shuttle you and the canoe to the river. When your journey is over, they will pick you up at the downstream pull-out point. For more details, call the Livery at (540) 626-7189.

When you tire of water sports, there's a tennis court. Volleyball, croquet, badminton and horseshoes are also available. Spectators have a particularly delightful vantage point. The picturesque gazebo, at water's edge, is a good place to sit, put your feet up, and observe everything around you. Or you may take a gentle cruise on a pontoon boat, where you'll learn about the geology and geography of the lake. Art lovers can have their day in the sun, too. The resort's artist in residence (Victoria Jordan Stone in 1994/95) will teach you how to reproduce the beauty around you, using watercolors and her special drawing techniques. Regular classes are conducted for a modest extra fee. Indoor games are plentiful here, too; you may even indulge in your own (in the privacy of your room, of course).

After all this activity, you may need to work a few kinks out of your body. A relaxing Swedish-style massage might do the trick. A full body massage takes approximately one and a quarter hours, and at $40 is well worth the effort, or rather the lack of it. Do your nails need attention as well? A manicure will make you feel especially pampered. Treatments, which are performed by a licensed technician, range from $17 to $55.

Now that you are relaxed and well-groomed, a pre-dinner shopping spree might be in order. Local Appalachian artists display their work in **The Gallery,** while **The General Store** offers a variety of Mountain Lake and *Dirty Dancing* souvenirs,and **MKW Antiques** carries a wide selection of antiques, jewelry and collectibles.

Whatever you do, or don't do, there is one thing you must not miss. Make sure you have that horse drawn carriage all to yourselves. Then you can snuggle up with your arms around each other and enjoy a romantic 40-minute trip through the enchanted forest.

You could say that Mountain Lake is the place for lovers, whether they are interested in dirty dancing or good clean fun. Telephone (540) 626-7121 or (800) 346-3334 to make your reservations.

Breaks Interstate Park

A Break for All Seasons

This will be a different kind of chapter – very short – as there is not much to write about. In this spot, you'll have no choice of restaurants and very little choice of things to do. Nor is there a choice of accommodations; the only option is booked far in advance for most of the year.

So what is attractive about this remote part of the world, over 425 miles from Washington, D.C.?

Research for this guide has taken us into the four corners of Virginia and Maryland. More often than not, the itineraries for such research trips have been planned; we have known in advance where we were headed, and had a reasonable idea of what to expect. However, on some occasions, the adventurous spirit has taken hold. We scoured the countryside for lesser known, or even unknown, places that might prove ideal for a romantic break. More often than not, these trips yielded little. The scenery was certainly memorable, but what accommodations there were could not be recommended; and restaurants, let alone nightlife, were virtually non-existent. There are exceptions to every rule, however. Breaks Interstate Park straddles the borders of Virginia and Kentucky and it is definitely an exception.

The scenery here is unparalleled in Virginia. The Russell Fork River has carved out of rocks a totally natural canyon, over five miles long and up to 1,600 feet deep. Nicknamed the "Grand Canyon of the South," it is the largest gorge east of the Mississippi River, and is said to be some 250 million years old. Today, this magnificent work of nature serves as the centerpiece of the park. Views from the Towers Overlook are the most spectacular, and what makes them even more spectacular is that the area is absolutely devoid of the commercialization that so disfigures much of the American countryside – and this is deliberate. In a joint action of the Virginia and Kentucky legislatures, Breaks Interstate Park was formed in 1954 to oversee 4,500 acres of some of the most diverse and interesting scenery you could ever hope to see. Here, today's hustle and bustle give way to the pleasures of a simpler time as you ponder the area's rich history and local myths. Go on a treasure hunt for the fortune in silver said to be hidden here by Englishman John Swift. Mentally dodge the bullets flying between the Hatfields and McCoys during their legendary feud. Explore the caves used by Shawnee Indians, first for shelter, and later to make potent "fire water."

Think of wandering the miles of trails surrounded by majestic trees dressed in their seasonal garb, and gathering an impromptu bouquet from the abundance of bright, delicately scented wild flowers. You may enjoy fishing, or maybe boating, but what you will cherish the most is just getting away from all the hassles that bombard you in day-to-day life. If this scenario appeals to you, then Breaks Interstate Park is, more than any other destination described in this guide, the place for you.

Besides the time it takes to get to the Breaks (even in the best of conditions), there is the problem of accommodation. The nearby area offers little choice. In any event, why come such a distance and not stay in the park itself? But therein lies the problem. As most activities within the park are seasonal (April 1 through October 31), the 34-room motor lodge is open only during those months. It doesn't really inspire romance and it's likely to be booked anyway, especially on weekends. But there is a solution: four totally detached two-bedroom cottages, real gems, set in beautiful woodlands and featuring all the modern conveniences. True, they aren't decorated with the latest furniture, and they are a bit love-worn, but they are the perfect complement to this environment. What could be more romantic for nature lovers than sitting outdoors, enjoying a picnic, with curious wild animals dropping by to see what you are up to — maybe even sharing your food? It is amazingly affordable; just $65 a night or $275 a week. As with anything, there are a couple of drawbacks; first, there is a minimum booking period of one week in the season; and, secondly, they are almost certainly going to be booked solid between June and early October, and difficult to reserve at other times as well. Out-of-season, ensure you'll get one by calling (800) 982-5122 many months in advance. In season, simply book it for a whole week, and just use the weekend. At these prices it is not such an extravagance to do so. If your schedule is flexible enough to wait until the last moment, call on Monday. If there have been any cancellations for the following week, they will take a reservation for just a weekend, even in season. Whichever way you do it, you will not have any regrets. Pack up your casual clothes and walking shoes, extra sheets and towels and, of course, as much food and drink as you'll need.

Each season has its own unique beauty and nowhere are the changes more dramatic than here. The spring's wildflower carpets and flowering shrubs give way to sun-dappled trails and hot days perfect for enjoying the park's water activities. In the fall, lush forest greens yield to a brilliant palette of red, yellow, gold, orange, scarlet, and brown. Finally, winter's blanket of snow makes a beautiful, yet stark, contrast to the dark trees against the cold grey sky.

If you visit "in season," there is a restaurant with a panoramic view, gift shop, swimming pool, a boating dock with pedal boats for hire and a stable where horses and ponies may be rented for a nominal fee. You can fish all year round, using your own boat (no gasoline motors allowed); picnic in one of the many shelters located throughout the park; or walk along the approximately 12 miles of hiking trails, detailed on maps available at the park headquarters.

There is one other leisure activity nearby, but it is recommended for experts only, and is an option for just one month. During October, on weekends, water is released, if rainfall has been adequate, from the nearby John Flanagan Dam. This makes for excellent white-water rafting on the Russell Fork River but, again, we emphasize that it is strictly for experienced rafters aged 16 or older. Arrange your trip by calling **Laurel Highlands River Tours**, at (800) 4 RAFTIN. On Saturdays the cost is $175.95, with Sunday excursions a little less at $150.95. This is the same company that runs the trips on the Upper Yough, in western Maryland, also designed for advanced to expert level rafters. The folks at Laurel Tours pride themselves on their commitment to their clients' well being, and potential raftersare evaluated to determine if they possess the skill necessary to make the journey safely.

All these attractions aside, you are primarily going to come this distance for the wild, magnificent scenery which this park offers. It also offers a very rare chance to be alone, together, away from the complications and worries that have become a part of modern life.

When you want a really unusual break, head for Breaks Interstate Park.

Tidewater & Hampton Roads, Virginia

Norfolk
Anchor Here for a Maritime Mood

The presence of an important naval base is sure to have a profound impact on the character of a city. This is most certainly the case with Norfolk. A place full of shipyards and servicemen would not strike you as a destination for a romantic weekend. Yet because and in spite of these influences, Norfolk is a city of pleasant surprises. Equally surprising is its sister town, Portsmouth, just a short ferry ride across the Elizabeth River.

Oddly enough, one of the most difficult things to find here is a charming place to stay. Certainly there is no shortage of hotels, but the majority of them offer nothing remarkable in the way of either location or amenities. In fact, Norfolk is the only full-sized city we've explored in which a bed and breakfast is one of the best places to stay. Not surprisingly, this is located in a historic district.

Located on a tract of farmland originally known as Pleasant Point, this district was far removed from the downtown area at the time that its owner, James Morgan, renamed it Ghent. This was done in honor of the Treaty of Ghent, in Belgium, which ended the War of 1812. By the latter part of that century, the district's growth into an exclusive area had begun. Through the period that ended with the Second World War, this was the fashionable place to live. The post-war era, however, brought a sustained period of decline; before long, the area had degenerated into an undesirable neighborhood. Fortunately, recent "regentrification" has returned the area to its former splendor. Today, stately homes on quiet, tree-lined streets exude a delightful Old World charm.

 It is at 323 Fairfax Avenue, in the heart of this Ghent Historic District, that one finds **The Page House Inn Bed & Breakfast**, (804) 625-5033. This gracious three-story Georgian Revival house was built at the end of the last century by Herman L. Page, a prominent real estate developer of the day, for use as his family residence. It is constructed of brick laid in the interesting Flemish bond pattern. By the time that Stephanie and Ezio DiBelardino first came upon the house, it had been neglected for an extended period its condition was so poor that it faced demolition. The DiBelardinos, whose family roots were entrenched in the area, had more productive ideas. Following strict guidelines established by the U.S. Secretary of the Interior for the rehabilitation of historic properties, Ezio used his skills as a professional builder and master craftsman to restore the house to its former beauty. The work was completed in 1991 and The Page House Inn, furnished with 19th and early 20th- century antiques, art and reproductions, opened for business.

Guests may choose from one of the two suites or four guest rooms and each one offers a distinct personality uniquely its own. **Miss Diane's Suite** is spacious, with a sitting room that features a wet bar and stocked refrigerator, and a bedroom with a queen-sized white iron bed. Both rooms boast a romantic gas log fireplace. There is a private dining room, as well, where (if you are still in the mood for privacy) an optional in-room breakfast may be served. This room overlooks The Chrysler Museum and rents for $145 per night. **Mistress Adela's Suite** is delightfully decorated with deep green English florals. The bedroom has a queen-sized canopy bed, a chaise longue which sits lazily by the gas log fireplace, and an inviting whirlpool bath. The sitting room boasts a bay window, an antique oak table for that optional in-room breakfast, a wet bar and stocked fridge. This rents for $135.

Mr. Herman's Room is decorated in deep greens and burgundies, with puddled drapes and handmade oak venetian blinds. The focal point is a very romantic canopy bed hand carved of black walnut in the 1830s. In addition, there are a converted fireplace with its original coal basket; a whirlpool for two; and a delightful location, just across from the rooftop garden. This room can be yours for $120 per night. **Master Percy's Room** has matching twin-size mahogany four-poster beds. (With a little advance notice, these are convertible to king-size.) The Williamsburg blue decor is done in the English floral style, and enhanced by a lovely skylight. A soaking tub of the European genre is a nice touch as well. For $95 per night you may enjoy these amenities while overlooking The Chrysler Museum and The Hague. **Master Lawrie's Room** is decorated in deep corals and furnished with rare turn-of-the-century birds-eye maple furniture. It features a European king-sized bed and skylight, and also overlooks the Chrysler Museum. The private bath, however, offers only a shower. The tariff, once again, is $95. **Miss Hulda's Room**, the only feminine offering, is appropriately finished in soft pinks and greens. Here you will retire to a full-sized mahogany sleigh bed, wile away the afternoon relaxing on the Victorian loveseat, or soak to your heart's content in a claw-footed tub with shower. The rate for this room is fixed at $85.

The rates quoted are for weekends and holidays, and include a delicious home-cooked breakfast served in the formal dining room on fine china, with crystal and silver. Along with hot or cold drinks, fresh-baked oatmeal cookies are available for afternoon refreshment. That's if they haven't been stolen by Charlie and Tootsie, two friendly Boston terriers. There is ample off-street parking and Stephanie will be more than happy to arrange for flowers in the room of your choice. The ambiance of the Page House Inn is absolutely delightful. If you want to sample it, book well in advance.

Just next door you will find the famous **Chrysler Museum**. Founded in 1933, this was renamed in 1971 after one of its major benefactors, automobile empire heir Walter P. Chrysler Jr. Its impressive collection consists of over 30,000 pieces dating from 2,700 B.C. to the present and ranging from French and Italian painting to an internationally famous glass collection. It has been ranked by *The Wall Street Journal* as among the top 20 collections in the country. Noted, too, for its architectural design, the museum is open from 10 a.m. to 4 p.m. Saturday and from 1 p.m. to 5 p.m. on Sunday. Telephone (804) 664-6200 for information or (804) 622-ARTS for a recorded message detailing weekly events. For a listing of other attractionsin close proximity, procure a copy of the **"Ghent Guide."** This also gives you some valuable insight into the surrounding area.

Norfolk is, first and foremost, a maritime city. As in other such cities, it is difficult to get a realistic perception of the area from the ground level or at any distance away from the waterfront. However, there are two hotels in the same general vicinity that enable you to get a real "feel" for the town.

At 235 East Main Street, just across the road from the Waterside Marketplace, is the **Norfolk Marriott Waterside Hotel,** telephone (804) 627-4200. The lobby and public rooms are particularly sumptuous, and we would recommend that you take the time to relax in the second floor lounge area. Here, you'll be treated to the sounds and easy showmanship of the house pianist. His reputation is far-reaching, and his talent absolutely riveting.

The rooms are all of a good standard, but the building's high-rise construction is its main attraction. To take full advantage of this attribute, request a room on one of the upper floors, preferably a corner one. These feature large picture windows on two sides, allowing for a wonderful birds-eye view of the area. By day the rivers and bays spring to life, with ferry boats and naval vessels of all shapes and sizes forming a kaleidoscope of action. By night, the light and the colors are spectacular. When booking your reservation, inquire about the "Honeymoon" or "Two for Breakfast" packages. These ensure you a river view and king-sized bed and include breakfast for all, with champagne for honeymooners. They range from $109 to $124.

Across the road, adjacent to the Waterside Festival Marketplace at 777 Waterside Drive, is the **Omni Waterside Hotel**, (804) 622-6664. This is the only hotel in Norfolk situated on the banks of the Elizabeth River, whose working seaport it overlooks. There are 446 rooms and 19 suites, half of which boast delightful views of the river. From this vantage point, or when dining on-site in the Riverwalk Restaurant or the Veranda Café, you'll have a panoramic view of the vessels passing your window. You will watch cruise ships, naval vessels, tall ships, and the tiny Elizabeth River Ferry craft as they float past.

One unusual feature here is the "hotel within a hotel" located on The Omni Club level. This section provides the finest rooms, separate check-in and express check-out, access to the club lounge, a complimentary daily national newspaper delivered to your door, and the services of a club concierge who will personally attend to all your needs. As an alternative to booking à la carte, consider one of the two "romance packages": a deluxe room on the club level, champagne in your room, complimentary valet parking and Continental breakfast for two, at $119 a night; or the "Suite" Romance, which includes a deluxe suite, champagne in the room, complimentary valet parking and a full breakfast for two (taken at the buffet or served in your room) for $189.

Norfolk's history is inextricably linked to its geographical position and the fact that it boasts a naturally deep, ice-free harbor, one of the largest in the world. In 1607, members of the Virginia Company, traveling in the vessels *Godspeed, Discovery* and *Susan Constant,* landed near the present-day Cape Henry in Virginia Beach. (They would continue upriver to Jamestown, where they would found the first permanent English settlement in America.) By 1636, Charles I had granted 200 acres of land in this area to Thomas Willoughby; later, in 1682, 50 acres of that grant were used to lay out the town of Norfolk. In 1754, Lt. Governor Robert Dinwiddie, presented the borough of Norfolk with a sterling silver ceremonial mace, said to be one of only two Colonial maces owned by U.S. localities. This is one of the items on display today in The Chrysler Museum.

This is a city that, for obvious reasons, has seen much fighting. During the American Revolution, Lord Dunmore's ships fired on Norfolk, causing considerable damage. In the War of 1812, the outcome was more favorable, with Virginia troops winning the Battle of Craney Island. Civil War history was made when Hampton Roads witnessed the first battle of ironclad ships; by 1863, Union troops occupied the city. The Second World War saw dramatic growth in the local naval base, today recognized as the largest such installation in the world. Commercially, the port of Hampton Roads – a name given to the point where the Chesapeake Bay, the Elizabeth River, the James River and the Nansemond River meet – links the port cities of Norfolk, Newport News and Portsmouth to major markets throughout the world.

It should come as no surprise that, of the many things to see and do here, most revolve around the water. A wise way to begin discovering Norfolk would be to take a tour of both the harbor and naval base aboard the *Carrie B.*, (804) 393-4735. A reproduction of a 19th-century Mississippi-style paddlewheeled river boat, she offers a close look at vessels in the powerful Atlantic Fleet from her open top deck or air-conditioned lower deck. Two types of daytime cruises are offered. One cruises the inner harbor and highlights the Norfolk Naval Shipyard, while the other takes you to the Norfolk Naval Base and Hampton Roads. These run between April 1 and October 31, with sunset cruises also available from June 1 to Labor Day. All set sail from The Waterside.

A bus tour of the **Norfolk Naval Base** will give you an even closer look at the fleet but, as the schedule is varied, it's best to call (804) 444-7955 beforehand. On the weekends, the base offers free "open house" tours of selected ships. To take advantage of these, you need to drive to the Naval Base Pass Office to get a pass and guide map. For security reasons, you must produce your valid driver's license and car registration as identification. A more graceful way of touring the harbor is "under sail."

Also departing from The Waterside is the largest three-masted passenger-carrying top sail schooner under the U.S. flag. Modeled after the Chesapeake Bay cargo schooners of the 19th century, the 135-foot *American Rover*, (804) 393-4735, offers three cruises a day between early April and late October.

The **Elizabeth River Ferry** operates between Norfolk and Portsmouth, as her forerunners have done for centuries. A trip on this charming pedestrian-only boat – which features an imitation paddle-wheel at the rear – is a lot of fun, cheap (only 75 cents each way), and gives you the chance to compare modern, bustling Norfolk with its neighbor across the river. The ferry departs from Norfolk's waterside at intervals of 30 minutes on the quarter-hour. It docks at Portsmouth's portside, which is next to the Olde Towne Historic District.

Before setting out to explore this enchanting area, stop at the **Visitor Information Center**, (804) 393-5111, directly in front of you. We suggest that you pick up the "Visitor's Guide" and "Old Towne Walking Tour" brochures. The Olde Towne is a real delight, with its numerous Colonial, Federal, Greek Revival, Georgian and Victorian structures. Both elegant and diverse, this is one of the largest collections of antique homes in Virginia.

If you don't feel like walking this mile-square area, you may choose to take an **Olde Towne Trolley Tour**, (804) 393-5111. That is, if you are visiting between Memorial Day weekend and Labor Day weekend. If you are feeling really romantic, look into **Chariots for Hire**, (804) 421-7750. They offer a most charming way to tour this delightful district from a slightly different perspective. You and your partner will be served a light supper while being leisurely escorted in a unique white vis-a-vis (face to face) horse carriage of French vintage. These depart at 5 p.m., 6 p.m. or 7 p.m. during the months of May through September. The rate is $85 for the nearly hour-long trip.

Visiting here will teach you much about the rich history of Portsmouth, a history which dates to its settlement as a plantation community around 1620. Seventeen years later, a county government was established here. In 1659, the

Portsmouth tract was granted to Captain William Carver, but subsequently confiscated after his execution in 1676 for his role in Bacon's Rebellion. The town was established in 1752 and the Gosport Shipyard instituted a decade and a half later, in 1767. The town was in the thick of the action during the Revolutionary War until late in 1781. At that time, Lord Cornwallis evacuated Portsmouth to relocate in Yorktown, the site of his surrender on October 19 of that year. Along the water, and within a few hundred yards of Portside, the **Naval Shipyard Museum** and the **Lightship Museum** chronicle this city's maritime traditions.

Museums aren't always romantic in nature, but when you return to downtown Norfolk, there is one you will want to see. Housed in a very modern building is **Nauticus**, the Nation's Maritime Center. An imaginative interactive showplace, this museum allows you to experience the power of the sea firsthand. Touch a live shark, or observe a high-tech naval battle simulated by the use of computers, videos and special effects. "Plunge" to a depth of 900 fathoms, where you will discover new life forms while watching *The Living Sea*. Meet Captain Nauticus, who teaches the importance of protecting the world's oceans. Descend into a 3-D underwater environment, where you'll be expected to carry out your own scientific mission. And the list goes on. At night you'll be enthralled by the powerful laser light show, which is set to musical accompaniment. The Nauticus is closed January through March, but open 9 a.m. to 5 p.m. on weekends for the remainder of the year. Call (804) 664-1080 for information on the museum's many special events.

There are a variety of land-based activities in Norfolk that do not revolve around the water but deserve mention, too. If your visit falls between May 23 and September 25, then by all means take the **Norfolk Trolley Tour**. Trolley cars depart from the Waterside Drive side of The Waterside Festival Marketplace at frequent intervals between the hours of 11 a.m. and 4 p.m. In the "off-season" (after Labor Day), the first trolley does not depart until midday. The tour encompasses the historical area of downtown Norfolk and makes scheduled stops at seven of the more important attractions: The Chrysler

Museum; the Douglas MacArthur Memorial, which houses 11 galleries of memorabilia, as well as his tomb; the Moses Myers and Willoughby-Baylor houses; St. Paul's church, the oldest building in Norfolk and the only structure to survive the British destruction of the city on New Year's Day in 1776; the d'Art Center; and the Hunter House Victorian Museum. Just get off wherever you choose and hop on a later trolley to continue your trip. If you can resist the temptation to make a stop — and you shouldn't — the tour will take about one hour.

The two houses included on the above itinerary are the property of the City of Norfolk and are operated by The Chrysler Museum. The Federal Period **Moses Myers House** dates from 1792; it was built by one of America's first millionaires, who was also Norfolk's first Jewish settler. Furnished with essentially original pieces, it is the only historic house in the U.S. with exhibits reflecting the traditions of early Jewish Immigrants. The second residence, the **Willoughby-Baylor House,** was constructed just two years later and features an absolutely delightful garden. Today it offers an interesting perspective of a middle-class family's lifestyle during the 18th century.

No visit to Norfolk would be complete without a stop at **The Waterside Festival Market Place**, built next to and overlooking the Elizabeth River. Although many local businesses use this as a base of operations, it is an attraction in its own right. Opened in 1983, it houses more than 120 shops and eateries, including five full-service restaurants. Its outdoor amphitheater and brick promenade reach to the river's edge, providing a stage for spring and summer concerts.

Two other attractions might interest certain visitors. **Fort Norfolk**, (804) 625-1720, on the banks of the Elizabeth River near Ghent, is one of the best preserved War of 1812 battle sites in America. Located at 810 Front Street and open between 1 p.m. and 4 p.m. on Sundays, it hosts many special events throughout the year, including military re-enactments. The new **Harbor Park Stadium**, (804) 622-2222, is similar in style to — but much smaller than — Baltimore's Camden Yards. This is home to the Norfolk Tides, a top minor league farm team for the New York

Mets. Its riverside location makes it a delightful place to see a ball game.

A city of this size has many restaurants and, in most cases, comments on this topic will be somewhat subjective. The following list details a variety of choices, with something for everyone.

Like others in its chain, the **Phillips Waterside**, located within The Waterside, is a fun place to eat and has a great selection of food. If you want to eat and cruise at the same time, walk a little further down the waterside to the **Spirit of Norfolk**. Like its sister ships sailing from Baltimore and D.C., this state-of-the-art vessel offers "Fun & Sun Lunch Cruises" and evening dinner cruises. These are accompanied by entertainment from either live bands, playing hits of the 1940s to 1990s, or the talented crew, who offer a cabaret-style show. "Moonlight Party Cruises" begin at 11:30 p.m. on Friday and offer dancing to live music, as well as a snack and bar service. Reservations may be made by calling (804) 627-7771.

Back on land, dine in an environment that will raise your spirits. The building which houses this restaurant was built in 1873, as the Second Presbyterian Church. It continued to serve in this capacity until it was converted to the **Freemason Abbey Restaurant & Tavern** in 1988. Located at the corner of Freemason and Boush Streets, it's impossible to miss. Two false ceilings have been removed to expose the cathedral roof trusses; the resulting ambiance is both unusual and attractive. An extensive menu of traditional American dishes is offered daily. But it is the lobster that is truly heavenly. What began as a Wednesday night lobster special has snowballed until today, over 1,000 whole fresh lobsters are served every month. The meticulous care taken in the selection of these lobsters accounts for the success of this venture. Only the off-shore variety are considered and they are never stored in tanks for more than a couple of days. More often than not, they are shipped from New England on the same day they come off the boats. For reservations, call (804) 622-3966.

There is one restaurant in the area that is superb. Approaching it from the outside, you would probably miss it. Even if you didn't, you wouldn't give it much thought. The interior is far from ostentatious, with a small bar, a table area, and a few high-backed booths. Although smarter, cleaner and more pleasant, it resembles an upscale burger bar (something it was once rumored to have been). The waiters and waitresses are well-informed and show a healthy mix of respect and informality, something one usually expects, but doesn't often find. And the food, oh, the food – just thinking of it makes your mouth water. Absent are the usual huge mounds that either entice you to over-indulge or to waste your portion. Here chef and owner Todd Jurich, who with his wife Barbara operates the restaurant, makes good use of the knowledge he acquired studying Thai cuisine. His light touch with traditional American and Continental recipes results in some of the most delicate dishes you are ever likely to taste. Indeed, the **Bistro**, (804) 622-3210 at 210 York Street, is a truly exceptional restaurant. Be sure to book your dinner reservation well in advance; it is nearly always filled to capacity, particularly in the evening. This restaurant is not widely advertised, but it doesn't have to be; enough discerning people know about it already.

For some lighthearted after-dinner entertainment, head for the Wells Theater, at the junction of Monticello and Tazwell. Here you may enjoy productions by **The Virginia** **Stage Company,** the region's only fully professional not-for-profit theater. The company stages five major productions each season, as well as a holiday musical and a selection of more intimate "second stage shows." For information and ticket reservations, call (804) 627-2310. Alternatively try the **Norfolk Scope** and **Chrysler Hall**, (804) 441-2161, an 11,300-seat domed arena and 2,503-seat luxury theater, respectively, which may offer anything from ice-hockey to a Broadway- style show.

Norfolk is never short of special events. The **Norfolk Convention & Visitors Bureau**, 236 East Plume Street, (800) 368-3097, will be happy to send you a full listing. Among the more interesting: **New Art-New Wine** in January; the **Waterside Valentine Wine Tasting**, in February; the **Downtown Doo Dah Parade** at the end of

March; the widely-acclaimed **International Azalea Festival** during the last week in April; the **Ghent Art Show** and **Virginia Renaissance Faire,** on the middle two weekends in May; and the **Afr'am Fest,** celebrating the accomplishments of African-Americans on the last weekend in May. June is busy, too, with **Harborfest, Bayou Boogaloo & Cajun Food Festival** and **America's Sail Tall Ship Festival**. Come July, there's the **Town Point Air Show and Fourth of July Celebration** and, on the last weekend, the **Blackbeard Pirate Jamboree**. The **Annual Town Point Jazz Festival** is scheduled for the end of August and the **River Rib Fest** for the middle of September. October has several offerings. They are, in order: **The Chesapeake Bay Maritime Festival and Classic Boat Show, Stockley Gardens Fall Arts Festival** and the **Virginia Town Point Wine Festival**. The **Holidays in the City Grand Illumination & Lighted Parade**, in mid-November, kicks off Norfolk's festive winter holiday season. From then until the end of December, there are the **Wildlights at the Virginia Zoo** and the **Garden of Lights** at the Norfolk Botanical Gardens. At the end of November, the **Holiday in the City Lighted Boat Parade** illuminates the Elizabeth River, while December 31 is the date for the **Annual Waterfront New Year's Eve Fireworks**.

Virginia Beach
A Whale of a City

Most Virginia cities are knee-deep in history. An exception to the rule is Virginia Beach. The first permanent English settlers did land at nearby Cape Henry, but soon headed upriver to Jamestown, leaving the beach area unsettled. So, if you go there, it should be for relaxation only; no tours, no historic homes, no exercise for your mind. Just put all of your worries behind you and have fun.

A few years ago, Virginia Beach had a somewhat seedy reputation. Not so today. Although somewhat smaller than Ocean City – a similar resort also featured in this guide – Virginia Beach offers a much more interesting range of unusual and romantic oceanfront rooms. Our favorites are in the **Clarion Resort & Conference Center**, right on the southern end of the beach at 501 Atlantic Avenue, telephone (804) 422-3186 or (800) 345-3186. This is an impressively large and modern hotel, offering many amenities designed for fun. There's a rooftop pool; a poolside tropical bar and grill; a sundeck with a putting green; rooftop tennis courts; a health club with sauna, jacuzzi and resident masseuse; and the award-winning Captain's Table restaurant. Valet car parking service is available, as is free indoor parking. There are 168 rooms, with over 50 allotted to time-share owners. Although they are all nice, we suggest that readers of this guide choose from among the seven detailed here. Four of these are queen V.I.P. suites, each consisting of two rooms and featuring a queen-sized bed and double-sized private oceanfront balcony. Also included are two remote control color cable televisions (one with a VCR), two telephones, a fully-equipped kitchen with service for four, a clock radio and a modern bathroom stocked with complimentary toiletry items. These rent for between $70 and $225 per night, depending upon the season. More appealing still are the center's other three suites. Laid out similarly to the V.I.P.s, but with two-person jacuzzis, they are each decorated in a different fantasy theme. You might get a little bubbly in the **Champagne Suite**, located on the third floor. Feel like "monkey business"? Head for the **Safari Suite** on the eleventh floor. The eighth-floor **Roman Suite** is your best bet if you feel like "fiddling around" in your togas. With its Caesar-sized bed, this last one is our favorite. Just choose according to your mood. The rates vary between $100 and $300, according to season. Be sure to reserve early.

At Oceanfront and 12th Street there is another modern motel with an unusual distinction. Though it's not uncommon to find jacuzzis in a few hotel rooms, this unique 10-story motel has them in most – over 60 in all. Decorated in light airy colors with modern furniture, each room has a private balcony with oceanfront view; a mini-refrigerator; microwave oven; and color cable TV with complimentary

HBO and ESPN. Take a leisurely swim in the heated indoor pool, or lounge on the sundeck after a relaxing soak in its hot tub. For your convenience, there is a coin-operated laundry room that is perfect for rinsing out those sandy bathing suits. On-site parking is also provided, with one space allocated per room. All of these rooms are worth recommending, but a few are designed with romance in mind. Some have a king-sized bed and a large jacuzzi all in one room, while others have a king-sized bed with the jacuzzi in the bathroom. There are three that are particularly special. These are called "King Deluxes," and with good reason. Decorated in tropical splendor, they feature a king-sized canopy bed facing a large whirlpool tub with a gas fireplace tucked in between surrounding mirrors. Doesn't that set your imagination awhirl? When you are ready for a change, there is a double walk-in shower with two shower heads. No telling what you can get up to here, but you won't have any excuses for staying dirty. The **Newcastle Motel**, (804) 428-3981 or (800) 346-3176, is always striving to update its facilities and improve customer service. It is also in the process of opening a full-service, on-site restaurant. Multi-course room service meals are also in the works, should these rooms prove too enticing to vacate. Depending upon room and season, they cost between $50 and $200 a night. And in the unlikely event you have energy to spare, there are bicycles available as well.

Another hotel with spectacular rooms is **The Trade Winds Hotel** at 1601 Atlantic Avenue, telephone (804) 428-5370 or (800) 344-3342 and fax (804) 422-1821. Located closest to the oceanfront, it offers penthouse suites that include jacuzzis, kitchens and private balconies. Guests also have the use of a sundeck on a private key-access floor overlooking the Atlantic. One suite has a fireplace, while another features a private sundeck, a wet bar, a big-screen television and a larger jacuzzi. Other on-site amenities include an outdoor pool, a restaurant and parking. The rates range from $115 to $150 in the winter, $135 to $175 in the spring and fall, and $176 to $250 in the summer months.

The Breakers Resort Inn at 16th and Oceanfront also has interesting rooms. For newlyweds – whether in fact or at heart – there are two bridal suites. Each boasts a jacuzzi, a living room, and a kitchen. Twelve deluxe king rooms feature king-sized beds with a two-person jacuzzi in each room. Be sure to ask for the Anniversary Package, whether or not you're celebrating an anniversary. This includes two nights' accommodation, a full breakfast, a bottle of chilled champagne, and gifts from the hotel management. Depending upon the season and the type of room you select, the rates range from $152 to $292 per night.

What you do when you get to Virginia Beach depends upon the season. Although some of the most enjoyable activities are "seasonless," many local attractions are only open between the Memorial Day and Labor Day weekends. Unless otherwise noted, this is true of everything described here. In fact, romantic couples in search of solitude may opt to avoid the crowds and visit out of season. Soaking in a hot jacuzzi is especially wonderful when you're drinking champagne and listening to the wind howling outside. Far more romantic than the hum of an air conditioner!

For further information, stop by the **Visitors' Information Center** at 2100 Parks Avenue. Its hours are from 9 a.m. until 8 p.m. during the high season and from 9 a.m. until 5 p.m. for the balance of the year. If you would like information before you arrive, call (800) VA-BEACH. Make your visit even more inviting by calling (800) 446-8038 and requesting the free "$200 Off Virginia Beach" coupon booklet. This offers discounts on local restaurants; jet ski, sailboat and bicycle rentals; dive trips; and much more.

Why not consider a trip early in the year? After the hustle and bustle of holiday celebrations, most couples could use a brief break just to celebrate each other. This is also the perfect time to take a very special cruise. In fact, it's the only time of the year that the Virginia Marine Science Museum sponsors trips to sea for **whale watching**. Humpback whales, which grow up to 50 feet long and weigh up to 40 tons, congregate off the coast during this season. Besides offering the opportunity to see these magnificent creatures up close, museum staff members conduct educational programs and answer questions about them.

The cruise also affords glimpses of pelicans, gannets, and other wildlife, as well as local landmarks. (Cape Henry Lighthouse is one of these. Constructed in 1791 by America's first congress, it is the oldest government-built lighthouse in the U.S.) Cruises depart Friday through Monday, but are subject to cancellation in inclement weather. Remember, too, that sightings cannot be guaranteed, since the whales don't follow specific time schedules. Telephone (804) 437-4949 for up-to-date information. You can, however, be guaranteed admission to the **Virginia Marine Science Museum.** And you'll definitely like these "sightings." Located just off General Booth Boulevard, south of the Rudee Inlet Bridge, this museum features many interactive exhibits. Here you can learn about decoy carving; touch creatures in the Touch Tank; and "build" a fish on the museum's special computer. In addition to hearing many fishy stories, you will see the 50,000 gallon aquarium; tong for oysters like Chesapeake Bay watermen; find out how much salt is in a salt marsh or, maybe, make waves in the weather room when you start a storm. These and many other activities are sure to captivate.

Seeing all these fish may inspire you to put rod to water. If so, head for the Rudee Inlet at the southern end of the boardwalk, and look for the **Virginia Beach Fishing Center**, (804) 422-5700. Here you will find a variety of choices. During February and March, there are all-day Boston mackerel trips that leave at 8 a.m. and return by 4 p.m., at a cost of $30. In the spring, fall and winter you can fish for sea bass, tautog and blues on full- or half-day wreck fishing trips, for up to $35. During the season, you might feel adventurous enough to go deep-sea fishing. Half-day charters, which run either 7 a.m. to midday or 1 p.m. to 6 p.m., cost $525. A full-day charter running 6 a.m. to 5 p.m. will set you back $925. Expensive, yes; but you might come back with a shark, tuna, white or blue marlin, swordfish, sailfish, wahoo or mahi-mahi. Besides the personal thrill, you'll have stories to tell for years to come! If you'd like something calmer, board the *Miss Virginia Beach* for either an oceanfront whale or dolphin-watching cruise. While at the Fishing Center, you may also try **Skyrider** para-sailing, (804) 422-UFLY. They use Para-Nautique powerboats to launch a patented aerial recliner seat that allows two passengers to fly together. What a novel place to cuddle!

If you'd like to play captain for a change, look up **Laskin Road Water Sports** at 1284 Laskin Road (804) 428-6156. Here you may commandeer a wave runner, pontoon boat or speed boat, at rates ranging from $39 for a half-hour on a wave runner to $225 for eight hours aboard a pontoon boat (plus deposit). Stop by between 9 a.m. and 6 p.m., or call for a reservation.

If you prefer the calmer inland waters, then head to Browning's Landing at 600 Laskin Road. Here you may board the climate-controlled luxury yacht *Discovery*, (804) 491-8090, for a two-and-a-half-hour sightseeing, lunch or dinner cruise to Lynnhaven Inlet and back. Advance reservations are required.

Should you tire of all this water, consider taking to the air. **Horizon Aviation**, (804) 421-9000, at the Chesapeake Municipal Airport, operates year-round and will take up to three passengers on a 50-minute Virginia Beach oceanfront flight for $65. Or, for $82 per flying hour, you can devise your own trip. Though not to everyone's taste, there's another way to become airborne that looks even more thrilling. **Beach Bungee,** at 108 Atlantic Avenue, (804) 422-2700, will take you up 110 feet in a bungee arch elevator, after which you take the plunge. The first 30 feet is free-fall. After that, the elasticity of the cord stretches you two to three times further before springing you back 75 feet at an acceleration of 2G. Then you bounce up and down about four more times before becoming suspended about 50 feet above the ground, to which you are then lowered. For some it might be the thrill of a lifetime, but most will prefer just watching. You can also watch some terrifically fast planes. The **Oceana Naval Air Station**, (804) 433-3131, is one of the U.S. Navy's four master jet bases. It's home to 19 aviation squadrons, including the F-14 Tomcat fighter and the A-6 Intruder medium-attack bombers. Seasonal tours of the base are available, but at other times you can drive down Oceana Boulevard (Route 615) to the Jet Observation post.

Rudee Inlet has already been mentioned in relation to fishing boats. You will also find two attractive restaurants in this tranquil waterway. Located at 227 Mediterranean Avenue, (804) 425-1777, **Rudees on the Inlet Restaurant and Raw Bar** has been a favorite since 1983. The distinctive building, designed both as a bait and tackle shop and a replica of a U.S. Coast Guard station, overlooks the inlet and has two outdoor decks. The atmosphere is casual, airy and nautical. Seafood figures prominently, of course, but there are also great steaks, sandwiches and daily house specials. Rudees is open from 11 a.m. to 2 a.m., with Sunday brunch served between 10 a.m. and 2 p.m. There is also free valet parking. Rockafeller's Restaurant, (804) 422-5654, at the junction of Mediterranean and Winston-Salem, boasts a different style of architecture, with an inviting wrapround deck on its second floor.

For really delicious seafood, combined with a delightful environment, head for The Lynnhaven Fishing Pier. On top of the pier, overlooking the Chesapeake Bay, is the **Lynhaven Fish House Restaurant,** (804) 481-0003. Every seat has a bay view. Besides a stained glass back bar and lobster tank, there is a refrigerated glass-enclosed fish cutting room, where you can watch the day's catch being prepared for your plate. This restaurant has a high Mobil and AAA rating, is open from 11:30 a.m. to 10:30 p.m. seven days a week (with continuous service for lunch and dinner), and features the greatest variety of fresh fish in the region.

If you fancy a lighthearted trip back to 16th-century London, try **Rosie Rumpe's Regal Dumpe**, at 14th Street and the boardwalk in the Sandcastle Motel. Patterned after King Henry VIII's favorite tavern, this place has character to spare. You are met by Rosie, who commits you to the care of one of her trusted wenches. As you await your sumptuous five-course feast, you are entertained by the ditties of wandering minstrels. What follows is a fun-filled and bawdy evening of musical pleasure. Call (804) 428-5858 for show times and reservations; maybe you'll pick a day on which the king himself appears.

During the season, the beach trolley is a fun way to get around. There are several routes; you can get on and off wherever you like. A one-day pass costs $2.50, while for two days, it's $3.50. Not only is it cheap, this mode of transportation is much more convenient than continually looking for a parking space.

There are many exciting events that take place here year-round. They include: the **Flight Fair,** towards the end of March; the **Easter Weekend Celebration**; the **Eastern Surfing Association's Mid-Atlantic Regionals** and the **Cinco de Mayo** party during the first week of May, followed by the **May Beach Music Festival**; the **North American Fireworks Competition** and the **Annual Boardwalk Show** in June; the **Family Fun Day and Fireworks** every July 4; the **East Coast Surfing Championships** at the end of August; and in September the **Super September Tournament Series,** a round of nine fishing events, and the **Annual Neptune Festival Boardwalk Weekend**, which says goodbye to summer.

The Northern Neck
Fishing for History
& Gambling on Love

If there is one word that accurately describes this part of Virginia, it is "enigmatic." Certainly there are numerous places of historical interest, attractive shorelines and charming small towns. In general, however, it is rural and old-fashioned. Quality accommodations are, if not non-existent, certainly few and far between.

Still, the Northern Neck is worth a visit. It is best, however, to approach this trip in a different manner than the others. Basically, the further northwest you go (along Route 3 towards Fredericksburg), the fewer good hotels you'll find (with a couple of exceptions). The opposite end of the peninsula is a different story. Here, there are a variety of options offering both interesting activities and nice accommodation.

First, let's consider a particularly remote and isolated spot not even located on the Northern Neck. How's that for enigmatic? You'll come across **Deltaville** when taking Route 17 to Saluda, where you pick up Routes 3 and 33. For the most part, this is an area of marinas filled with private vessels. However, **Marine Resort Group, Inc. (MRG)**, which operates several such marinas, has had the foresight to address a related market. Accordingly, they have made two modern condominiums available. Situated at the Club on Fishing Bay, these are by far the best choice for many miles. Opened to the public in July 1995, each condo features two bedrooms, two full baths, a fully equipped kitchen, dining room, "great" room, living room, washer and dryer (with linen supplied). In addition, there is a private swimming pool and two decks overlooking the beautiful fishing bay. The rent is $360 for a period running from midday on Friday to 3 p.m. on Sunday. This is a bargain for a couple, yet these condos are large enough to accommodate two couples or even a family. Other options are available as well. For an "all-in-one price" of $660, MRG will include weekend use of a 20-22-foot runabout power boat. $150 will get you the boat for just one day. You may also rent Wet Jet Wave Runners at $65 per hour. For reservations, telephone Tom Facca, MRG's sales and marketing manager, at (804) 776-6463 or (800) 701-4MRG. So far, this is a well kept secret; but you can be assured that once the news gets around, these condominiums will be booked solid.

MRG offers another exciting option, but for this you will need maritime experience. If you possess the prerequisite knowledge, consider spending the weekend on either of the company's two models of houseboat. Choose between a Coastal Barracuda 380 (at $750) or an Aqua Home 39 x 14 Wide Body houseboat ($980).

On board, you'll want to try your hand at fishing. This is never as simple as it seems. What you need is someone with expert knowledge of the waters, and the patience to teach you how to handle your boat. Captain Gillie is just the man. A successful area fisherman for over 30 years, he now offers his services as a personal guide, giving on-boat instruction in the wheres, whens and hows of fishing. He specializes in rockfish, cobia, speckled trout, flounder and spade fish; following his advice might lead to that trophy. It will be an entertaining day and $125 well-spent. For information and reservations, telephone **Captain Gillie's Guide Service** at (804) 776-7398.

Two other styles of fishing, the fly variety and light tackle spin casting, are gaining in popularity. For assistance in these, call Captain Hank Norton of **Fly Fishing – Chesapeake Bay** at (804) 776-6807, between 7 p.m. and 10 p.m. Not only will he supply all the necessary equipment, he will take you out on the flats and grassbeds of the Chesapeake Bay (as well as the Rappahannock and Plankatank Rivers) in search of speckled trout, striped bass (rockfish), Atlantic croaker, puppy drum, flounder and gray trout, to name a few. This adventure costs $175 for a half-day, with one or two people. If you think that won't be long enough, he charges $200 for a full day with one person, and $225 for a full day with two.

If you decide to strike out on your own and need fishing gear or bait, visit **Chesapeake Bay Seafood**, (804) 776-6400 or (800) 332-9740. Not only will they address your every angling need, they sell an extensive selection of seafood as well. After all, it's best to have a back-up, in the unlikely event that you come home empty-handed.

If you don't feel like cooking, help is just around the corner – although, at first glance, you wouldn't necessarily recognize it. The unusual colors with which the **Red Sky Restaurant** is decorated are meant, perhaps, to reflect both its name and culinary style. The menu leans toward Cajun and southwestern, with dishes that are unusually sophisticated for this part of the world. The surroundings are pleasant, too; altogether, a great surprise that shouldn't be missed. Oh, and by the way, if you'd rather "eat in," the Red Sky Restaurant's courtesy car will bring your dinner selections right to you. They're busy on weekends, so reservations are recommended. Call (804) 776-9183 or fax (804) 776-7335.

The next destination – across the wide Rappahannock River – is Irvington. This town is reached by following Route 33 back to Route 3 north, which will take you over the bridge. But first, take a peek at a small town on the south side.

Urbanna's current claim to fame is its sponsorship of the Oyster Festival, held the first weekend in November. But it has a history, too. Urbanna is one of the four remaining sites – out of the original 20 – designated by a 1680 act of the Assembly as primary ports for the shipment of tobacco, imports, goods, and slaves. The town was laid out the following year and remains the same today. It derived its name – which means "city of Anne" – in 1704, from the reigning monarch, Queen Anne. Urbanna's location made it susceptible to attack during the Revolutionary War, the War of 1812, and the Civil War. Even as late as the 1930's, it was a port of call for commercial vessels and steamboats from Baltimore and Norfolk. Today, however, the protected harbor is home mainly to recreational boats and the vessels of local watermen.

Yes, Urbanna, listed on The Virginia Landmarks Register and the National Register of Historic Places, is certainly worth a visit. One would even be tempted to linger a while longer, if it weren't for the chronic lack of decent accommodation. Surely, someone will one day open a B&B in this charming town. In the meantime, though, you'll have to improvise.

As you are exploring, go down Virginia Street, towards the water. The first sign you will see reads **Payne's Crabhouse**, (804) 758-5301, but don't let that confuse you; it isn't a restaurant. In season, however, you'll see wooden troughs brimming with crabs – a sight that will surely tempt you to take some away. After all, you'll know they're fresh. Turn left and follow the road to the end, where you will come across an actual restaurant, and a most charming one at that. The **Bay-Watch Res-**

taurant, (804) 758-4047, is housed in an unusual round wooden building that, as the name implies, affords a marvelous view of the bay (either from indoors, or on the outside deck). Get set for a marvelous seafood lunch, the caress of a gentle breeze and a serenade from the nesting birds. You're virtually assured of an afternoon pleasantly spent.

Once on your way, cross over the bridge, turn left at White Stone and follow the road to Irvington. Then follow the signs to **The Tides Inn**, (804) 438-5000 or (800) TIDES INN. Without a doubt, this is the premier hotel on the Neck. In fact, it is more than a hotel; it is a small resort. Though somewhat old-fashioned, it's not the least bit run-down. Both style and ambiance are rather conservative but, then again, many people like that. Indeed, the inn has enjoyed many repeat visitors since its opening in 1947.

Perched on the shores of historic Carter's Creek and the two-mile wide Rappahannock River, The Tides Inn sports unprecedented views of delightfully calm backwater bays and inlets from almost every room. These make for a feeling of timelessness and peace. Within the boundaries of the extensive grounds, you will find a sandy beach, salt water pool, putting green, croquet pitch, tennis courts and a par-3, nine-hole golf course. Nearby are two other, more challenging 18-hole courses. Small sailboats, canoes and paddle boats are available on a complimentary basis, while small outboard motorboats and larger sailboats may be rented from the dockmaster. For the ultimate in relaxation, take a cruise on either the 127-foot classic yacht *Miss Ann*, named after the original proprietor's wife, or the 60-foot *High Tide*. There is no charge for these trips, but if lunch is included, $12 will be added to your account.

Rates are based on the Modified American Plan (MAP) and, depending on which of the three seasons you visit and which of the four room styles you choose, range between $112 to $175 per person, per day. Bedroom plus parlor suites are also available with rates from $175 to $355 per person. When you call, inquire about the Anniversary Package, which includes a reserved table in the dining room, use of the fitness and health facility as well as new bicycles, evening music and dancing, nightly parlor games or a movie and, in season, oyster roasts. Once at the Tides Inn, you won't wander far. Its peaceful atmosphere and complete range of activities are more than enough to keep you moored.

Our last suggestion is a curious little town at the eastern end of Route 360. The area's prosperity during the Victorian era is evident in the mansions of that period, which line Main Street. This economic success was based upon the Atlantic menhaden fish, which are found in estuarine and coastal waters from northern Florida to Nova Scotia. Even today, a major landing site is here at **Reedville** – obvious enough, when the wind is blowing inland! Of course, other varieties of seafood are also available at one of the town's many fisheries.

At the end of the street, to your right, is an imposing three-story Victorian edifice. Built as a sea captain's home in 1895, it is now the **Elizabeth House – A Bed & Breakfast on the Water**. Though there are four bright and spacious rooms, one in particular is worthy of serious consideration. The entire third floor has been transformed into the Queen Elizabeth Suite, which overlooks the water in both directions. It consists of a sunny sitting room with a queen sleep sofa, natural wicker furnishings, bright prints and plants, a wet bar with refrigerator, and (at the top of the turret) a game table. You'll also find a bedroom with a queen-sized bed, and a large bathroom with an oversized jacuzzi and separate shower. The rate is $110 a night, double occupancy. Included in the tariff are breakfast in the formal dining room, use of the TV and games room, volleyball, croquet and badminton, free use of bicycles and, for the waterbabies among you, use of the skiff. If you fancy crabs, drop a line from the dock; with a little luck they will be complimentary as well. Those intent on taking it easy may watch all of this activity from the porch, or take it a step further and doze in the hammock.

Of the handful of bed & breakfasts in and around Reedville, there is one more worth recommending. Across the bay at Fleet's Point is **Cedar Grove**, telephone (804) 453-3915. An affluent factory owner built this Colonial Revival style home in 1913 as a wedding present for his daughter, Miss Virgie. There are three spacious bedrooms tastefully decorated with period antiques. The suite also offers a private balcony furnished in wicker. Here, you're blessed with a panoramic view of the lighthouse guarding the entrance to the Great Wicomico

River. From this vantage point, you may also study nesting ospreys and arctic swans, who winter in these coves and marshes. If you crave outdoor activity, start a game of tennis or croquet, or take a bicycle tour of the surrounding countryside. When you're ready to rest, swing in the hammock built for two, or relax in the rocking chair on the porch – provided the cat hasn't claimed it first.

While in the area, you mustn't miss the **Reedville Fishermen's Museum**, a portion of which is located in the oldest house in town. A visit here will give you a much better appreciation of the town's history.

Another summer sidetrip takes you to two Chesapeake Bay islands with unique ties to the past. The **Chesapeake Breeze** – which is owned by Tangier & Chesapeake Cruises, Inc., (804) 453-BOAT – sets sail at 10 a.m. daily (between May and October) for a narrated 1 ½-hour cruise to **Tangier Island**, at a fare of $18.50 per person. It was Captain John Smith who named the island when he landed there in 1608. At that time, it was used by the Pocomoke Indians as a fishing and hunting ground. In 1666, they sold it to a certain Mr. West – for the princely price of two overcoats. In 1686 he, in turn, sold a part of it to John Crockett, who subsequently settled there with his family. Then, as today, the island's rich oyster and crab grounds provided a good living. Although some of the modern world has touched the island, this is still a largely unspoiled fishing village full of romantic charm. The natives speak with a trace of an Elizabethan accent, and have no desire to leave their idyllic home. They won't mind at all, however, if you spend your two and a half hours getting to know them.

Offering similar daily cruises is Island & Bay Cruises, Inc., (804) 453-3430, which is based a little further out of town (and in a KOA Kampground!) Departing and returning at the same time aboard the **Captain Evans**, you'll visit the larger **Smith Island**, 13½ miles across the Chesapeake Bay. Captain John Smith also charted this island in 1608. Today this Methodist colony is one of the few remaining outposts of the original Cornish settlers who arrived here in 1657. You'll dock at Ewell, the largest of the three fishing villages, where the islanders' principal means of support is harvesting shellfish.

Once you've settled on a place to stay, you may consider the other attractions scattered throughout the Northern Neck. We feel that the following are the most worthwhile.

Begin by traveling north on Route 3, until you see signs for **Stratford Hall Plantation**. It is located in Westmoreland County, which was established in 1653 and, like most other places in the area, named after an English shire. It has the distinction of having produced more statesmen than any other county in the country. Many of these were active in Revolutionary politics. In fact, it was here at Leedstown that the first organized resistance to English oppression of civil liberties occurred. That was in February 1766, when the Leedstown Resolutions were signed by 115 patriots who bound themselves together "To Prevent The Execution of the Stamp Act." Among the "bound" were six Lees, five Washingtons, and the father of President James Monroe.

Although not as well-known as others of its type, Stratford Hall is truly magnificent. It was prominent Virginia planter Thomas Lee who built this unusual home in the late 1730s. Using bricks made on the site and timber cut from virgin forests, he created an H-shaped manor house with four dependencies, a coach house and stables. The house has an architectural style uniquely its own. The Great Hall – connecting each side of the H – is considered one of the most significant surviving rooms from colonial America. You'll be enchanted, too, by the spectacular location; Stratford Hall is situated high on a hill overlooking the Potomac River.

Thomas was successful in his personal life, too. He fathered eight children, the eldest of whom was Richard Henry. Born in 1732, his accomplishments were numerous and varied. He was a Justice of the Peace, a member of the House of Burgesses for 17 years, and a member of three Virginia Conventions. He exerted his influence on the Revolutionary movement by preparing and signing the Leedstown Resolutions; helping to shape and signing the Declaration of Independence; and serving as a member of the committee that awarded George Washington command of the Continental Army. During and after the war, he served as a Colonel in the Westmoreland Militia; was a member of the Continental Congress for nine years, serving as its president in 1784; was a member of the House of Delegates, for which he was speaker in 1784; and, finally, was elected to serve as a U. S. Senator from 1789 to 1792. His brother, Francis Lightfoot, was born in 1734 and achieved many of the same honors. He, too, signed the Declaration of Independence; the Lees were the only brothers to do so. Their cousin, General Henry "Light-Horse Harry" Lee, was one of George Washington's most trusted officers. After the war, he married the heiress to Stratford Hall and subsequently served three one-year terms as governor. Their son, Robert Edward Lee, was born at Stratford in 1807 (his crib is still displayed there.) Soon after, however, the family moved to Alexandria. After receiving his education there. Lee graduated, in 1829, from West Point. He was second in his class. He went on to become the only man ever offered command of opposing armies in the same war. It makes one wonder why no member of such a prominent family ever aspired to the presidency.

Back at the plantation, you will find gardens that vary from formal to vegetable. There is also a reconstructed mill that operates on Saturdays, weather permitting, during the months of May to October. Its products are available for purchase at the Stratford Store. From April through October, you may even arrange for a plantation lunch, served in a log cabin. The Hall itself is open for tours every day of the year, except Christmas, from 9 a.m. to 4:30 p.m. Call (804) 493-8038 for information during weekdays or (804) 493-8371 on weekends and holidays.

A few miles further north, turn off Route 3 onto Route 204. Continue to Popes Creek, where George Washington was born in 1732 on his father's tobacco farm. The original house was destroyed by fire in 1779; today, a memorial house marks its approximate site. **George Washington's Birthplace National Monument** is operated by the National Parks Service and, in addition to the memorial house, features a visitor center, weaving room, farm workshop and a colonial farm. Visit between 9 a.m. and 5 p.m. daily to learn much about 18th century plantation life, and the ways in which it influenced the young Washington. Admission is free.

By now you will have had enough of history lessons. It's time to relax. Carry on north along Route 3 until you reach Oak Grove. Head south on Route 638 for two and one half miles and turn in at the sign for **Ingleside Plantation Vineyard.** Your visit begins with an informative introductory movie, followed by a tour of the winery and, of course, tastings. Actually the tasting here is made into a game in which you are asked to rate each wine individually. If you and your partner agree, it makes it easier to decide on which varieties to take home. If you don't, you'll just have to buy more bottles. One thing you must agree on is the kind of wine you'll take to your picnic that afternoon. This will give you a good excuse to buy a pair of glasses and a corkscrew, for practical use now and as souvenirs later. These and many other attractive items are available from the well-stocked shop. The winery is open daily and you may telephone (804) 224-8687 if you need more information.

Next, go back the way you came, crossing Route 3. Half way between there and **Colonial Beach** you'll pass another historic site, the birthplace of James Monroe, the fifth President of the United States, and the author of a long-respected doctrine on international law. It is really not worth a stop. However, as a matter of interest, you may be surprised to learn that, like Thomas Jefferson, Monroe died on July 4, but in the year 1831.

Before you settle on the beach, buy some snacks to complement that wine, and then relax for awhile on the banks of the Potomac. What you see around you will lead you to believe, and rightly so, that this was once a popular resort. Originally incorporated in 1892, it prospered much during the Victorian era, when one of its more famous residents was Alexander Graham Bell. The early part of this century brought large numbers of tourists who frequented the river boats, dance halls and enjoyed a period of legalized gambling. All this made it a favorite weekend retreat for residents of the D. C. area.

Those days are long gone, however. Though the area still enjoys a modest popularity, its charms are somewhat anachronistic.

Colonial Beach does have something no other place in Virginia can claim: a piece of Maryland – well, almost. Before you make a bet on the reason, let us explain. Most people logically assume that whenever states are separated by a river, state lines run down the middle of the water. Whatever the case elsewhere, this state line is drawn where the Potomac River meets the Virginia shoreline. This means that **Riverboat on the Potomac** – which is built on pilings sunk into the Potomac – has a Virginia address, 301 Beach Terrace Drive, and a Virginia phone number, (804) 224-7055. Yet it is legally located in Charles County, Maryland.

Don't worry, though, you won't have to swim there. The boardwalk leading to the riverboat is legal also. What you'll find is quite fascinating, and even more so if you are a gambler. This is one of Maryland's off-track-betting parlors; horse races are simulcast from numerous locations to literally dozens of televisions spread throughout the building. Other games of chance are available, too, including "Keno," the Maryland lottery game that gives players a chance to win every five minutes. If you get hungry, the Potomac Room has fine dining. Or you may choose just to sit on the deck and watch the "birds." For those who wish to imbibe, there's also a liquor store with stock offered at Maryland prices. Whatever your inclinations, it's worth the trip, if only for the novelty.

Smithfield
Light Up Your Life in the
Town That Ham Built

Have you ever fantasized about spending a romantic night alone in a lighthouse? Perhaps you will also

have considered the possible drawbacks: being ma-
rooned in a dangerous storm, or the discomfort of truly
spartan accommodation. Maybe it would be better to opt
for a modern hotel? Well, don't abandon your fantasy;
you **can** have the best of both worlds. Tucked away on
the Pagan River, a few miles from its confluence with the
James River and not far from Hampton and Norfolk, is
an in-water Chesapeake Bay-style lighthouse, complete
with cupola. It has two luxurious suites. It is, in fact, the
only lighthouse in Virginia that offers overnight accommodation. But the good news doesn't end there. It is a
part of a modern hotel, restaurant and leisure facility
that was built to resemble a Victorian Coast Guard
Station. The charming small town of Smithfield, in
which it is located, is traditional, peaceful and historic.
Once there, you will definitely want to stay awhile.

Although some towns on the James' north shore are
better known (Williamsburg comes to mind), those on
the south side have an equally colorful history. As early
as 1608, Captain John Smith crossed over from the
Jamestown Colony, bringing corn to barter with the
Indians. However, not until 1619 was the first English
settlement established on the southern shore by Captain
Christopher Lawne and Sir Richard Worsley. In 1634,
the colony was divided into eight shires with the one on
the south bank originally called Warrorquoyacke, the
name of the indigenous Indians. In 1637, it was renamed
Isle of Wight in honor of the English island that had been
home to many of the county's principal settlers. These
men worked hard to establish themselves, putting up
elegant brick buildings which are some of the oldest
standing structures in North America today. The first of
these settlers to own land – in what would later become
Smithfield – was Arthur Smith. In September 1637, he
patented 1,450 acres described "as a neck of land running south-east along a creek behind the Pagan Shore."
It was not until 1750, however, that a descendant, Arthur Smith IV, had the land formally surveyed and laid
out as a town. It is from him that the town derives its
name. The settlers brought hogs with them and found
that the climate was in fact ideal for curing hams and
bacon. The first curing and shipping business was established in Smithfield by Captain Mallory Todd, a native
of Bermuda, as far back as 1779. Today the name Smith-

field is known the world over for succulent dry-cured hams. These owe their distinctive flavor to hogs fed on another famous local product, peanuts.

History is important but, to inspire romance, a town must also have fine hotels. Smithfield has three, each with its own individual style.

The **Smithfield Station**, at 415 South Church Street, telephone (804) 357-7700, is home to the lighthouse. Of the three hotels, this is by far the most visible and unusual. It features wraparound porches on the first and second levels, and a period-perfect "widow's watch" tower. Though all the rooms are pleasant, the one on the corner overlooking the marina is worth requesting – that is, if you can't get a reservation in the lighthouse itself.

Connected to the main building by a wooden walkway, the lighthouse sits right out in the river, supported by stilts. It houses two immaculately furnished suites in which nothing is overlooked (except the peaceful river marshes)! Guests are welcomed with a basket from Basse Choice that contains wine, peanuts, ham, and napkins. Other special touches include large thirsty bath sheets, fluffy bathrobes, a hair dryer, and Crabtree & Evelyn bath supplies. The lower suite, Room 100, is handicapped-accessible and a bit larger, though slightly less intimate. It has a fold-down king-sized Murphy bed, several seating areas (one with a fireplace), a kitchen, a large bathroom with a steam shower, and a private wraparound porch which seems tailor-made for romantic moonlit nights. It rents for $195 per night on Fridays and Saturdays.

This is all quite delightful, but Room 200 upstairs is even more charming. Slightly smaller, yet still quite spacious, it is laid out in a circular floor plan with views to all directions. This results in a feeling of total seclusion and warm intimacy. A short climb up the circular staircase puts you in your own private cupola. This suite is quite impressive. Of the many wonderful rooms we've visited, this one is a particular favorite. Modern, but discreetly so, it boasts a king-sized bed and fireplace, as well as a double whirlpool tub and shower. The dining area is of an unusual, raised "booth" style. Located next to a window, it is an intimate place to share a glass of wine while basking in the moonlight. This room also rents for $195 per night on Friday and Saturday, but to avoid disappointment, book far in advance.

No need to travel far for good food, either. The Station's restaurant is excellent. Beautiful views of the surrounding water enhance your meal, whether you dine indoors in the dining room, with its large picture windows, or outdoors on the terrace. Summertime visitors should not overlook the Outdoor Bar and Grille, located next to the marina. Seafood features prominently on the menu, but the burgers and salads are equally delicious, and everyone will want to cool off with the Station's frozen specialty drinks. Perhaps the "Pagan River Pain Killer" will be to your taste. The inside bar is another cool place to hang out, and you won't have to worry about displacing the locals – their seats are permanently reserved with brass nameplates.

Depending on what weekend you visit, you may find an art show, a fishing tournament, or a concert on the marina boardwalk. You will be tempted to take a picnic basket and venture out onto the river. The energetic may opt for a canoe, while those who prefer a more leisurely approach may want a skiff. The front desk will be happy to supply details on how any of these crafts – as well as bicycles – can be rented.

If you can't get a reservation at the lighthouse, there is another option well worth consideration. The setting is not as dramatically beautiful, and it is slightly hard to find, yet it offers some marvelous rooms. The **Isle of Wight Inn**, outside of town at 1607 South Church Street, telephone (804) 357-3176, is easily missed because it resembles an office building – which it once was. Looks can be deceiving and, in this case, they certainly are. You'll never find an office building that looks like this one inside. Although there are numerous rooms, the two on the end are the best. Large, with a comfortable mix of furnishings, each features a queen-sized bed, fireplace and double jacuzzi tub. These rent for $110, including a Continental breakfast, year 'round. Be sure to stop by the house antique shop, where you may enjoy some leisurely browsing or purchase a keepsake of your visit.

If you love the countryside, drive four miles out of town on Route 258, turning onto Route 620 (Four Square Road), and continuing until you come to number 13357, the **Four Square Plantation Bed & Breakfast**, telephone (804) 365-0749. There, you will find a charming house surrounded by lovely countryside. Dating from 1807, it has been authentically restored to include modern conveniences, yet retain its original ambience. Of the three rooms, all are furnished in country style antique furnishings, and two have four-poster beds (one king-sized and one queensized). The price is $65 for the queens and $75 for the king, including a full breakfast, the use of a canoe to explore the stocked fish pond, and the company of some very friendly cats.

When it's time to dine, remember that Smithfield is a small town and the choices are limited. So don't expect great culinary delights. The aforementioned Smithfield Station is the best selection for both food and location; but if you feel like a change of scenery, we suggest **Angelo's**, located at 1804 South Church Street, across from the Isle of Wight Inn. Rather oddly-shaped on the outside, Angelo's has an extensive menu. The fare includes seafood, every variety of steak, deluxe sandwiches, and an interesting mix of Italian and Greek dishes. Whatever your desire, Angelo's prides itself on the quality and quantity served.

Nightlife isn't Smithfield's claim to fame, either. However, the **Smithfield Little Theater**, at Commerce Street, (804) 357-7338, waits to romance you. The Cotton Gin theater building, originally a hay and grain store and warehouse, is over 100 years old. It was the only building to survive the great fire of 1921, after which it was used as a cotton gin (hence its name). In 1966, the Smithfield Little Theater company moved in, paying a nominal $1 a year rent. The building was donated to the company in 1973. If theater isn't what you had in mind, don't despair. With rooms such as those at the Smithfield Station and Isle of Wight Inn, it won't be hard to create your own entertainment.

The place to begin your tour of the town is **The Old Courthouse of 1750**, located at 130 Main Street. Built, as the name implies, in 1750, it has a unique rounded end room that was copied from the old capitol in Williamsburg. It served as the courthouse until 1800, when the county seat was moved to Isle of Wight. After an intervening period, during which it saw a variety of uses, the courthouse was given the dual purpose of housing the Chamber of Commerce and **The Visitors' Center.** Visit between 9 a.m. and 5 p.m daily, or telephone (804) 357-5182 or (800) 365-9339 for information. The center offers many interesting brochures but the one that is most helpful with regard to the town's history is the **"Old Towne Walking Tour."** A quick perusal will clarify why Smithfield is designated a Historic Landmark and has a place on the National Historic Register. Take a stroll around with brochure in hand, following the numbered instructions. A kaleidoscopic mix of Colonial, Federal and Victorian architectural styles will unfold before you. The size and embellishment of a number of these structures bears testament to Smithfield's former affluence, an affluence that peaked after the end of the Civil War, when the income from steamboats and the peanut industry resulted in the construction of some especially extravagant homes.

As you come full circle, returning to the courthouse, take a few minutes to look around. You will see some surprising things. What is a traditional English telephone box doing on Main Street? Those people resting on the bench, haven't they been there since you passed by sometime ago – like a similar scene across the road? Well, yes, they are motionless, and they will remain so. Such statues, although pleasing, do seem somewhat incongruous in this environment. But that's Smithfield for you: a small town full of surprises.

This is a place conducive to pure relaxation. There's no need to go rushing around, as all of the places you'll want to see are in the immediate vicinity. You may decide to see a little or a lot, depending on your mood and preferences. We'll tell you what is available and let you take your choice.

While on Main Street, you may dig further into the town's history by browsing through the **Isle of Wight Museum**, at 103 Main Street, telephone (804) 357-7459. Though a museum since 1978, it was originally built in 1913 to house the Bank of Smithfield. It was decorated with imported marble and tile and a large Tiffany-style dome skylight – all in keeping with the area's affluence. Current resident exhibits include fossils from the banks of the James, Indian artifacts, Civil War memorabilia and, of course, a history of the ham industry. Hours are from 10 a.m. to 4 p.m. on Saturday and from 1 p.m. to 5 p.m. on Sunday.

There is one place we strongly recommend you include on your itinerary. Travel two miles south of town to the junction of Routes 10 and 32. Make your way to 14477 Benn's Church Boulevard and, as the name implies, you will find a church. This is no ordinary church, however. In fact, it looks rather out of place. Its natural home would appear to be one of those picturesque English villages so often seen on postcards. Which is not surprising, considering that the settlers who built it came from just such a place. The best estimate of its age comes from a brick dated 1632. But there is no question that **St. Luke's Church**, or "Old Brick," as it is affectionately known, is the oldest existing church of English foundation in America. In addition, it is the nation's only original Gothic church. Its present good condition belies its tumultuous past; this church survived both the Revolutionary and Civil Wars, only just avoiding falling into total disrepair on several occasions. Abandoned in 1785, when the Church of Virginia was disestablished, it lay deserted until 1821. At that time, it was used to temporarily house a congregation until the new Christ Church was completed in Smithfield. In 1887, a violent storm caused damage that took three years to repair. Subsequently, it was again deserted. By 1953, it was almost in total ruin. Then the town's interest in the structure was rekindled, and great efforts were made to organize and finance a restoration. This movement resulted in the designation of St. Luke's as a National Shrine. In spite of many different restorations, the building retains much of its original structure. A good number of the church's 17th century artifacts, previously removed for one reason or another, have now been returned. All in all a fascinating place, it's open for tours between 9:30 a.m.

and 4:30 p.m. on Saturdays and from 1 p.m. to 4:30 p.m. on Sundays. It is closed, however, in January. For more information, call (804) 357-3367.

With afternoon coming on, a relaxing picnic might suit. There are two delightful locations, both beautiful and historic, from which to choose.

Perhaps you would like to continue your "history lesson" by seeing how rural Virginians once lived and worked. If you also fancy some physical exercise – a hike, a bike ride, or a relaxing swim – head north on Route 10, take a right on Route 634, and look for **Chippokes Plantation State Park**, (804) 294-3625. The original 550-acre Surry County tract, located across the James River from Jamestown Island, was granted to Captain William Powell (who in 1617 became Lieutenant Governor of Jamestown). One of the local chiefs, Chippokes, made friends with the colonists and Powell named it in his honor. A succession of owners, some of them famous, increased the tract's size to its present 1,400 acres. One, Governor William Berkeley, even owned it twice. Albert Jones, who purchased it in 1837, was one of the first owners to live there. In 1854, he constructed a magnificent mansion, one of the two plantation homes now on the property. The Stewarts purchased it in 1918. After Mrs. Stewart's death in 1967, it was willed to the state, with one proviso: that it be continuously farmed. Thus was a unique legacy continued. Possibly beginning with the Algonquin Indians, (and definitely as early as 1617), the land has been perpetually worked, making it one of the oldest continuously-farmed plantations in the nation. Modern-day visitors will find the plantation a unique combination of educational and recreational facilities. The Chippokes Farm and Forestry Museum's exhibits show how difficult it was for these early settlers to survive. They also display an interesting selection of artifacts, including a rare early-17th century oxen-drawn plow. The recreational area is spread over 280 acres of adjacent land, and includes a Visitors Center, picnic shelters that may be rented with advance notice, trails for hiking, and an Olympic-size pool. Bicycles may be rented for $2.50 an hour. Canoe rentals are also offered. You may prefer to take it easy and stroll on the beach looking for fossils. Whatever you choose, you are sure to enjoy Chippokes. As many activities are seasonal, be sure to call ahead for current information.

Another ideal picnic spot, a bit closer to town but also on the banks of the James River, dates from the same period but is historic in a different manner. On Easter Friday in 1622, Indians led by Chief Opechancanough launched attacks throughout the young colony, killing over 50 settlers on the land that was later to become a part of Isle of Wight. Shortly after this incident, the House of Burgesses voted to build strategically-located forts to defend the colony. On May 11, 1623, Captain Roger Smyth was entrusted with overseeing this task and commissioned to protect the colonists against "Spaniards by sea and Indians by land." Choosing a site high on the bluffs overlooking the James River, with naturally deep ditches, his men constructed a fortification called "The Castle." He couldn't foresee that his creation would, over the next 250 years, be involved in every military campaign fought on American soil. During the Revolutionary War, it was refortified and used to defend the James against British attacks. It was at this time that it was renamed after Major Francis Boykin, who served on George Washington's staff and whose family owned the land on which the fort was built. Another member of the Boykin family, Brigadier General Francis M. Boykin, fought there in the War of 1812, during which it was redesigned into its present seven-pointed star shape. British attempts to capture it were unsuccessful and it was abandoned when the war ended in 1815. Nearly 50 years later, in 1861, Virginia had joined the secession of southern states, and it was time to reinforce the fort once again. The work was still in progress when, in 1862, three Union gun boats (the USS *Galena*, USS *Minnesota,* and USS *Susquehanna*) steamed upriver and attacked. The fort's batteries of guns proved only partially successful. They were powerful enough to fend off two of the gunboats. But when all three backed down the river out of the range of the fort's guns, the strength of the Galena's long-range guns, after a fierce fight, overcame all resistance from **Fort Boykin**. On a more romantic note, the famous poet Sidney Lanier was stationed at the fort during the Civil War. It was within these walls that he wrote "Beautiful Ladies" and "Hoe Cakes" and began his novel, *Tiger Lilies.* Another period of desolation followed until it was purchased by Mr. and Mrs. Herbert Greer, who spent the remainder of their lives landscaping the grounds. Subsequent owners continued to improve the property, which was eventually donated to the state for use as a public park. Visitors should take Route 10 to Blounts Corner Road and follow the signs to Fort Boykin, 7410 Fort Boykin Trail, (804) 357-2291.

When packing for your picnic, you'll want to get the real flavor of the area by including some Smithfield Ham, this is the town's most famous product. Despite the preeminence of the industry – one factory outside of town is huge! – retail outlets are few, and factories selling directly to the public are practically nonexistent. Yet on your walks along Main Street, you will probably have noticed the **Joyner's Smithfield Ham Shop** sign, at number 315, telephone (804) 357-2162. So when you are ready to make your purchase, head in that direction. Behind the shop is the original Joyner's factory, first opened in 1889. The way things are done hasn't changed much in the century since. Time is not important here; every aspect of production from salt-curing, natural wood smoking and natural aging is done the traditional way, with no shortcuts. The results are genuine Smithfield hams, with the same deliciously distinctive taste that they had back in 1889. The factory is interesting but, because of health and safety precautions, is not open to the public. Fear not, the shop is the next best thing. Choose, if you can, from a complete selection of Smithfield hams, country hams, and honey-glazed hams, as well as peanuts, sauces, gift packs, and gift baskets. If you want your purchases shipped somewhere, they'll do that too. Opening hours are 9 a.m. to 5 p.m. on Saturdays and, between April and December only, 1 p.m. to 5 p.m. on Sundays.

Smithfield hams are sold worldwide, but there is an unusual "foreign" market right here in the United States. It was the Chinese who, millennia ago, first discovered the art of curing ham. (The Spanish are no slouches at it, either.) Because of strict food laws, however, these large immigrant communities cannot import ham products from their country of origin, so Joyner's comes to their rescue. If you look closely in the shop, you might see examples of the cloth bags printed especially for those markets.

Other places to comb for souvenirs include **The Collage Studios and Galleries**, at 346 Main Street, telephone (804) 357-7707. Here, between 10 a.m. and 5 p.m. on Saturdays, you can watch and chat with working artists, view the regular exhibits, or choose unique hand-crafted gifts for the special people in your lives. At **Southern Accents**, 913 South Church Street, (804) 357-2724, you will find handmade pottery from the Isle of Wight and Smithfield, as well as the obligatory T-shirts.

There are two other buildings of historical importance worth visiting. They are a little farther afield in Surry County, north-west of Smithfield. In fact, they are not far from the Jamestown-Scotland Ferry, and, if you are re-turning home by way of Williamsburg, this is the most interesting way to go. If not, you may still consider taking a little side excursion. After all, how many opportunities are there to put your car on a boat these days? You can then get out, let the wind blow away the cobwebs, and admire the wide expanse of the James River with its accompany-ing wildlife. These boats run every half an hour for most of the day, take a similar time to cross, and cost $4 per car each way. Not much to pay for such a relaxing form of travel, and one that is now all but lost to modern culture.

About half-way along Route 31, between the small town of Surry and Scotland, the Jamestown Ferry Landing on the south bank of the James, you will come across **Smith's Fort Plantation**, (804) 294 3872. Here, the early Ameri-can saga continues. In 1614, colonist John Rolfe married Chief Powhatan's favorite daughter, Pocahontas. As a dower gift, the chief gave Rolfe a 2,000-acre portion of a neck of land on the south side of the James River. Since the couple moved to England in 1616 (where Pocahontas died at an early age), they never actually lived here. But there's more to this story. Their son Thomas Rolfe returned in 1635 to claim his inheritance. In the late 1640s, he sold the property to one Thomas Warren, who reportedly built a brick house on the site in 1652. This particular edifice was then subsequently replaced by the existing 18th-century

structure, which is thought to have been built by Jacob
Faulcon, a wealthy merchant and Surry County court
clerk. Copied often in later centuries, this one-and-a-
half-story brick building is particularly beautiful, with
dormer windows and tall chimneys. Inside, where much
of the original pine woodwork survives, there are early
English and American furnishings. Of particular interest is the "Blue Room," with its unique chimney piece,
fluted pilasters, cornice, butterfly shelves and paneling.
There is also an English boxwood garden, designed and
planted by the Garden Club of Virginia, and the earth-
works of an early 17th-century fort, all within just 16 of
the original 2,000 acres. It was from the fort that the
plantation got its name. In 1609, Captain John Smith
built the fort as a retreat for Jamestown settlers in the
event that Jamestown was attacked, either by the Indians or raiding Spanish ships. The site is located in the
woods behind the house.

Not far away, on Route 10 towards Smithfield, is an even
older and more fascinating house. Located near Chippokes State Park in a hamlet of the same name, **Bacon's
Castle** is a National Historical Landmark with an intriguing history. Oddly, it is named after a man who
probably never went near the place. Arthur Allen was a
wealthy man who owned 10,000 acres of land. In 1665,
he built himself an amazingly intricate high Jacobean-
style house that, today, is the oldest documented brick
house still standing in North America. It was also one of
the earliest in Virginia to be constructed in the cruciform
style, where the two parts of the house, front and rear,
are connected by a porch tower and stair tower. In
addition, it features curvilinear (Flemish) gables and the
unusual triple chimney stacks that have become its
trademark. The third floor has the best-preserved woodwork, including original 1665 floorboards in its two bedrooms, one of which was used by the family and one by
the slaves. The first floor has been altered more extensively, with most of the changes dating from 1774 when
the last of the Allen family died and ownership was
transferred. The name is derived from events that were
unfolding just after the house was constructed. In 1676,
nearly a century before the American Revolution, anger
over the tyrannical rule of Royal Governor William

Berkeley resulted in a colonists' rebellion. The leader of the rebels, Nathaniel Bacon, took on first the Indians and then the government, burning its houses in Jamestown to the ground. Then, directing the rebel forces from Gloucester, he authorized one of his Surry County followers, William Rookings, to fortify an outpost there. He saw Mr. Allen's house as a natural target, besieged the home and ruled the county from there for four months – hence the name "Bacon's Castle." There is an interesting love story associated with the house, as well. The Georgian poet Sydney Lanier, mentioned earlier in relation to Fort Boykin, also visited here. But he was not just enamored with the house. Virginia Hankins, daughter of the house's owner, also caught his eye. Romantic attentions soon followed. In recent years, much effort has been expended in the archaeological excavation and restoration of the castle's gardens. The resulting finds are exciting for the botanically inclined, as they include previously-hidden gardens dating from the 17th, 18th and 19th centuries. Many special events are held year-round at Bacon's Castle, including an occasional ghost tour. Telephone (804) 357-5976 for more details.

Both Smith's Fort Plantation and Bacon's Castle are owned and operated by the Association for the Preservation of Virginia Antiquities. They are open weekends between March and November, from 10 a.m. to 4 p.m. on Saturdays and from noon to 4 p.m. on Sundays.

Williamsburg
Travel Back in Time
for Some Colonial Romance

Virginia was a vast and prosperous colony that stretched west to the Mississippi River and north to the Great Lakes when, in 1699, the Virginia Assembly voted to move the capital from Jamestown to a new site, Middle Plantation. The new capital was renamed after the reigning British monarch; hence, Williamsburg. This was not the first honor bestowed on the town. In 1693, a Royal Charter had been granted for a college, only the second such established in the colony. This was named after the British sovereigns, William and Mary. Williamsburg soon became a powerful center for commerce, and culture blossomed here as the first colonial theater was opened. Perhaps most importantly, it became the seat of power for colonial politics. It was the place where George Washington, Thomas Jefferson, Patrick Henry and others argued the cause of American independence. The events that transpired here during these years literally changed the course of the nation's history. Ironically, this also caused the city's decline. In 1780, during the Revolutionary War, the threat of British attack was great and the location of Williamsburg so vulnerable that the capital was moved upriver to Richmond. Merchants, tradespeople and tavern keepers followed; as a result, the town drifted back into obscurity.

It remained so until the 1920s, when the Reverend Dr. W.A.R. Goodwin, then pastor of Bruton Parish Church, shared his vision of restoring the colonial capital of Williamsburg with one John D. Rockefeller, Jr. Captivated by the idea, the philanthropist summoned an impressive group of archaeologists, architects, historians, antique furniture experts, landscape architects, and other experts. He then entrusted them with a huge task: re-creating an entire colonial town from a collection of maps, drawings, correspondence, diaries and expense accounts of the period.

After decades of work, Williamsburg has evolved into a completely-restored 18th-century city. Its more than 500 buildings – including 88 original structures, authentically furnished colonial homes, stores, trade sites, and taverns – make it the country's largest living museum. That it is successful is self-evident, as over a million visitors from all over the globe visit Williamsburg every year. More importantly, this has been achieved with the maximum of good taste and style. The Colonial Williamsburg Foundation, the city's owners and operators, have ensured that the 173-acre historic area remains an island of peace and tranquility, never encroached upon by the crass commercialism that has grown up around it.

Indeed, greater Williamsburg has become, in many ways, a satellite that exists to service Colonial Williamsburg. As a consequence, it has become a tourist attraction in itself – but for very different reasons. If you like theme parks, water parks, potteries, modern hotels and motels, every type of fast food restaurant you can imagine and outlet shopping centers, then you will feel at home here. Of course, these exist all over America and discerning visitors will treat them for what they are: peripheral distractions. In any event, to visit these, you will need a car. Better to dispense with your car altogether, travel back two centuries, and stay in Colonial Williamsburg itself.

Colonial Williamsburg Hotel Properties, Inc., a subsidiary of the Colonial Williamsburg Foundation, operates four hotels. One, in particular, is very special. **The Williamsburg Inn** is a magnificent five-star hotel that combines old-world graciousness with world-class resort facilities. Since its opening in 1937, it has played host to presidents, prime ministers, and royalty. Its design was inspired by the great 19th-century "springs" hotels and, grand though it is, the inn's furnishings and service are based on a very humble philosophy expressed by Williamsburg's earliest benefactor, John D. Rockefeller Jr. He dictated that the inn be "absolutely unlike a hotel, but rather like a private home away from home."

The inn's public areas and guest rooms – there are 102 of the latter, with no two quite alike – are decorated in the Regency style. This, combined with the magnificent grounds and adjacent golf courses, creates the feel of a beautiful country estate. The rooms are spacious enough to get lost in, and are elegantly, if conservatively, furnished. "Conservatism" is in vogue here and, at times, renders the atmosphere somewhat formal. This is especially true in the Regency dining room, where masterpieces of Continental cuisine are created daily. It's also apparent at the traditional high tea, served daily at 3 p.m. in the East Lounge.

If you fancy some activity, sportswise that is, you may partake of a genteel game of lawn bowling or croquet; play tennis; take a dip in the large spring-fed outdoor pool; or make use of a complimentary pass to the Tazewell Club Fitness Center. There, after a workout, you may treat your aching bones to your choice (or a combination) of sauna, steam room, whirlpool, or massage. Not to be forgotten is the renowned championship Golden Horseshoe golf course, designed by Robert Trent Jones Sr. and his son, Rees. This course has earned accolades from *Golf Magazine,* which has labeled it one of "the nation's best."

That is not all – far from it. The Williamsburg Inn has a very well-kept secret that further fuels the romantic imagination. Sprinkled in amongst the restored houses are three taverns – Market Square, Brick House and Chiswell-Bucktrout – as well as 23 guest houses. An integral part of the hotel, they offer a rare chance to experience the restored capital's 18th-century charm. In fact, these are the only accommodations within the boundaries of the historic area. Each of them has its own history, which you can share in. For example, Thomas Jefferson stayed at the Market Square Tavern while he studied law under George Wythe, while Patrick Henry opened an account here on the very day he was inaugurated as first governor of the Commonwealth of Virginia. If you are looking for something a little more secluded, try one of the smaller houses. You might find a canopy bed and a sitting room with a fireplace that, like your passions, is just ready to be lit. And, if your fires outlast the wood, there is be plenty more stacked outside your door. Of all the experiences we have outlined in this guide, none beats wandering around Colonial Williamsburg at Christmas time and then returning to your own cottage. Of course, it helps that there is champagne cooling. And just one match will bring forth a crackling fire to warm your chilled bones. Naturally, guests in the colonial houses and taverns can enjoy all of the amenities available at the inn proper.

The tariffs here are complicated somewhat by the inn's division of the year into four seasons. And some of these have their own sub-divisions. For the inn itself, expect to pay upwards of $125 in the low season and $235 in the high season. The colonial houses and taverns cost upwards of $99 in the low season and $157 in the high season. Keep in mind that the inn's suites, as well as the larger colonial houses, are substantially more. For exact prices during the season of your visit and details of all the available rooms, write to The Williamsburg Inn, 136 East Francis Street, Williamsburg, VA, 23185; telephone (804) 229-1000 or (800) HISTORY; or fax (804) 220-7096.

Before setting out to enjoy the historic area, it is advisable to obtain a general admission ticket. Although there are two options, the best value is undoubtedly the **Patriot's Pass**. This not only gives you unlimited admission to all exhibits, it is valid for one year, and may be purchased at the Visitor Center, the Merchants Square Information Station, or the Greenhow Lumber House ticket office on Duke of Gloucester Street. In 1995, the cost was $30. **The Colonial Williamsburg Visitor's Companion**, which comes as a benefit of your ticket purchase, is issued weekly and gives you complete, up-to-date information on all of the day's activities, along with a helpful street plan. On this plan, the red line indicates the route of the all-important shuttle bus. As no cars are allowed in the historic area, you'll need to become familiar with the bus's scheduled stops – unless, that is, you don't mind long walks. The good news: unlimited use of this service is another benefit of your pass. A wise place to start is **The Visitor Center.** Here, you can take in the orientation program and see the film **Williamsburg – The Story of a Patriot**, which will give you insight into the years that preceded the American Revolution.

Afterwards, take the bus back and disembark outside the **Capitol** (at Christiana Campbell's Tavern) for the tour, which details how patriots of the day fashioned the fundamental concepts of self-government and individual liberty. Look carefully and you can just see George Washington making a well-reasoned argument, or Patrick Henry stoking the fires of revolutionary passion with an inflammatory speech. You'll exit on the other side of the building, where you may begin a stroll down the main thoroughfare, **Duke of Gloucester Street**. It is there that you will begin to sense the real colonial atmosphere. Wherever you wander, you will find faithfully-recreated historic trade sites buzzing with activity. The tradespeople, attired in traditional costume, will be making items intended for use in the historic area. These same items are available for sale in one of the nine restored shops that recreate the world of the colonial merchant.

Historic monuments are open to visitors as well. The **Governor's Palace** was home to seven British governors, as well as the first two elected to represent the newly-formed Commonwealth of Virginia. Then there is the **Courthouse,** and the destination for those convicted therein, the **Public Gaol.** This last was home not only to lawbreakers, but to the gaolkeeper and his family as well. If you've ever wanted to put your partner in stocks, this could be your big chance! And if that makes you feel guilty, a visit to **Bruton Parish Church**, active since 1715, may ease your conscience. While there, be sure to take note of the gravestones in the churchyard. Their inscriptions will give you incredible insight into the lives and family histories of the city's past residents.

Wherever you go and whatever you do, you cannot escape a unique and particularly innovative Colonial Williamsburg phenomenon. These are the **"people of the past,"** living people portraying colonial residents, from the humble to the mighty. These people conduct their daily business as they would have done 200 years ago, but with an interesting, yet sometimes embarrassing, difference. They bring you into the conversation as though you were their contemporaries and are conversant with their problems!

An appropriate method of transportation here is the carriage or wagon ride. Tickets are available at any of the regular ticket sales locations, on a first-come, first-served basis. If you are still curious about anything, you can partake of the **Orientation Walk** that leaves on the hour between 10 a.m. and 3 p.m.

Museum lovers won't feel neglected here; Williamsburg offers at least three excellent choices. **The Abby Aldrich Rockefeller Folk Art Center**, established by Mrs. Rockefeller in the 1930s, houses the country's premier collection of American folk art. In addition to special exhibits, the **DeWitt Wallace Decorative Arts Gallery** features a permanent collection of English and American decorative arts. This last is located in the reconstructed building which once housed the first hospital in the country dedicated solely to the care of the mentally ill. **Bassett Hall** is the 18th-century house adapted in the 1930s by Mr. and Mrs. John D. Rockefeller, Jr., as their Williamsburg residence. Tours guided by audio tape are offered each day except Wednesday; reservations must be made by calling a ticket sales location. There are so many attractions that it is impossible to list more than the highlights here. Consult your Visitor's Companion for full details of other options that might interest you, as well as the times and places where "people of the past" make their appearances.

All of this activity will make you hungry and thirsty, two conditions that are well-addressed by four authentic colonial taverns. Indeed, no visit is complete without lunch and dinner in the colonial fashion. **Christiana Campbell's Tavern**, located behind the capitol building, was George Washington's favorite. It specializes in seafood served in the colonial tradition. A most popular dish with its diners is Jambalaya, which consists of shrimp and lobster and is served with sweet potato muffins. **The King's Arms Tavern**, on Duke of Gloucester Street, is as genteel today as it was in the 18th century. Next door, **Shields Tavern** is the oldest in Colonial Williamsburg, with both food and decor characteristic of the late 1740's. Also on Duke of Gloucester Street, next to Market Square, is **Chowning's Tavern.** This has the more rough and ready atmosphere of an 18th-century alehouse. In fact, it is a great place for a snack, day or night. Besides full fare in the dining room, there is a light menu served in the "tavern." Here you'll sit (not necessarily alone) on rough wooden benches and at well-worn wooden tables set with pewter utensils and lit by candlelight. A bowl of potato and leek soup and a crock of cheddar cheese with sippets, washed down with Old Dominion Lager, should be enough to satisfy anyone's hunger. After 10 p.m. you will be entertained, and encouraged to join in, as musicians play and sing bawdy bar room ballads of their day. A local magician will even teach you to play 18th-century games. Though each has a slightly different atmosphere, none of these taverns will disappoint. The ambiance is enchanting, the food wholesome, the service good, the musicians entertaining and everything done in good taste.

One thing that may surprise you is the array of alcoholic beverages available. If you're a student of history, you know that early Americans were fond of drinking. They quenched their thirsts with a variety of imported and locally-produced drinks, such as Madeira wine and rum. Though not terribly fashionable today, authenticity rules; so why not try a Madeira cobbler or rum toddy. Today's favorites are not ignored, however; besides the normal offering of mixed drinks, there are numerous American and European wines.

If you need a reality check, or a change of fare, historic restaurants aren't the only game in town. Across from the Merchants Square Information & Ticket Booth, at 110 South Henry Street, you'll find **Seasons Cafe**, (804) 259-0018. This is one of the most delightful restaurants you are ever likely to set foot in. There are other, and nominally more famous, restaurants in this tastefully-organized shopping area. But in our opinion, none have the style and easy-going feel of Seasons. In fact, it has many styles, with each room decorated in a theme reflecting a different season. In the appropriate season, there is a large outdoor patio as well. The menu is particularly extensive. You may choose from light fare, specialty platters, sensational salads, fine beef and seafood, old favorites, or simply sandwiches and burgers. The proprietor – who also runs the Cheers and Beacon Street chains – has achieved something many others attempt but usually fail to attain. Impeccable service, plentiful and delicious food, and a superb environment, all at a reasonable cost. Admittedly, it is not at all colonial. But sometimes even the most ardent tourists want a change.

One of the delights of this particular trip is the opportunity to get away from the pressures of our 20th-century lives. However, don't completely exclude all the other things the greater Williamsburg area has to offer. Some of these are not in the least bit commercial, and will certainly appeal.

The first of these is another restaurant. **Ford's Colony** is a prestigious community that has been the recipient of many awards, and so has its restaurant, **The Dining**

Room at Ford's Colony. Elegant and beautiful, this is the centerpiece of the Ford's Colony Country Club and has been described as one of the finest dining experiences in all of Virginia. It has received the coveted Distinguished Restaurants of North America award, and *The Wine Spectator* has given it the "Best Award of Excellence." But with the largest collection of wine in Virginia – over 1,000 domestic and imported selections – that should come as no surprise. Executive chef David Everett holds many awards himself (including Chef of the Year in 1991), and you will delight in his **Signature Dish**. This five-course dinner, the menu for which changes daily, includes the chef's choice of appetizer, salad, two petite entrées and dessert. If you so desire, you may also have a different wine with every course. The price for this four-star extravaganza is just $48 per person, excluding wines, and $74 with them. One innovation here simply cannot go without mention. Unassumingly named The Kitchen Table, it is located just inside – you guessed it – the kitchen. Here you may watch your food being prepared, while other diners observe you from behind the glass window separating the kitchen from the dining room. To make your reservation for this very special dining experience, call (804) 258-4107.

It may intrigue you to see where some of the wines you are imbibing originate. Take the short two-mile drive from Colonial Williamsburg towards the James River and visit **The Williamsburg Winery**, (804) 229-0999, located at 5800 Wessex Hundred. Winemaking was encouraged in the early days of the colony, but it wasn't particularly successful. A period of success came later, at the end of the 19th century, when American hybrid grapes were substituted for the European varieties. A hiatus of many decades followed until, in the late 60s and 70s, there came a renewed interest in Virginia wines that resulted in the birth of this winery. Surrounded by peaceful countryside are more than 50 acres of vineyards. A visit here is really enchanting. After a tour outlining the basics of winemaking, you are invited to enjoy a sampling of these fine wines in the great hall accompanied by, of all things, knights in armor. Before leaving, a visit to the shop is a must. You'll want to take home a few bottles of your favorites, or choices from their wide selection of French wines.

On the way to the winery, you will pass two other, very different points of interest. At 1022 Jamestown Road there is the **Liberty Rose,** which enjoys a well-deserved reputation as Williamsburg's most romantic bed and breakfast. Brad and Sandi Hirz fell in love with each other and this house – then abandoned – in 1986. What they have done to the house since then is a marvel to see. The two-story white beaded clapboard house has a dormered slate roof, flanked by two chimneys of Jamestowne brick. It has been filled with an eclectic mix of English, Victorian, French country and 18th-century antiques, accented by wall coverings, fabrics, and collectible treasures that appeal to the romantic in everyone. Furthermore, this house has become a home filled with love and life. Warmth permeates the atmosphere, and it's emanating from more than the fireplace in the elegant guest parlor (where, by the way, you may serenade your loved one on the grand piano). Each of the bedrooms has its own unique decor and is just as inviting.

The **Savannah Lee** has a "hearts & carving" antique mahogany bed, rosy peach wall covering and an old-fashioned clawfoot bathtub (with lots of bubble bath, of course). It rents for $110. You will find a canopied rice-carved queen-sized bed in the **Magnolias Peach** room, along with lots of light from five double-hung windows. The private bath and shower are walled with black marble. For your entertainment, a TV-VCR and a selection of movies are hiding in the cherry armoire. This room rents for $145 a night.

Most everyone's favorite room is the **Rose Victoria.** Call Brad or Sandi at (804) 253-1260 if this is the one you fancy; it's available for $175 a night. The centerpiece of this first floor suite is a cherry French canopied queen-sized bed embellished with fringed and tasseled bed curtains. The deep red damask wall covering contrasts with the ivory woodwork and tin ceiling. Alternatively, you may relax on the seven-foot sofa while you view a movie on a TV-VCR cleverly concealed in the antique armoire. The bathroom's Victorian "wall" was taken from a turn-of-the-century townhouse, and the heart-pine floor from a 1740's plantation. When it's time to bathe, take your choice of a leisurely soak in the oversize clawfoot tub or some good clean fun in the red marble shower.

The **Suite Williamsburg** is the newest renovation. Its magnificently carved ball-and-claw queen-sized poster bed boasts elaborate hand-stitched coverings of reproduction silk and jacquard. Six windows offer pleasant views of the garden. You may enjoy these while sitting on the French sofa, warmed by the working fireplace. If you can't find the TV-VCR, take a look inside the Habershams doll mansion. Glass doors lead into the most romantic private bath you are likely to see anywhere; embellished by cherry panelling, a Monticello floor, and porcelain candelabras, it features an Italian tile shower and clawfooted tub. Plush bathrobes are provided, making you feel really pampered. Altogether perfect for a romantic break, and not unreasonable at $175 per night.

No matter which room you choose, you will find that nothing is wanting. Upon retiring for the evening, you'll even find a rose lying on the bed. It is this attention to detail that has gained Brad and Sandi the AAA Four Diamond Award. If you stay anywhere outside the historic area, consider the Liberty Rose.

Before ending your visit, why not get a bird's-eye view of the area you've just explored. This will give you a much better perspective and understanding of the region. Contact **Historic Air Tours**, (804) 253-8185 or (800) VA BY AIR, located at the Williamsburg-Jamestown Airport. Weather permitting, you may book a peninsula tour, which will fly you over the historic triangle of Jamestown, Williamsburg, and Yorktown. This company operates on the principle that "the most exciting and educational tour of Virginia's history isn't in Virginia.... it's above it."

Colonial Williamsburg is always a delight, but particularly so during the Christmas season. This is also by far the most romantic time of year here. The town is transformed as doorways and windows are bedecked with fresh fruit, ribbons and, of course, the traditional greenery. The holiday season begins on the first Sunday in December when a cannon blast signals the **Grand Illumination** of the city. This is a "grand" affair in a very different sense. Don't expect millions of brightly colored lights; you won't find that here. After all, there were none in the 18th century. Like everything else here, this is accomplished authentically. On the blast of the cannon, candles are lit in more than 400 restored and reconstructed public and private buildings in the historic area. What follows is an evening of merriment with singing, dancing, and musical performances on outdoor stages, themselves illuminated only by fiery cressets. Oh, and be sure not to miss the 18th-century firework displays. What could be more grand?

All manner of festivities and special events are scheduled throughout the month. More than ever, you will think that you have been transported back in time as you stroll arm-in-arm through the historic streets. Carolers in period dress sing traditional holiday songs, while the buildings echo the trills of fifes and rumbles of drums. Add to this the rich aroma of wood-burning fireplaces wafting through the crisp air. Savor the incomparable atmosphere as you sit around one of the large open-air fires and warm the cockles of your heart with a festive drink. Don't forget, either, to reserve a place in one of the taverns for a seasonal banquet.

Colonial Williamsburg – truly a place to raise your Christmas spirits.

Washington, D.C.

From Politics to Passion & Everything in Between

We are taking a different approach to things in this chapter, for reasons that will become apparent. So far, we have aimed to showcase a place that is not necessarily well-known, detail a little of its history and describe whatever nearby attractions we deemed most enjoyable. Even in cases where the area is well-traveled, there are choice spots that remain unfamiliar to potential visitors. Washington, D.C. doesn't fall into either of these categories. For obvious reasons, this city has been an entity unto itself, constantly in the limelight, and familiar to most everyone, from the time of its very formation.

The attractions here are so well-known that, in our opinion, it is superfluous to detail them. Cases in point: the White House, the Capitol, and the Mall; museums such as the Smithsonian Institute and National Gallery; theaters like those found in the Kennedy Center; or the many monuments. Even if your knowledge of these is limited, the tourist information available locally is quite comprehensive. We are not suggesting that you avoid these places; we are sure you will want to visit them. Rather, we intend to concentrate on the more practical matters – hotels, restaurants, interesting means of transportation – things that have the potential to make or break your romantic weekend. Because of the vast number of options available, we will detail some of the more esoteric choices. Though this is a highly subjective approach, that has made it great fun for us. We hope it will do the same for you.

The most difficult decision has been which hotels to recommend; the choice is simply overwhelming. We decided to narrow things down by applying the following criteria:

they should be in close proximity to the downtown area, and preferably near the White House; they should reflect the grand character of the city; and, finally, they should have political connections – after all, this is the nation's capital. This process eliminated most of the options that, while otherwise nice, just didn't suit our purposes. We finally settled on two that are institutions in their own right. In fact, we were so taken with one that we spent the first two nights of our recent honeymoon in one of them.

A little later, a place that approached the epitome of romance came to our attention. It couldn't be more different from the other two, yet it sometimes shares the same clientele. Suffice to say, nothing prepared me for this. The place is truly extraordinary.

Before continuing, though, let us add one proviso. If you prefer your hotels to be prominent, grand, maybe a little conservative and serviced by numerous personnel in uniformed attire who tend to your every need – this is not the place for you. But read on: one of the other two will be.

H.H. Leonards Inc./The Mansion on "O" Street

In truth, you may have trouble just finding this place, or any information about it. They don't advertise because they don't have to. There is no sign hanging outside, or any other indication that it is other than a residence. Nor is there a reception desk, with staff to answer the phone. Rather, an answering machine leads you into E-Mail and, sometime later, your call is returned. We can almost hear you thinking "what kind of a place is this?" Well, we'll tell you: a place so confident of its own attributes that it can afford to be this way. In addition, they service a clientele that prefers such anonymity and seclusion.

Located just south of Dupont Circle, this hotel actually consists of townhouses linked together. One of these dates from 1892 and was designed by Alan C. Clarke for his brother Champ, then Speaker of the House. It is believed to be the last private residence of that period which is still virtually intact. It features 14 fireplaces and an authentic Tiffany window. It also contains the room and actual table where President Theodore Roosevelt played snooker. The house next door, which was owned by the Clarkes' "artist" brother, was originally linked to the former house via archways on both the first and second floors.

Nearly a century later, a Miss H. H. Leonard saw the potential here to exercise what must be considered a fertile imagination. Keeping the exteriors intact, she gutted the insides and created a wonderland reflecting contradictory (but surprisingly complementary) eras and styles. Inside the home-cum-hotel you will find 21 unique bathrooms and eight highly imaginative, and extremely well stocked, kitchens. These are shared between just 12 suites and rooms. Trying to describe the latter would take pages of text and would prove an exercise in futility, as few things stay the same. "H" likes to change things around now and then and the guests often take things away with them. That, however, is a part of her plan — because absolutely everything here is for sale!

When walking through the door, which will be opened electronically, you will enter into the dimly-lit interior, reminiscent of the Victorian era. Soon you will learn that this theme is often repeated throughout the establishment. When your eyes have acclimatized, however, you will notice that things aren't at all what they seem. It is a marvelous renovation but it is not, and isn't meant to be, authentic; it is much more innovative than that. Wherever you look, your eyes will be drawn — and then drawn back again — to a kaleidoscopic mix of furniture, antiques, modern prints, collectibles from different eras, and dolls, just to name a few. There is so much to see here that it is truly impossible to take it all in immediately. You will be encouraged to wander around the house. As you proceed from room to room and floor to floor, you will feel as if you are journeying through a three-dimensional maze, passing through two centuries concurrently. Victoriana is mixed with avant garde, topped by Art Deco and embellished with much more than a splash of high tech.

One thing you won't see is conformity; except in the sense that everything adheres to the highest standards, and no detail appears to have been overlooked. The rooms and suites vary considerably in size and style. In some you will find a classical turn-of-the-century French ambiance; in others you may be transported back to the 20s and 30s, and the secluded penthouse on the fifth floor is pure Art Deco. More often than not, there's a touch of some other style or period tossed deliberately into the mix — just to keep you on your toes. For a change, there is the cabin suite. Wooden beams on the walls and ceilings lend a rustic feel, while the salt-water fish tank built into the bed's headboard is almost surreal. The bathroom runs the width of the room behind the bed and features everything you could possibly imagine. The over-the-bed loft houses a living area and full kitchen that would be at home in the pages of any design magazine.

In some rooms, it is a game just to find the television; or televisions, because, more often than not, there is more than one. (The Penthouse Suite has no fewer than six!) Space here is at a premium and the design has been cleverly crafted to maximize it. To this end, the television sets are often in unusual places. Some rooms have a bank of two or three stacked over a wardrobe or even built into the wall of the bedroom. Earphones are provided so you won't disturb each other while watching different programs. This may not sound very romantic, but at least it will avoid an argument. Sometimes there is an additional large-screen television in the living area; in the log cabin's bedroom, the picture is projected onto the wall opposite the bed from above the headboard. Modern technology doesn't end there — each room has its own modem and phone messages may be left on your own private E-Mail.

Last but not least is the even more eclectic range of bathrooms. Some are not attached to any particular suite or room, giving you a choice of bathing options. There are showers, showers with two seats and numerous jacuzzis, some of which are an integral part of the room. One is surrounded on three walls by mirrors and glass shelves holding all kinds of knick-knacks. Don't be embarrassed by the dolls looking down on you. They modestly turn their heads — at least most of the time! In reality, there is nothing about H. H. Leonards Inc./The Mansion on "O" Street that is run of the mill.

The tariff runs from $100 to $500 a night for the Art Deco Suite. You may telephone (202) 496-2000 or fax (202) 659-0547 to make a reservation. Don't ask for a brochure, though; they don't need them. Just remember this address: 2020 "O" Street NW. On your next visit to Washington, let the Mansion on "O" Street give you a welcome you'll never forget.

If you are looking for something a little more formal – as we were when looking for a honeymoon spot – then you would do well to opt for one of the following two hotels. Either, in its own way, will fit the bill.

The Hay-Adams House

In 1884, John Hay, who served as President Lincoln's private secretary and Henry Adams, the great grandson of Revolutionary statesman John Adams, purchased adjoining lots at the corner of "H" and 16th Streets, facing the White House and Lafayette Square. The homes that Adams commissioned for each of them were elaborate and Romanesque in design, and destined to become the social centers of Washington. Indeed, both saw numerous visits from presidents, artists, writers, politicians and other such notables of the age. After John Hay's death in 1905, that home was acquired by his son-in-law Senator Wadsworth. The wedding reception he gave for his daughter in 1924 (following her marriage at St. John's Church to Senator Stuart Symington) was the last social occasion there before the house was demolished. Adams' house was used as the Brazilian Embassy after his death in 1918.

Both properties were purchased in 1927 by developer Harry Wardman, who commenced building a 200-room apartment hotel in the Italian Renaissance style, to be named The Hay-Adams House. It opened the following year, with a dazzling array of architectural styles, including Doric, Ionic and Corinthian orders, walnut wainscoting and intricate ceiling patterns with Tudor, Elizabethan and Italian motifs. Some of its more pleasing offerings were the large suites overlooking the White House, Lafayette Square and St. John's Church. In 1930, it boasted the first air-conditioned dining room in D.C. Like the houses that preceded it, this establishment attracted an influential clientele until the economic difficulties of the 30s cut short the era of elegance in Washington. Remarkably, the Hay-Adams managed to retain its reputation even though it changed hands numerous times over the next 50 years. In

1983, its fortunes turned when David Murdock acquired and totally renovated the property, upgrading it to the highest of standards. Today, what you'll find is unmatched classical elegance and the gracious yet unobtrusive service that comes only from a thoroughly trained professional staff. When they welcome you home, they really mean it.

With only 143 guest rooms, there is more time for them to become personally involved. The rooms, as you might expect, are immaculate – and spacious. We would particularly recommend the **Junior Suites**. There are six, measuring a generous 476 square feet. The regular rate for these is $480 per night, but you may get a price break if you keep a lookout for specials and weekend packages. If you fancy something a little smaller, and less expensive, a regular room ranges from $210 to $360 a night. Each of these features a king-sized bed, an elegant sofa, a fully stocked mini-bar (quite a rarity), and a large bathroom, with all the accoutrements you would expect. You may even leave your shoes outside the door and find them shined the next morning.

It's true that other hotels can offer much of the same in terms of facilities, if not ambiance. But there is one thing that can't be matched – the view. This is because, as they like to boast, "nothing is overlooked but the White House." In this city, few views are more romantic at night than the floodlit White House, with the Washington Monument towering behind it and the constant air traffic slowly, and silently, forming a moving backdrop. If any scene deserves a champagne toast, it is this.

You will find the public rooms equally enchanting. From the time you enter the lobby, the flavor will envelope you. Polished walnut, fine English antiques, gilt mouldings and even a 17th-century Medici tapestry will hint of delights to come throughout the hotel. The John Hay Lounge is wood-paneled, with a 20-foot ceiling that gives it a feeling of grandeur and majesty, and two fireplaces that lend considerable warmth. A light menu is served for either lunch or dinner. Alternatively, you may visit just to enjoy the afternoon tea or cocktails. Live music is performed on the Steinway grand piano from 5 p.m. until late in the evening, every evening. It's also interesting to relax there in the morning, perhaps over a cup of tea, and amuse yourselves by watching the high-powered people who enjoy being watched. Dining in The Lafayette is a true experience; enjoy contemporary American cuisine, but make the most of the atmosphere by requesting a table next to one of the seven windows overlooking the White House and Lafayette Park.

Telephone (202) 638-6600 or (800) 424-5054, or fax (202) 638-2716 to make a reservation at **The Hay-Adams Hotel**. Don't worry about parking; just pull up at 1 Lafayette Square NW and everything will be taken care of. Should you need further assistance, the concierge is on hand 24 hours a day.

The Stouffer Renaissance Mayflower Hotel

The last hotel we recommend is not only the oldest and the largest, it is fondly referred to as Washington's second best address. Located at 1127 Connecticut Avenue NW, it originally opened in 1925 with 1,057 rooms, including 112 apartments composed of anywhere from one to nine rooms each. Needless to say, it was one of America's largest. Designed by the same architects who created Manhattan's Grand Central Station, no two of its rooms were furnished alike. Speaking of furniture, it took three months of round-the-clock work to set out the over 25,000 pieces of furniture that had been delivered from New York. Just two weeks after it opened on March 4, 1925, an inaugural ball was held for the new president, Calvin Coolidge. Since that date, only Presidents Reagan (for his second term), Bush and Clinton have not held a ball here. One of the most memorable inaugural balls occurred after John Kennedy's election in 1961, when a blizzard immobilized downtown Washington. The stranded guests, staff and others were forced to "camp out" at the hotel, sleeping wherever they could.

Since its opening, the hotel has hosted all of the presidents for one event or another. Dignitaries who have stayed here include the Duke and Duchess of Windsor, their Imperial Highnesses Prince and Princess Takamatsu of Japan (who stayed here on their honeymoon in 1930), Charles de Gaulle, Winston Churchill and Charles Lindbergh, to name just a few. FDR wrote the famous lines "we have nothing to fear but fear itself" in suite 776; Jean Harlow was so intrigued by the hotel's switchboard that she spent a morning here as a stand-in operator; and F.B.I. Director J. Edgar Hoover ate lunch here every day he was in Washington, for over 20 years.

In 1982, the hotel began undergoing extensive restorations. While its infrastructure and service areas were modernized, efforts were made to return the entire hotel to its original appearance. These efforts were rewarded when, in 1993, the hotel was listed on the National Register of Historic Places. In 1990, it was acquired by Stouffer Hotels and Resorts. Three years later, they initiated a multimillion-dollar refurbishment of the 330-room west wing. Today this Four-Star, Four-Diamond-rated hotel has 659 guest rooms that include 78 suites, two grand suites (The Presidential Suite and The Mayflower Suite) and two Hospitality Suites.

There is no shortage of places to eat and drink here, either. The Four-Diamond Nicholas Restaurant – there are only a handful of restaurants so rated in the city – is often frequented by the high and mighty. So, if you want to rub shoulders with the famous and have a great meal at the same time, it's the place to be. Look, too, for the Café Promenade, Town and Country Bar and Lounge and the Lobby Court. The latter is located just across from the front desk and is an ideal place to linger and watch the passersby. This is no ordinary lobby, either; besides being particularly elegant, the promenade is a spectacular one-tenth-of-a-mile long. It will also give you the perfect opportunity to observe the remarkable hotel staff, many of whom have worked at The Mayflower for over a quarter of a century. And do they have stories to tell! Stop and talk to them for a while. Martini lovers will also be in seventh heaven here. There is a totally separate menu offering a selection of 10 martinis and five Manhattans; surely one here will slake your thirst.

The Mayflower is not short on amenities, either. Maid service is rendered twice daily. There is 24-hour room service, same-day valet cleaning, 24-hour valet parking, a fitness facility with state-of-the-art equipment, saunas and/or a complimentary pass to the YMCA just two blocks away. The concierge service includes fax, message, secretarial services and city/restaurant information and reservations. In your room you'll find a two-line telephone with dataport and private voice mail. You will be pampered with other special complimentary services such as an overnight shoeshine and complimentary coffee and newspaper delivered with your wake-up call. There is one other service that will further ease your visit: complimentary limousine transportation to any destination within a three-mile radius of the hotel!

If all of this sounds attractive, take advantage of this hotel's special weekend package rate, which is $129 per night. There is no extra charge for parking either, a real bonus in the nation's capital. To make a reservation or obtain further information, contact the Stouffer Renaissance Mayflower Hotel by calling (202) 347-3000 or (800) HOTELS-1.

It's time now to consider restaurants, and there are plenty to consider. As with the hotels, any selection is subjective. So let's set some more criteria. One of the joys of eating in Washington is the variety of restaurants serving cuisine from all corners of the globe.

As aficionados of all things Spanish, the first thing we looked for was a Spanish restaurant. The obvious choice was **Taberna del Alabardero**, (202) 429-2200, at 1776 I Street NW. It was, admittedly, a calculated choice. Owner Luis Lezama Baranano, a charming urbane man who used to be a priest, owns similarly-named restaurants in Madrid, Puerto Banus and Sevilla, as well as a restaurant school (Escuela de Hosteleria de Sevilla) and a small hotel in the latter city. It would be an understatement to say that he knows a thing or two about food. Like all Spaniards, he believes that mealtimes should be more than a time to eat; they should be a social occasion, as well. He has successfully imported both the cuisine and that all-important "ambiente" to the Washington Taberna. To ensure that you are have the time to enjoy both, the Taberna is conveniently open until 11 p.m. on Friday and Saturday. Don't plan this experience for your Sunday itinerary, however, as they take this day off. A few weeks later, we were entertained by Sr. Lezama at his Taberna in Madrid, and what a pleasure that was. One interesting aside: in Spanish restaurants, alcohol of every description runs freely and without the complicated bureaucratic necessities required of liquor licenses here. It was absolutely hilarious, while dining in the Madrid restaurant, to hear Luis explaining his exasperation at dealing with the U.S. authorities on this subject. If you dine here, you may come away with more than a taste for the food; you may also have developed an appetite for the country, as we did.

There is another restaurant that all lovers of seafood — especially seafood cooked in the Mediterranean style — will want to investigate. Cross the Potomac and follow the Washington Memorial Highway; just 6.7 miles after the last traffic signal in Alexandria, you will arrive at the **Cedar Knoll Inn on the Potomac**. Housed in a quaint 18th-century home perched on the banks of the river, this restaurant offers elegant indoor and outdoor terrace dining with an unparalled view of the Potomac. What it has also is a Malagueno chef — and no city in Spain is more famous for its seafood than Malaga. If your appetite is whetted by thoughts of authentic Spanish tapas, paella Valenciana, roast duck Sevilla, or zarzuela de Mariscos (a kind of shellfish casserole), then this is the place for you. In the truest Spanish tradition, this is a meal over which you can linger, savoring delicious food and pleasant conversation. An extensive list of international wines also is available. The inn is open for lunch and dinner daily; a champagne brunch is served on Sunday. To avoid disappointment, call maitre d' John Reynolds for a reservation.

As a treat for both of you, call **Dominion Limousine Service**, (703) 281-1217, and arrange to travel to and from the Cedar Knoll in style and luxury. Alternatively, they can pick you up at your hotel and give you a narrated tour of the city before delivering you to your restaurant. Whichever way you do it, you'll have plenty of fun.

The next stop on our culinary tour is a small and unpretentious restaurant on "I" Street NW, between 19th and 20th Streets, close to Pennsylvania Avenue. Indian-style food has not yet gained widespread popularity in the U.S. As a result, restaurants of this genre are few and far between outside of the major cities. In D.C., of course, there are several – most of them larger and grander than this. Experience has taught us, however, that the quality of the food is generally in inverse proportion to the size of the establishment. This is particularly true of Indian restaurants, which often rely on gaudy decorations and overdressed waiters to draw a clientele. That's not so here. In fact, proprietor Daljeet Singh – who sports a full beard and turban that only accentuate his distinguished demeanor – managed the nearby Bombay Palace for seven years. In autumn of 1994 he opened the **Aroma**, (202) 833-4700. The menu offers the usual range of delights, spiced to suit your taste, with a full range of vegetarian dishes as well. Some of the latter are from Mr. Singh's family collection. Those not familiar with this cuisine (and hesitant about curries) may prefer the *tandoori* (Indian barbecue) style. But, whatever else you choose, by all means order one of the *tandoori* breads. Dinner is served from 5:30 p.m. to 10 p.m. on Saturday and Sunday, with an average meal costing $20 to $25 per person.

For a change in both continents and styles, go next to a place where you will not just be fed, but entertained. When you drive up to 617 New York Avenue NW, the outside doesn't look too impressive. After the valet service has parked your car, walk in to a big surprise. Instantly you will think you have been whisked away to North Africa, more particularly Morocco. At the **Marrakesh**, (202) 393-9393, you will be seated on cushioned banquettes and treated to an authentic seven-course Moroccan feast (which you will eat using your fingers, of course). When your stomach is full, you may feast your eyes on a delicious belly dancer. The Marrakesh is open from 6 p.m. to 11 p.m. nightly. Reservations are required and no credit cards are accepted.

By now, you may be "fed up" with all these different foods. So let's sample some exotic and interesting choices a little closer to home. Perhaps a champagne Sunday brunch will entice you, as it does a wide range of local celebrities. If so, a visit to the **Colonnade** – on the site of the ANA Hotel – is in order. For $35 a person, you may refresh your bodies and spirits while seated under crystal chandeliers in an elegant glass-domed gazebo overlooking a lovely garden with a sparkling fountain and shady trees. Included in the price are unlimited refills of French champagne. This delightfully relaxing ambiance is further enhanced by the gentle melodies performed by the harpist. One word of caution: sip slowly and make your menu selections carefully. Otherwise, you'll never get beyond the first courses – and you certainly wouldn't want to miss the Oriental station. Also try the innovative "Culinary Arts Gallery" for dinner; it offers pairs of delectable appetizers, a selection of salads and delicious entrées finished off with a sherbet intermezzo and dessert. Here, you need not worry about ordering a whole bottle of wine. Different wines are offered by the glass at $5.50 each, and matched to each course. Colonnade, (202) 457-5000, is located at 2401 "M" Street NW, midway between the White House and Georgetown. Reservations are suggested.

Generally speaking, the Phillips seafood restaurants aren't especially romantic. However, they can be fun. Especially the **Phillips Flagship**, (202) 488-8515, at 900 Water Street SW. It is large, innovatively-decorated, and offers panoramic views of the Potomac River. The range and quality of the food – and not just the seafood – are outstanding. Of particular interest is Sunday brunch, offered at a fixed rate of $19.95 per person, between 11 a.m and 4 p.m. A large majority of the patrons will have just come from church, dressed in their Sunday finest. It makes for a charming and colorful sight.

Next, walk off that lunch with a stroll around the nearby **fish market**. Right under your eyes are stalls displaying every kind of fish and shellfish you can imagine, up to and including fresh octopus. Many will want to take home delicacies not readily available elsewhere. Even if you don't buy, the sight (if not the smell) is fascinating. Having trouble making a choice? You may be swayed by free samples like spiced shrimp, served straight out of the pot!

Being so close to the water, you are bound to notice the passing boats. With a little planning, you too can be floating around out there. There are two recommended options. Your choice may depend on how you like to travel in the water – high or low? If it's the former, then you'll want to join a lunch, dinner or moonlight party cruise on

The Spirit of Washington, which departs from Pier 4 at 6th and Water Streets SW (just a short walk from the Green Line Waterfront Metro Station). This sleekly-designed vessel rides high in the water and features three fully-enclosed and climate-controlled decks, each surrounded by huge panoramic windows. Relax in comfort and enjoy the elegant decor. After dining, get a breath of fresh air on the outside decks before returning to the dance floor. On Saturday and Sunday, try a Fun-And-Sun cruise with a DJ, snacks and bar package included in the price. For information or tickets, call (202) 554-8000.

Alternatively, you may head to the nearby Gangplank Marina at 6th and Water Streets SW, where an entirely different style of vessel awaits you. The Odyssey is a floating glass atrium designed like the grand river barges in Europe. It has been specially-constructed to pass beneath the bridges that span the Potomac River. Seating over 600 people, in three different areas, the interior decks are climate controlled and boast a state-of-the-art sound system. Choose the dinner cruise and you will enjoy a sumptuous meal prepared by the in-house Four-Star executive chef, washed down with fine wines and/or champagne. Afterwards, dance cheek-to-cheek as you float over the Potomac. The rate on Friday and Saturday nights is $72 per person. The Lunch, Sunday Jazz Brunch and Midnight cruises are also interesting optionsthat fit nicely into a compact weekend schedule. These range from $25 to $38 per person. Telephone (202) 488-6000 for reservations and/or further information.

No matter where you stay or where you eat, there is one thing you can do to spice things up. Call **ROSExpress**, (202) 842-1000, and arrange for a tuxedo-clad messenger to deliver roses to either your room or table. The flowers offered by ROSExpress are the finest available and will take your breath away. Certainly, no other floral service offers such a wide range of colors. Even exotic hues, such as lavender, black and a variety of two-tones are available in the Rosexotica collection by special advance order. Appeal to all the senses and satisfy your partner's sweet tooth with chocolate roses. They come in three flavors – milk, dark, and white chocolate. Though delightful enough on their own, they make an unforgettably exciting gift when mixed with real roses. To keep the romantic fires burning once you are home, enroll in the Rose of the Month Club. This ensures that a dozen of the same quality super-select roses will be delivered to your love, at the location of your choice, each month for a year. This package will cost you a one-time fee of $300.

Moving on from the subject of food, we'll explore a topic that seldom concerns Americans – railway stations. Since few Americans have even ridden on a long distance train, they hardly worry about where they stop. In other countries, people are accustomed to taking the train to most any destination. As a result, many of the stations – particularly those in major cities – are social centers in their own right. We were pleasantly surprised, therefore, to discover that **Union Station** has characteristics that place it continents away. This is not your typical plain American station. It is bright, airy and architecturally pleasing, with shops of every nature, restaurants and bars, and a simply awesome central concourse. At the center of the latter is a café which offers open-air dining on its upper level. This is a delightful place to head on a Sunday morning. Grab a newspaper on the way and catch up on current events over coffee. If you so desire, you may leave your car back home and come here by train – a far more romantic prospect.

Once in D.C., you must navigate around the city yourselves. This is not so simple, although it is supposed to be logical. Washington is divided into four quadrants – Northwest (NW), Northeast (NE), Southwest (SW) and Southeast (SE) – with the Capitol at its center. The divisions are made by four streets: North and South Capitol Streets; East Capitol Street; and the National Mall. These are at right-angles to each other and radiate outwards from the Capitol building. Which is why every address here has a quadrant designation; and it's an absolute necessity to ask for one if you need to get anywhere. Then there are the in-between streets. Numbered ones run north and south, parallel to North and South Capitol Streets, with the numbers increasing sequentially the further east or west you travel from the Capitol. Lettered streets run east and west, parallel to East Capitol Street and the Mall, ascending through the alphabet (up to W but not including J) the further north or south you travel from the Capitol. After W, this east-west series continues with two-syllable names, then names of three syllables, and so on. If you've got that, you're fine so far – but here comes the curve ball. There is a series of diagonal avenues named after states. Where they cross other avenues, you will often find traffic circles. If you are not confused already, you certainly will be when you get to D.C. To drive here, one needs to have not only eyes in the back of one's head, but in the sides as well; traffic comes at you from every angle!

Amusingly enough, that brings us to our next – and last – subject. How best to get around D.C.? For obvious reasons, we don't recommend using your car. Even if you did, the chances of finding a parking place are next to zero, any day of the week. Public transport is a good option; the **Metro** (five lines identified by different colors) and the extensive **bus system** are both affordable and easy. **Taxis** are a little different here, though. There are no meters; fares are determined by zones, with a base rate – in 1995 – of $3.20 for one zone. Zone maps and fare schedules are posted prominently in each cab. Curiously enough, taxis are allowed by law to take on additional passengers going to different destinations. But the driver must get your permission first, and there can be no more than a five block diversion.

In a city with this many attractions, there are plenty of operators running tours. These come in a variety of forms: trolleys, buses and even boats. Unfortunately, these modes of transportation are generally limited to either land or water. There is one company, however, that gets around that problem in a very nifty way. **DCDUCKS**, (202) 966-DUCK, uses amphibious vehicles – boats with wheels – to take passengers on land and water tours. This is probably the most creative transportation idea we have encountered, and one worth experiencing. Buy your ticket and board at 1323 Pennsylvania Avenue NW.

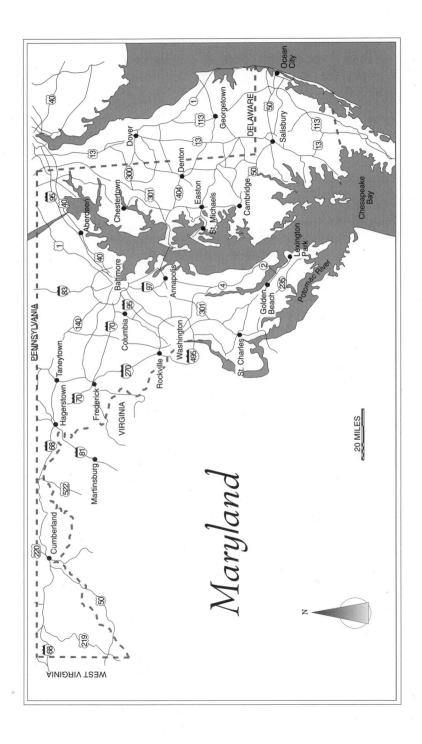

Maryland

20 MILES

Maryland's Capital Region

Buckeystown
Where the Accommodation is Divine

*M*any couples get married in a church, but how many spend their honeymoon in one? Well, we did – part of it, anyway.

Located in a charming nationally-registered historic village, with pre-Revolutionary roots and a strong Civil War influence, is a brick structure dating from 1884 and once known as St. John's Reformed Church. As the congregation consisted of only 27 people, the church they built and consecrated on June 9, 1885 was not very large. Nonetheless, it was adorned with traditional stained glass windows, arched doorways and high ceilings. Its time as a church was short-lived, however. In 1929, the building was sold to a private individual. In 1950 it was purchased by Philip and Margaret Lee, who transformed it into their home. The one large room on the main floor was divided into several smaller ones: a large sitting room with a cathedral ceiling and raised hearth fireplace, a master bedroom, a smaller bedroom and a bathroom. A balcony became a loft bedroom overlooking the sitting room. The Lees lived there until their deaths, after which it was bequeathed to their daughter, Georgine, who lived there until her death. In 1985 it was acquired by the present owner, Dan Pelz. Mr. Pelz had recognized the building's potential and wanted to incorporate both the church and the parson's cottage – also located on the grounds – into his village-based business, **The Inn at Buckeystown**. After some tasteful conversions, he furnished the rooms with delightful period antiques and paintings, beautiful lace window treatments, and novel curios. Also added were a grand piano and a secluded hot tub on the deck outside the main entrance, which faces away from the street and overlooks the garden and fields beyond. These, combined with the stained glass windows and other church features, make for an atmosphere that is incredibly charming and very intimate, if somewhat surreal. This is an ideal place for either a honeymoon or romantic break. How nice to relax in the tub, listening to your partner playing the piano and waiting for him or her to join you. A bottle of champagne awaits you both as you dry off in front of a real wood fire. For the finishing touch, call **ABLOOM Ltd.** (301) 898-5550 for a dozen long-stemmed roses.

If St. John's Church is booked, you should consider the main building housing The Inn at Buckeystown. It offers a different yet delightful alternative. Built in 1897 on twoand one half acres of land, this beautiful 18-room Italianate house has a wraparound porch, widow's walk and random-cut chestnut floors and woodwork. Ownership of the building has changed frequently; at one time, it was so neglected that it was dubbed "the flea's nest" by local residents. Daniel Pelz and his lifelong friend Maty Martinez, who wanted to open a full-service country inn together, discovered and purchased the house in 1981. By the time the Inn opened, in the spring of 1982, they had created an absolute gem. The house already had character galore, with high ceilings and original mouldings; the addition of distinctive chandeliers and lighting fixtures, modern facilities and a tasteful mix of furniture, decorations and personal artifacts made for sheer perfection. The ambience here is marvelously relaxed. There are five guest rooms – three doubles and two queens – each with a private bathroom and lovely period furnishings. You'll find a stocked medicine cabinet, an electric blanket, and a bottle of sherry with two crystal glasses for those loving toasts. Also evident throughout the inn is Dan's love of clowns. Their images are displayed throughout the house in an impressive collection of paintings by various artists, in different styles. Antique Valentines and postcards abound as well. You may even purchase one of your own in the gift shop next to the dining room.

Rates include not only a delicious breakfast, but the evening meal as well. Dan is an accomplished chef who is featured in Gail Greco's *Great Cooking With Country Inn Chefs*. The inn's delightful accommodation and fine cuisine has been applauded elsewhere, too. In 1990, The Inn at Buckeystown was named the "Best Inn of the Year" by Uncle Ben's Country Inn Rice. Subsequently, one of Dan's recipes was featured on the back of their rice boxes. The inn is open Wednesday through Sunday nights, with rates of $225 for doubles, $250 for queens or the Parson's Cottage, and $300 for St. John's Church. On Valentine's Day, Easter, July 4th, Labor Day, Thanksgiving and Christmas, Dan creates special holiday evening meals. Prices are increased accordingly, (by $50 a couple). Dan, his partner Chase Barnett (Marty Martinez passed away in 1988), or innkeeper Rebecca Smith will be happy either to take your reservation or answer further inquiries. They may be reached at (301) 874-5755 or (800) 272-1190, between 8 a.m. and 8 p.m.

The Village of Buckeystown, on the banks of the Monocacy River, has some fine examples of Federal and Victorian homes, a few local craft and antique traders, and some historic sites and monuments. It is small, however, and most visitors will want to explore further afield. There are plenty of options. The surrounding scenery is particularly picturesque, and a terrific way of getting a birds-eye view is to take an air tour. We suggest starting your Saturday morning this way. It will also give you an opportunity to take note of places you might like to explore further, such as **Harper's Ferry,** West Virginia. This last is a very unusual town, rich in history and dramatically situated on a promontory at the confluence of the Potomac and Shenandoah Rivers. **Frederick Aviation,** located a few miles north at Frederick Airport, will be happy to arrange your flight. These may be booked by calling (301) 662-8156 or (800) 545-9393. The more daring romantic purists will consider accomplishing the same thing in a different way. **Adventures Aloft**, at 1938 Lewis Avenue, Rockville, Maryland, 20851, telephone (301) 881-6262, specializes in sunrise fantasy flights for two – weather permitting – in a hot air balloon. For one hour you will float above the tree tops, captive to the whim of the wind as you sip champagne. Upon landing, you will be presented with a "first flight" certificate and returned to your starting point by the chase vehicle crew. Balloons are FAA certified and piloted by a certified commercial pilot. The cost is $150 per person.

Once your feet are back on solid ground, a good first stop is Frederick. A charming town with much historical interest, this county seat celebrated its 250th anniversary in 1995. Begin with a visit to **The Tourism Council of Frederick County & Frederick Visitor Center** at 19 E. Church Street, (301) 663-8687, open from 9 a.m. to 5 p.m. (except for January through March, when they close at 4:30). The staff are knowledgeable and most accommodating; many interesting brochures are also available. Two we found most helpful were "Frederick County, Maryland – So Proudly We Hail," one of the better produced guides and maps of its kind; and "A Tour of Historic Frederick Maryland," with planned walking and driving tours.

For such a small town, Frederick has a rich and diverse history. Founded as Frederick Town in 1745 by one John Schuley, it was originally a largely German settlement. Growth was rapid; by 1748, there was a large enough population to create Frederick County. As in most early American settlements, religion played an important role. Lutheran, Anglican and Reformed churches were soon established. Irish immigrants constructed America's oldest consecrated Roman Catholic church here in 1837. The proliferation of churches – many dating from the mid-19th century – have become the city's trademark. (Their steeples are now known as the "clustered spires.") Frederick's location as a gateway to the west made it a strategic point during the French and Indian War. It was the launching point, in 1755, for a failed expedition by the British General Braddock to capture Fort Duquesne – now Pittsburgh – from the French. A decade later, in 1765, Frederick was home to the first act of rebellion against the British: the defiance of the despised Stamp Act, when residents hung an effigy of the tax collector and the act was repudiated by the Twelve Immortal Judges.

Though it didn't see any action during the Revolutionary War, Frederick was home to a notable patriot, Thomas Johnson. It was he who nominated George Washington for commander-in-chief of the Continental Army; served as Maryland's first elected governor (1777-79); and greatly assisted the new Federal government. Johnson eventually retired to his daughter's home, **Rose Hill Manor**. Now a Children's Museum with displays of period furniture, this home is featured on the driving tour.

After the war, Frederick continued to grow and develop. It was home to two notable lawyers of the post-war period. One of these was Francis Scott Key, the author of the national anthem, who now liesburied in Mt. Olivet Cemetery. A monument was erected in his honor in 1898. His brother-in-law, Roger Brooke Taney, served as chief justice of the young republic between 1815 and 1823. He is probably best remembered for his decision in the famous Dred Scott case, which subsequently led to the Emancipation Proclamation. He also had the distinction of swearing in no fewer than seven U. S. presidents. His home, at 121 S. Bentz Street, (301) 663-8687, now houses the **Roger Brooke Taney House & Francis Scott Key Museum**.

The city was incorporated in 1817. The next year saw the advent of both the railroad and the C & O Canal. Three of the banks established during this period are still in operation today. The ownership of slaves was widespread, and not just on the farms; even city dwellers like Brooke Taney had slave quarters in their homes. Yet when the Maryland Legislature met here in 1861, it decided not to secede from the Union, but to cast its lot with the Northern forces. Its proximity to the Mason Dixon line made it a crucial area for both sides. Residents were pressed for supplies and two major battles were fought nearby. After the Battle of Antietam, local churches and other buildings were used as hospitals; here, local women rallied to nurse the wounded. On July 9, 1864, Confederate General Jubal Early marched into town and gave an ultimatum: pay $200,000 in ransom or he would torch the city. After urgent consideration, officials saved the town by raising the money from local banks. Early left town peacefully, but he was subsequently defeated at the Battle of Monocacy, which stopped the advance of the Confederate Army and saved

Washington from capture. Frederick was immortalized in John Greenleaf Whittier's famous poem about Barbara Fritchie, who waved her Union flag in rebellion when General Stonewall Jackson marched his troops past her house. A replica of her house at 154 W. Patrick now serves as a museum in her honor.

The best place to get a feel for this intriguing background is within the 33-block historic district. This is where the aforementioned guided map "A Tour of Historic Frederick Maryland" is invaluable. You may prefer accommodation in this area of town. If so, indulge yourself with a night in one of the more gracious old houses. **The Tyler-Spite House**, at 112 West Church Street, telephone (303) 832-4455, is a classic three-story Federal-style mansion dating from 1814. The "Spite" in the name stands for just that. Dr. John Tyler had the foundation of the house built literally overnight, with the sole intention of "spiting" the town authorities by preventing the extension of Record Street through to West Patrick Street. Dr. Tyler, thought to be the first American-born ophthalmologist, made his residence at number 108. He is credited with having performed the first cataract removal operation in the United States. Now a delightful bed and breakfast, the Tyler-Spite is decorated with elegant period pieces, richly-hued oriental carpets, and spectacular chandeliers (which compliment the house's high ceilings). Also featured are intricate moldings and a majestic winding staircase. There are five rooms, one being a honeymoon suite with a king-sized canopy bed, brick fireplace and whirlpool bath. Four additional rooms are available next door. Rates range from $150 to $200 a night and include a sumptuous breakfast, a decanter of sherry, and high tea at 4 p.m. In the winter, this last is taken in front of a roaring fire in the library or music room. In warmer seasons, it's served in the beautiful English garden overlooking the swimming pool. Resident hosts Bill and Andrea Myer will be happy to arrange for you to take a romantic half-hour carriage tour, ascending and descending from the original 18th-century block in front of the house.

Across the road in Court Square is the Frederick City Hall, which stands on the same spot as the city's original

c. 1756 log court house. It was in that structure that the Stamp Act was repudiated in 1766, and seven Tories were condemned to be hanged, drawn and quartered in 1781. The historic area has so much to offer that you should consider taking a **Guided Walking Tour of Historic Frederick**. The tours are led by certified guides who bring to life the city's colorful past. They depart at 1:30 p.m. from the visitors' center between the months of April and December, lasting approximately one and one half hours and costing $4.50 per person.

When exploring Frederick, be sure to go to the junction of Route 15 and Rosemont Avenue. Here stands a house considered to be the finest example of German colonial architecture in America. Its builder, Joseph Brunner, immigrated to Philadelphia in 1729. He later found his way to Frederick, where he purchased, for 10 English pounds, 303 acres of land. **Schifferstadt**, named after his birthplace near Mannheim, Germany, was completed in 1756 and still stands on its original site. This unique structure is the oldest house in Frederick. It boasts walls that are two and a half feet thick, hand-hewn beams of native oak, a vaulted cellar with winding staircase and a perfectly-preserved five-plate stove, dated 1756 and bearing a German inscription which translates "where your treasure is, there is your heart." It is open between April and mid-December. The hours are from 10 a.m. to 5 p.m. on Saturday, and from mid-day to 4 p.m. on Sunday. End your tour with a visit to the museum, where you may choose a remembrance of your trip from their selection of books, crafts and gourmet treats. More details may be obtained by calling (301) 663-3885.

Sightseeing can be tiring business. By now your thoughts will have turned to the business of refreshing and refueling your bodies. On your way back into town, stop at **Jennifer's Restaurant**, 207 West Patrick Street, telephone (301) 662-0373. Here you will find a delightful pub-like atmosphere and an unusual decor. Brightly colored flags and banners hang from the ceiling, while the cozy wooden booths tucked in along the walls are perfect for couples. An unusual wood-burning fireplace opens to both rooms, warming your tingling toes during the winter. The food isn't bad, either. Choose from a multi-faceted menu with many original dishes. Jennifer takes special pride in her selection of beers. With 42 bottled, six on draft, and occasional specials from which to choose, you will surely find one to tickle your palate.

If one beer leads to a craving for another, stop by the **Frederick Brewing Company**, 103 South Carroll Street, (301) 694-7899. Though this company has only been in operation three years, brewing beer is hardly new to Frederick. Between 1792 and 1939, 10 breweries were located in the city. In 1992, a group of entrepreneurs with a common appreciation of full-flavored beers and dedication to traditional brewing methods decided to revive an old tradition. Their creations are marketed under the name "Blue Ridge." Tours and tastings are conducted at 1 p.m. and 2:30 p.m. on Saturdays, and 1:30 p.m. on Sundays. You will find that their seven very different varieties are quality beverages indeed. You may even buy a T-shirt advertising your favorite brew or a Blue Ridge mug as a "tasteful" souvenir.

Since most shops are closed on Sunday, it might be best to spend the rest of the afternoon walking around town. The atmosphere is refreshingly relaxed and you will enjoy visiting the many antique, arts and crafts, and specialty shops, as well as galleries and studios. As you're strolling about, you'll want to discuss your plans for the evening. Besides dining out, the options in Frederick are rather limited. There is, however, one place worth consideration: **The Weinberg Center for the Arts**. This building, located at 20 West Patrick Street, (301) 694-8585, opened in 1926 as the Tivoli Theater Movie Palace. It has now been fully restored with the elaborate decor characteristic of the period. Performing and visual arts programs are offered year-round by The Fredericktowne Players, the resident company since 1978. Occasionally, there are performances by touring companies. The theater is also used as a "warm-up" for Broadway-bound productions. Refreshments are served from "gourmet" concession stands, and a variety of tasteful and interesting souvenirs are offered for sale. All told, a possibly delightful evening at the theater, without many of the usual hassles.

If you are not staying – and therefore eating – at The Inn
at Buckeystown, there is an interesting selection of restaurants from which to choose. By common consensus, **The
Brown Pelican**, discreetly located in a basement at 5 East
Church Street, is among the best. Diners descend the
stairs to stone-walled rooms with exposed wooden beams,
apparently lit only by candles. It's no wonder local residents voted it their favorite for a "romantic dinner." It is
not overly expensive either. Fish is often featured in the
pastas, salads or entrées, which are quite imaginative in
their presentation. If you prefer lighter fare, you won't lack
for variety; The Brown Pelican offers 15 delicious sandwiches.

A few blocks north at 6 East Street is a restaurant of a
different style. **Tauraso's Ristorante & Trattoria**, (301)
663-6600, is located in the oldest part of a historic manufacturing complex that has been imaginatively re-created
into Everedy Square. Here you will find shops, offices and
Tauraso's. Within the one restaurant are three distinctly
different atmospheres. Depending upon your mood, you
may wish to dine formally, in the casual pub environment
or outdoors in the Patio Café. As you might have guessed,
the flavor is heavily Italian. Seafood, meat and pasta are
united with an enticing array of other traditional and
not-so-traditional ingredients to form mouth-watering
dishes. If you fancy something more mundane, there's
Tauraso's own Wood-Burning-Stone-Oven-Cooked Pizza.
As you might expect after such a preamble, the desserts
are delectable. To wash it all down, they offer an equally
eclectic range of drinks.

What is left to do on Sunday? We would suggest getting out
and exploring the beautiful surrounding countryside.
Where you go and what you do when you get there depend
entirely upon your mood, however. If you are feeling particularly "together," you might try traveling in tandem –
literally. One visit to **The Tandem Center**, 503 South
Market Street, (301) 694-2944, and "you'll look sweet upon
the seat of a bicycle built for two." The fee includes not only
rental, but comprehensive hands-on instruction (including
mounting and dismounting) and private cue sheets for
routes of 10 to 50 miles (round-trip) on either the C&O

Canal, area roads, or both. More adventurous cyclists may opt for full-day or even overnight trips.

If you seek a saddle of a different type, give **Sunshine Riders**, (301) 869-3777, an advance call. Jim Finigan, an experienced guide, lets you fulfill your "wild West" fantasies on a true Western-style trail ride. You'll don outback jackets and cowboy hats, mount beautiful Appaloosas outfitted with Western saddles, and journey to tranquil places with clear mountain streams, waterfalls and hidden valleys. The price of $70 per person includes soft drinks, a snack and a new understanding of Jim's motto, "only a cowboy knows the feeling."

Those whose inclinations don't run to the equestrian may wish to head southwest out of Frederick on Route 340 for about 18 miles. After crossing the Potomac River into West Virginia, you will see a dramatic and beautiful sight. On a steep promontory that falls away to the confluence of the Potomac and Shenandoah Rivers is one of the most picturesque towns you'll ever see. Following the signs, cross the Shenandoah River to **Harper's Ferry**. The site of John Brown's famous 1859 raid is now a national park with interpretive living history programs and many private shops. It is open year-round; for more information, call (304) 535-6298.

On your return trip, cross back over the Potomac River and turn right onto Route 478. After a minute or two, you will reach Knoxville, Maryland, the home of **River & Trail Outfitters**, 604 Valley Road, (301) 695-5177. This company organizes a variety of water activities between April and October, and offers cross-country skiing in the winter. The North Branch Dam on the Shenandoah releases a rush of white water with rapids and large waves that provide plenty of thrills for water enthusiasts. A half-day raft trip, picnic lunch included, costs $45 per person. Or, for the same fee, you may choose canoeing or kayaking on either scenic flat water or challenging white water. More appealing to most romantics is the laziest option: idling away the hours tubing on Antietam Creek at $24 per person (or $26 with picnic).

Those uninterested in hard physical activity should definitely choose this last option. To add to the experience, head east on Interstate 70, take Route 75 north and then turn to the east again on Glissons Mill Road. Continue until you see the sign for **Linganore Winecellars** at number 13601. There, at the end of a winding shaded lane, you will come to a winery in the middle of a picturesque 230-acre plantation. The Aellen family, who moved here from Pennsylvania with their six children in 1971, had always dabbled in home wine-making. Their hobby grew past their original expectations until, in 1976, they opened the winery. By 1983, they had defined and registered Maryland's vinicultural area. Many of their wines win awards at national and international competitions, but it is their berry wines that are really different. Like many families, they had tinkered with fruit wines at home. But, with access to large quantities of local produce, they began to experiment with commercial production. The results are tastefully unusual. As you sample the many different varieties, the winemakers will delight you with lighthearted and humorous tales of the winery's history. Be sure to ask them how they came to produce dandelion wine. Whether you choose traditional grape or berry, these wines make excellent gifts. For those who time their visit just right, Linganore also hosts a series of outdoor festivals with different kinds of music on certain weekends during the summer.

Next, take a slow, relaxing detour back to Frederick, through the lovely Maryland countryside with its unusual covered bridges. There's no need to outline the routes here. Refer to the guide and maps in the "Frederick County, Maryland – So Proudly We Hail" brochure for a comprehensive detailing of the area.

Whatever you have chosen for your afternoon activity, plan to be back in Frederick before 5 p.m. so you may round out your weekend with a visit to **The Tea Room at Lindentree Designs** on 238 North Market Street. If you don't fancy tea, you may have coffee or cocoa with your choice of scones topped by jam and cream. Also available are tarts and assorted tea cakes.

Maryland's Central Region

Baltimore
Crustacean Central... and Much More

Over the past two decades, many major cities have under-taken major revitalization efforts, with varying degrees of success. Of all the places mentioned in this guide, none have transformed an unsavory image as completely as Balti-more. As late as the 1970s, this city would have been an improbable choice for a romantic weekend. Not so now. An enlightened development of the old and decaying harbor area has since yielded results that attract visitors from far and wide. The now famous Inner Harbor area is, however, just one of the many attractions that Baltimore has to offer. Above all, Baltimore is comfortable and down-to-earth, without pre-tensions about its status. In fact, this is still very much a working-class city where the residents take pride in their ethnically diverse neighborhoods. Here you can really enjoy yourselves without necessarily getting fancy.

Baltimore is located in the northern part of the Chesapeake Bay, which gets its name from the Algonquin Indian word meaning "Great Water." Of course, the Chesapeake Bay is "great" in size – the nation's largest bay, in fact, with a shoreline that approaches 6,000 miles long (tributaries included). Indeed, the bay's 25-mile-wide confluence with the Atlantic Ocean lies many miles south. It's great in a different sense to Baltimore, as it has been the city's commercial lifeline for over three centuries. Over

45 rivers flow into this virtually tideless bay, which is also a major fishing ground.

You'll want to get a clear perspective of this intriguing city before beginning your explorations. There's no better place from which to see it than the **Top of the World**, (410) 837-4515, which is on the 27th floor of Baltimore's World Trade Center. You won't be able to miss this building. The only one on the Inner Harbor's waterfront that boasts any real height, it holds the distinction of being the world's tallest pentagonal structure. In addition to offering a panoramic view of Baltimore's dramatic and rather unusual skyline, the surrounding city and the Chesapeake Bay beyond, the Top of the World acquaints you with the city's history through multi-media presentations and hands-on displays. It is open from 10 a.m. to 5:30 p.m. Monday through Saturday, and from midday to 5:30 p.m. on Sunday. Tickets are on sale up to a half-hour before closing.

As you look out over the harbor, it will become apparent that Baltimore is very much a marine-oriented city. You will surely be fascinated by the kaleidoscopic mix of vessels, each going about its own business. Your attention may first be drawn to one of the majestic sailing vessels. This could well be the *Clipper City,* which departs for a two-hour sailing excursion of Baltimore Harbor at noon and 3 p.m. on Tuesday through Saturday, and at 3 p.m. and 6 p.m on Sunday. The trip costs $12 per person. Or you can party to the sounds of calypso and reggae music on trips that feature live Caribbean bands. These run from 8 p.m. to 11 p.m. on Friday and Saturday nights, for a reasonable $20 per person. If you fancy something a little more peaceful, the Sunday sailing brunch – from 11 a.m to 2 p.m., at $30 per person – is just the thing for you. Reservations for these trips, which run between mid-April and mid-October, may be made by calling (410) 539-6277.

Different in style – but equally graceful – is the sleek and modern *Spirit of Baltimore*. Choose from a variety of cruises originating from this vessel's home base at Harbor View in The Inner Harbor (next to the Rusty Scupper Restaurant). Lunch cruises are offered between midday and 2 p.m. from Monday to Saturday, and between 1 p.m. and 3 p.m. on Sunday. Every evening from 7 p.m. to 10 p.m. you may enjoy a dinner cruise. Or you may opt for what is probably their most romantic proposition, a moonlight party cruise. These are available from 11:30 p.m. to 2 a.m. on Friday and Saturday. During lunch and dinner cruises, you'll feast from a delightful buffet of delicious foods, all freshly prepared on board, and washed down with cocktails or other beverages from full-service bars. As you sail slowly along, the captain will offer an informative commentary on the city's many interesting landmarks. Live musical entertainment and a cabaret-style show performed by the *Spirit's* talented waiters and waitresses round out the evening. Regardless of the weather, you can relax in total comfort on one of the two fully climate controlled decks, each of which are surrounded by huge windows affording lovely panoramic views of the harbor. And what could be more romantic than stepping outside for a crisp breath of air on the outdoor decks? Whatever your choice, ensure a reservation by calling (410) 523-7447.

You'll also see strange little covered pontoon boats flitting around the harbor. These are Ed Kane's **water taxis**, the most interesting and practical form of transportation in Baltimore. These vehicles are continually darting between 16 scheduled stops throughout the harbor, making them much more like "waterbuses" than taxis. There are several different routes and not every one of these blue-and-white water taxis stops at each landing, so be sure to tell the "mate" your destination before boarding. Though they run year-round, much longer – and more frequent – service is offered between April and October. A one-time charge of only $3.50 buys you unlimited access on the day of purchase. In season, you will have only an eight-to 18-minute wait between taxis. But between November and March, expect delays of up to 45 minutes. Be sure to pick up a copy of "Ed Kane's Water Taxi Waterfront Guide To Baltimore" which, apart from helpful maps and schedules, includes anecdotes and notes on all of the landings and nearby attractions. Note, too, the little crabs dotted around the maps. These denote locations where you may purchase steamed crabs. For more information on this unique method of transport, call (800) 658-8947.

If you are unfamiliar with the area, you may wonder why such a map would include information on crabs. In fact, these crustaceans are one of Baltimore's many claims to fame. The Chesapeake Bay is the largest producer of blue crabs in the world. These migrate up the bay during spring and early summer to mate, after which the females return to the bay to spawn. Out of the up to two million eggs produced by each fertilized female, only two to three grow to maturity. To accommodate their growing bodies, the young crabs shed their hard shells from time to time. Remarkably, the soft shell underneath hardens within two hours when the creature remains in the water; it is when they are harvested during this short period that one gets the prized "soft shell" crabs. Hard shell crabs are sold live or already steamed at numerous locations throughout the area from April to year's end.

One place you'll surely pass, no matter what boat trip you take, is **Fort McHenry**. Originally known as Fort Whetstone, it was constructed during the American Revolution. But the event that catapulted it to fame did not occur until the War of 1812. In the heat of this conflict, the British laid siege to Baltimore, bombarding the fort from gunboats to render it useless to colonial forces. However, the crafty rebels had littered the harbor with sunken boats. These impeded the gunboats' approach and kept the British vessels far enough off shore to thwart their plan. It was during this attack that Francis Scott Key, deeply moved by what he had seen, drafted a poem that would later become world-famous. Prior to the onset of the bombardment, Key – a lawyer from Frederick, Maryland – had sailed out to the British fleet with an American officer. Under a flag of truce, they sought to repatriate a Maryland physician who had been captured previously. The request was rejected and Key and his colleague were denied permission to return to shore while bombardment of the fort was in progress. The next morning came and, by some miracle, the American flag was still flying over the fort. Key was so overwhelmed with emotion that he began composing a poem on the back of a letter he was carrying in his pocket. He completed it when back in Baltimore that evening. It was his uncle, Judge Joseph H. Nicholson, who first had the poem printed on a handbill at the offices of the *Baltimore American*. He subsequently discovered that the verses fit quite naturally to the tune of an old English drinking song. "The Star-Spangled Banner" became on overnight sensation and was sung by both sides during the Civil War. However, it was not until March 4, 1931 that Congress officially adopted it as the national anthem. Today the spot from which Key observed the battle is marked by a red, white and blue coastguard buoy. The home of the lady who created this particular flag – one Mary Pickersgill – now houses the **Star-Spangled Banner Flag House & War of 1812 Museum**. The original "Star Spangled Banner," which measured a sizeable 42 by 30 feet, has been preserved at the Museum of American History, part of the Smithsonian in Washington, D. C.

Let's go back up to the **Top of the World** and complete our overview of the harbor. Continuing on the theme of warships, look for the U.S. Frigate *Constellation,* the first ship ever commissioned by the United States Navy. Built in 1797, it is also the oldest U.S. warship continually afloat. Call (410) 539-1797 for more information.

Down and to the left are two thoroughly modern buildings with a different sort of maritime emphasis. **The National Aquarium in Baltimore** is a place that will fascinate everyone, no matter their age. Moving belts on ramped bridges transport you between such diverse habitats as a frosty Icelandic coast and a steamy tropical rain forest. Tanks with a capacity of over two million gallons of water house in excess of 5,000 creatures. Participate in your choice of many interactive exhibits and marvel at the ImaginOcean, a "fanta-sea" of whimsical creatures from the deep. For prices, hours and up-to- date information about seasonal discounts, call (410) 576-3800.

Before you leave the Top of the World, take a long look at the Baltimore skyline. Some of the buildings you'll see are unusual indeed. One of the strangest resides back in the business district at Howard and Lombard. Isaac Emerson, who relocated his Bromo Seltzer company to Baltimore early in this century, constructed a 357-foot high building, the **Bromo Seltzer Tower**, in a fashion similar to the Renaissance Tower at the Palazzo Vecchio in Florence, Italy. Construction was completed in 1911. As a finishing touch, he topped the edifice with a giant, revolving bottle of Bromo Seltzer. This was illuminated by floodlights and often used as a navigational aid until its removal in 1936, due to high maintenance costs. Today this 14-story tower — now topped by a working clock — is still a prominent landmark.

Cast your eyes to the left, where you'll see another prominent building. Located only 960 steps from the Inner Harbor, **Camden Yards** is the new home of the Baltimore Orioles baseball team. Highly acclaimed as a modern version of an old-fashioned ballpark, this has a seating capacity of 46,000 and has sparked a trend in stadium design around the country. Touches of "old-time" Baltimore include the brick facade of the old B&O warehouse, located behind the right-field fence, just 432 feet from home plate. And you can't miss the old-fashioned clock on top of the scoreboard. Accessible by Metro, Light Rail, Park and Ride and even water taxi — which offers special late night services on game nights — this is a marvelous place to enjoy America's favorite sport. If you fancy spending an afternoon or evening at the ball park, call the box office at (410) 685-9800 to order your ticket. If you're really a fan, you may want to go "behind the scenes" to the clubhouse itself. If so, join one of the tours. They take about an hour and 15 minutes, departing every half-hour between 11 a.m. and 2 p.m. Monday through Saturday, and between 12:30 p.m. and 3 p.m. on Sunday. More information may be obtained by calling (410) 547-6234.

While on the subject of baseball, one must note that Baltimore was the birthplace of America's most legendary sports figure, **George Herman "Babe" Ruth.** "The Babe" came into this world on February 6, 1895 in a modest 12-foot wide "rowhouse" that still stands on 216 Emory Street. His father ran a saloon which was located, appropriately enough, in what is now Camden Yards' right field. Ruth's birthplace now houses the **Babe Ruth Birthplace/Orioles Museum,** (410) 727-1539.

Rowhouses are one of Baltimore's architectural trademarks, with a history all their own. Originating in Holland, this type of narrow, elongated structure was widely used in London after the Great Fire of 1666. It was

English settlers who introduced the idea to the new world. Rowhouses became popular in Baltimore during the late 18th and early 19th centuries, when the burgeoning middle classes wanted homes with individual doorsteps of their own. Typically, these consisted of two rooms down and two rooms up, with a passageway down the side. In Baltimore, they often boasted white marble steps as well. Many examples of these are still found in the Park Avenue and Bolton Hill sections of town. As an interesting aside, many of these houses are still standing in the working class districts of northern England. Many more existed there until the last 30 years or so, when they were demolished and replaced with that modern monstrosity, the high-rise apartment building. But things have come full circle. These towers have since caused many urban problems, both here and in the United Kingdom. Now they, in turn, are being demolished − and replaced with single family homes again.

Once back on ground level, you'll want to wander a bit around the Inner Harbor. On one corner you'll find the **Harborplace Amphitheatre,** which offers daily activities of interest to everyone. There might be band music, folk dancers, mime artists or jugglers; on some nights, onlookers are even treated to a firework display. Two large and airy structures − the Light and Pratt Street Pavilions − form the core of this complex. They offer a wide-ranging choice of eateries and unique shops. Across the road, in the Stouffer Harborplace Hotel, you'll find an unusual six-level atrium with an array of top-flight shops.

By now you may be wanting to branch out a little and explore some of those fascinating places you saw from the Top of the World. You are well-served in this respect by the **Baltimore Trolley Line,** the city's only regularly scheduled, ground-based tour. Operating seven days a week between April and October, service begins at 10 a.m., with the last trolley pick-up at 4 p.m. Hours are extended in July and August, but limited between November and March. You can catch the trolley every 30 minutes, at any of 20 locations. A $12 ticket − available at 10 of the 20 stops − allows you unlimited same-day access. Baltimore is a city that is known for its diverse and very distinct neighborhoods; taking the full fascinating tour will give you real insight in this regard. These guides, all Baltimoreans, have an in-depth personal knowledge of the area. When combined with the company's extensive training, this results in a unique, personalized introduction to the city – no pre-recorded commentary or standard script here. If you don't fancy sharing this experience with a trolley full of people, then you may charter one just for yourselves. For $105 per hour, you will receive the same delightful tour – in romantic privacy. For detailed tour, ticket and charter information, telephone (410) 752-2015.

Before setting out on any trip, take time for a quick visit to either the **Baltimore Area Visitors' Center,** (410) 837-4636, on the corner of Pratt and Howard Streets; or the **Visitors' Information Kiosk,** on the western shoreline of the Inner Harbor. One brochure you should definitely request is the "Baltimore Street Map & Visitors Guide." In addition to detailed street plans and interesting anecdotes about the city's history, it features advertisements for many services and places of interest – some of which carry discounts.

Those of you who crave a more personal and luxurious tour should consider taking a chauffeur-driven "stretch" limousine from **Carey Limousine,** (410) 837-1234. For $50 an hour (plus taxes and gratuities), they will conduct a tour of the city according to your specifications. They'll also deliver you to your choice of restaurant and, after you have dined, carry you back to your hotel in style. Maybe a shade expensive, but certainly a special treat for a special occasion – and lots of fun. A word to the wise: this indulgence carries a three-hour minimum.

The Inner Harbor development has brought a variety of new hotels to the area, and the choices of accommodation are numerous. There are also many interesting places in the more traditional parts of city. As with other towns of this genre, our selection must be rather subjective. We would like to think, though, that our recommendations provide an eclectic and colorful mix. We will begin with the Inner Harbor area. Here, we have chosen only hotels overlooking the harbor. After all, the main attraction is the harbor itself. It's peaceful and romantic to peer out from your hotel window – especially at night – and watch both boats and lights slowly and silently weave their patterns on the water.

Some hotel architects choose to draw attention to their structures with a flourish of exterior design. All too often, however, the follow-through is lacking, and the interior proves less grand. So experience has taught us to rely on our "sixth sense." When we first chanced upon the distinguished – but nevertheless low-key – **Harbor Court Hotel,** our instincts told us this was something special. We certainly weren't disappointed with this Four-Diamond and Four-Star-rated hotel, located at 550 Light Street. Ideally sized at 203 rooms, it is large enough to offer exceptional facilities but small enough to offer personal service. The Harbor Court also boasts unparalleled views of the Harborplace complex and the National Aquarium – both a short walk away – as well as the Inner Harbor itself. From the moment you enter the lobby, which is accessed from the cleverly designed forecourt, you will be impressed by the richly conservative decor. Featured are oak paneling and marble floors that enhance the unusual floorplan. Two focal points are the library, which is filled with volumes collected from all over the world; and the gently curving staircase that leads upstairs to a series of public rooms.

The Four-Star **Hampton's Restaurant**, overlooking the Inner Harbor, epitomizes the gracious style found throughout the hotel. Its fine American cuisine is highly rated, and Hampton's was listed as a "top 10" restaurant in *Condé Nast Traveler*'s 1995 Restaurant Awards. A favorite here is the traditional Sunday champagne brunch. For a more informal atmosphere, head to **Brightons**, another in-house option for breakfast, lunch, dinner or tea. You'll also want to relax in the **Explorers Lounge.** Here you can become an armchair adventurer and dream of far-away places. The decorationsin this lounge are really most unusual. One large hand-painted mural depicting African scenes converges with a ceiling work in the 19th-century Italian style. Formal furniture, informal cane furniture and exotic *objets d'art* make for an ambience that would be difficult to recreate elsewhere. Nightly piano music and weekend jazz serve as a background. Between the hours of 11:30 a.m. and 10:30 p.m., light dishes are available to accompany your favorite beverages. Until 1 a.m., lingerers or latecomers may enjoy cocktails.

A variety of rooms and suites are offered here; in fact, there are a myriad of combinations. To wit:regular guest rooms with your choice of a harbor or city/courtyard view; executive staterooms; one-bedded suites; two-bedded suites; the Clipper City Suite; and the Harbor Court Suite. Obviously, these vary to some extent in size and style. But in each and every one you can expect a level of quality and taste that is seldom surpassed. The staterooms, for example, are enhanced by colorful hand-painted wallpaper, polished marble vanities, and a luxurious five-foot tub in which you (both?) may soak. Especially delightful are the rooms overlooking the harbor. The most luxurious choice is the harbor court suite, which sits elegantly on the top floor and boasts a breathtaking view of the Inner Harbor. In fact, the entire suite is breathtaking. Covering 2,600 square feet, it is spacious, to say the least. Featured are a living room; dining room with seating for 12; two bedrooms; and two-and-a-half baths. Other highlights include a marble wet bar, working fireplace, butler's pantry, and a baby grand piano. There is just one catch: it rents for $2,000 a night. Although this is beyond most peoples' reach, it suits Frank Sinatra and his ilk very well indeed.

On the rooftop you will find a beautifully landscaped fitness center that offers tennis, croquet, swimming, racquetball, aerobics, weight training, and a sauna and whirlpool. One of the unique features of this hotel is the fact that all rooms face outwards, allowing each a beautiful view of the surrounding area. When walking to your room, be sure to look down into one of the inner courtyards. You'll be in for a surprise; there are live peacocks "strutting their stuff."

The Harbor Court offers couples an array of weekend packages, all of which include breakfast, valet parking and personalized concierge service. For $300 a night you can set your "Hearts Ablaze" in a stateroom equipped with a complimentary bottle of champagne. If you fancy some "Deluxe Romance," add $175 a night, and you'll dine on fine cuisine either at Hampton's or, should you prefer, in the privacy of your room. "Bon Appetit" features accommodation in a guest room, as well as a full breakfast for two at Brightons at a nightly rate of $275. If you are in a rush, there is a "Quick Getaway Rate." At $140 per night, this covers only the cost of a guest room. If you choose to extend your stay, this can be arranged for as low as $99 a night. The helpful staff will be most happy to take your reservation or provide additional information when you call (410) 234-0550 or (800) 824-0076, or fax (410) 659-5925.

Located in the Harbor Court building is **Flowers by Chris**, (804) 727-3434 and fax (410) 727-0110. Herein lies a fascinating and courageous tale. Back in 1978, Chris Psoras' husband George – a prominent Towson trial attorney – was dying of cancer. With the family's finances in a precarious state, she had to find a way to earn money; but how? It so happened that a family friend sold flowers on a street corner. He suggested that Chris and her two sons do likewise. Though she had no experience, she gave it a try. She had little initial success. However, the perseverance and hard work of all three eventually paid off and, to cut a long story short, business began to bloom. Chris now runs two locations – here in the Harbor Court and at Marriott's Hunt Valley Inn – with future plans to open even more. When planning your visit to Baltimore, call or fax ahead to Chris. She will arrange for a wonderful bouquet of roses or other flowers to be waiting in your room, or on your restaurant table. Another unusually nice surprise is a bottle of champagne tucked into an ice-filled crystal top hat – a classy way to "top" off the evening.

For those who prefer a larger hotel, the **Stouffer Renaissance Harborplace Hotel** is the obvious choice. Centrally located by the main side of the Inner Harbor, it is connected to the Gallery and Harborplace Malls. Not surprisingly, it is also Four-Diamond and Four-Star-rated, with 622 deluxe rooms, including 60 suites. Each of these offer the latest in modern conveniences, including cable TV with movie channels and a mini-bar. Many sport marvelous harbor views. A full range of services is available. Coffee and newspapers are complimentary with your wake-up call. Also *gratis* are shoe shine, valet parking and 24-hour room and concierge service. Guests also have access to the on-site health and fitness center, which includes an indoor swimming pool, Nautilus equipment and a cardiovascular machine. After your workout, you may enjoy the jacuzzi and sauna.

The management understands that those escaping for a weekend have a different agenda from most travelers. To this end, they have developed a series of special packages. The Precious Memories Package, at $199, is a special one-night getaway including a chilled bottle of champagne and a buffet breakfast for two. If you fancy a deluxe room with a view of the harbor, choose the Room With A View Package. In addition to the chilled bottle of champagne, you will enjoy a candlelit dinner for two, served either in your room or in the award-winning Windows Restaurant overlooking the Inner Harbor. The tariff for this package is $315 per night. To double your pleasure, opt for a special two-night package. The Sights & Sounds Package gives you two nights in a deluxe room and breakfast on each morning of your stay. Also included in the $475 price tag are admission tickets to both the National Aquarium and the Maryland Science Center, as well as dinner for two at Windows. If you really want to splash around, then you should definitely take the Harbor Hideaway Package. Your $540 will give you two nights in a fabulous harbor-view room, with champagne upon arrival; breakfast each morning; all-day passes for the water taxi; and a romantic candlelit dinner for two, either at Windows or in the privacy of your room.

Just nine blocks away from the Inner Harbor – but an age apart – is the historic Mount Vernon district. Here, in this European-style section, you may wander down cobblestone streets and browse through shops in the famous Antique Row. You may also visit Mount Vernon Square, with its impressively tall column supporting the city's monument to George Washington. Here you'll also find a hotel with more traditional leanings, in perfect harmony with its surroundings. Constructed in 1927at 612 Cathedral Street, **The Latham Hotel**, (410) 727-7101 or (800) LATHAM-1, underwent extensive renovations in 1994. As a result, it has earned a Three-Diamond rating from Mobil and four stars from the AAA. Its 104 rooms and 25 suites are decorated in a most comfortably traditional manner and feature a remote-controlled color TV, a fully stocked mini-bar and marble bathrooms with European-style towel warmers and plush robes. The tariff card details three categories of room, but we would suggest you consider the Private Reserve with its relaxing and romantic jacuzzi (at $170 a night). After leaving your automobile for valet parking, you will return to your room to find imported chocolates waiting onyour pillows. The next morning, you'll awake to find a newspaper outside your door. If you are in need of some exercise, you may take advantage of complimentary entrance to the Downtown Athletic Club, Baltimore's premier health facility two blocks away.

The Latham offers you a choice of two delightful restaurants. Of particular interest is the **Citronelle**; a magnificent glass-enclosed dining area atop the hotel, it affords breathtaking views of the city. This is the brainchild of Michel Richard, the highly-acclaimed chef of Los Angeles' celebrated Citrus Restaurant. The Citronelle showcases his creative but light approach to food, which you will enjoy in this casual yet elegant atmosphere. This is further enhanced by music from a jazz duo. Recently, *Bon Appetit* magazine named the Citronelle one of America's top 25 hot new restaurants.

Be sure to ask the concierge for your complimentary copy of the self-guided "New Historic Mount Vernon Walking Tour." This includes a packet of up-to-date information on the various sights; discount coupons for many stores in the Mount Vernon area; and, if you've forgotten your camera, a chance to purchase an inexpensive Konica disposable model. For those preferring to take it a little easier, The Latham's complimentary van service will get you wherever you need to go.

Back across town is **Fell's Point,** a charming neighborhood that blends well-preserved history with a cosmopoli- tan smattering of specialty shops, restaurants, markets and hotels. And everywhere you look are residential streets replete with the city's most delightful rowhouses. The area was purchased in 1730 by William Fell, a Quaker and shipbuilder who hailed from Lancaster, England. Fell's chosen trade began to flourish here, and by the end of the century there were 16 shipyards on the waterfront.

This natural deep-water port saw the building of speedy Baltimore clipper ships, schooners and, perhaps most notably, the aforementioned *Constellation*. It was also used as a commercial port, as well as an entry point for wave after wave of immigrants. Today it is recognized as one of the nation's oldest working waterfront communities. At night, the giant neon Domino Sugar sign on the far bank of the Patapsco River reminds you of just one company that calls Baltimore home. This is one of the world's largest such signs, and the bill for the electricity that feeds it is said to be immense. All in all, this is a fascinating area, and as you stroll around admiring the late 18th and early 19th-century architecture, take note of the street names. Monikers such as Thames, Fell, Bond, Wolfe, Lancaster and Shakespeare serve as a reminder of this area's roots. If you visit in October, be sure to inquire about the annual Great Chesapeake Bay Schooner race. In this event, old and new schooners ranging in size from 34 to 156 feet begin a race that will finish in Norfolk. If you don't want to drive back to town, simply hop on either a trolley or water taxi.

If you're so inclined, you can lodge in Fell's Point as well. On the corner of South Broadway and Thames Street, by Market Square, is an attractive hotel. One of the taller buildings in Fell's Point, this has served the area in a variety of different ways over the past century. In 1889, the Women's Auxiliary of the Port Mission established The Anchorage – a now-legendary seaman's hostel – here. This functioned until 1929, when it was acquired by the YMCA. That organization converted and expanded the building into a 105-bed Seaman's YMCA. Between that time and its demise in the mid-1950s, it is estimated that this YMCA provided a home for over 50,000 sailors a year. Comfort, however, was not the main aim back then. The rooms were so tiny that it was nicknamed "the doghouse." The structure's next stint was in the commercial arena; the cellars of the four interconnected buildings were transformed into a cider and vinegar bottling factory known as the Vinegar Works. This venture did not fare well, however. After closing its doors in the mid-'70s, the buildings remained unoccupied until 1985 when, like a phoenix, **The Admiral Fell Inn** rose from the ruins.

Quality accommodation is offered in any one of the inn's 80 guest rooms and suites, each bearing the name and displaying the biography of a prominent Baltimore figure. Period furnishings – including a four-poster bed – complement the custom-designed Federal-style decor. The baths are modern and some feature whirlpool tubs.

The cellars of the old vinegar plant have been transformed into The Admiral Fell Restaurant, which is renowned for its creatively prepared seafood, meat and poultry. Nearby is an English-style pub that supports its bistro-type menu with a wide range of domestic and imported wines and beers. This last place is particularly interesting during the Thanksgiving and Christmas periods, when you may sip on traditional seasonal drinks (like hot buttered rums and mulled wine) and enjoy what has become a hotel tradition: readings from Charles Dickens' classics works.

In 1995, the regular rate here was $165 for a double room. That included a Continental breakfast, transport by courtesy van to various spots around town, and self-parking in a nearby lot. Valet parking is also available for a charge of $6. Special winter rates were as low as $109 for one night, with a $10 discount per night for stays of two nights or more. These rates will be valid at least through early 1996, and possibly beyond. Telephone (410) 522-7377 or (800) 678-8946, or fax (410) 522-0707 for your reservation. The address, by the way, is 888 South Broadway.

A short walk away at 1714 Thames Street is a most unusual bed and breakfast. The sidewalk is narrow indeed, so it may be easiest to look for the distinctive wrought-iron gate that opens onto the narrow passageway leading down to **Celie's Waterfront Bed & Breakfast**, (410) 522-2323 or (800) 432-0184 and fax (410) 522-2324. For those seeking something more intimate, this provides quite a delightful contrast to the larger hotels. There are two harbor-front rooms, one on the second floor and one on the third floor. Furnished with king-sized beds and wicker furniture – and featuring wood-burning fireplaces and whirlpool tubs – these rent for $160 a night. Each of the upper two floors also has an atrium room overlooking the courtyard with a queen-sized bed ($115 per night); and a garden room with a view of the city, queen-sized bed, private balcony and whirlpool bath ($135 per night). The seventh room next to the ground floor courtyard is furnished with either a single bed or two twin beds, with a private courtyard and handicapped accessibility. The charge for this is $100 a night.

Whichever room you choose – and each one is delightfully different – it will be tastefully furnished with antiques and lovingly filled with both collectibles and freshly cut flowers. The effect is both warm and inviting. The modern conveniences have not been overlooked, either; these include, among other things, air-conditioning; private baths with terry robes; televisions; ceiling fans; refrigerators; and (with the exception of the ground floor courtyard room) coffee makers. The public rooms are equally well-appointed and welcoming. In addition, Celie's boasts one quite unexpected surprise: a roof deck and garden. From here you will have sweeping views of both the city skyline and the busy harbor. This is a fantastic place to partake of your complimentary Continental breakfast.

All room rates include off-street parking, but be aware when making your reservation that the harbor front and garden rooms have a two-night minimum booking on any weekend. This is a stipulation which is extended to all of the rooms during holiday and "special event" weekends. As you might expect from this cosmopolitan and ethnically-rich city, there is a wide range of restaurants from which to choose. We will detail here what we feel are some of the highlights; but you may want to do some research on your own.

Nearly everyone loves Italian food. Therefore, few will want to miss the opportunity to take a short trip – just a few blocks from the Inner Harbor – to Little Italy. Of the many restaurants there, few have received such accolades as **Da Mimmo**, (410) 727-6876, at 217 South High Street. Here, you needn't worry about finding first the restaurant and then a parking space; they will gladly send a limousine to pick you up at your hotel and return you there at the end of the evening (complimentary, of course). In this casually elegant and intimate atmosphere, you will find all your favorite dishes (as well as unfamiliar ones that will likely become new favorites). Everything is prepared by Chef Mimmo, who oversees this family-run business and has been honored as "Restaurateur of the Year" by the Restaurant Association of Maryland. Chef Mimmo strives to cater to his patrons' every need, so should you have a particular craving, telephone ahead to order one or more gourmet specialties from virtually any part of Italy. You may also choose an accompanying wine from one of the finest wine lists in the area. Such a combination of virtues seldom goes unnoticed, so don't be surprised to find yourself seated next to one of the celebrities who often frequent Da Mimmo's. After an exquisite meal, head over to the Roman Cocktail Lounge for live entertainment.

A trip to Baltimore would be incomplete without a visit to an old-fashioned crab house, and they don't come any more old-fashioned than **Gunnings Crab House**, (804) 354-0085. This Baltimore institution is located just a few minutes south of the Inner Harbor at 3901 South Hanover Street, in the old neighborhood of Brooklyn. The only thing fancy here is the food, and there's plenty of that. Brown paper covers the tables, you'll be forced to don a bib, and the main eating utensil will be a wooden mallet used to crack open the crabs – which, incidentally, are some of the largest served anywhere. If you don't like crabs, the other seafood choices are vast. And if you prefer turf to surf, this establishment's steaks and chicken dishes are equally delicious. A casual atmosphere is pervasive, both indoors and in the outdoor dining area, with its unique "crab garden." Endowed with a different kind of magnetic charm, Gunnings is also popular with local personalities.

As we've already mentioned, Spanish restaurants are among our favorites. There's one in Baltimore that's certainly worth visiting. The **Tio Pepe Restaurant**, (410) 539-4675 and fax (410) 837-7288, is at 10 East Franklin Street, near the Mount Vernon neighborhood. It was started by Chef Pedro Sanz, who cooked at the Spanish Pavilion in New York's two world's fairs and later ran the esteemed Toledo Restaurant in that city. In December, 1968, Pedro and his fellow Spaniard Jesus Perez opened this restaurant. And it didn't take long for it to become a city favorite. Indeed, it's been recognized as the best restaurant in town for 12 straight years by readers of *Baltimore* magazine. (It's also received national recognition from, among others, *Travel Holiday* magazine and the *Mobil Travel Guide.)* After Pedro's death in 1989, the longtime *chef de cuisine* Emiliano Sanz and his nephew Miguel took over the restaurant. They have zealously maintained its sterling reputation, whipping up numerous traditional dishes that will be familiar to those acquainted with Spain, and pleasantly surprising to those who aren't. The wine list is extensive, too. As usual with a good Spanish restaurant, there is a wider range of reds than whites, as well as some great vintages (especially on the reserve list). Reservations here are definitely recommended.

If you like Chinese food, then head for **Uncle Lee's Harbor** at 44 South Street, right next to the Inner Harbor. In these unique surroundings, you can feast on your choice of Szechuan, Hunan or Mandarin delicacies. If you are a purist – or just feeling adventurous – authentic Chinese preparations are available as well. If you don't feel like getting dressed and going out, give Uncle Lee's a call at (410) 727-6666. They'll deliver your favorites right to your hotel door.

If you need a break, like southwestern and Mexican food, and would like to travel by water taxi, try **Lista's of Fell's Point**, (410) 327-0040. It's at 1637 Thames Street (just a few feet away from the water taxi stop), and dining here is really a treat. Restaurants featuring this style of cuisine can vary as to quality and style, but no need to worry here. For more than 50 years, the name Evangelista has been associated with original and exciting food in Denver, Colorado. Florencio's children have followed in their parents' footsteps. After opening their first Lista's in Virginia Beach, his youngest son Ruben teamed up with wife Kathy to start this one. The saloon-like interior transports you back to the days of the Wild West. There is an abundance of Tex-Mex furnishings, with all the appropriate trappings. The major sources of illumination are candles and – believe it or not – strings of "chili pepper lights" draped from the ceiling and across the vast expanse of windows overlooking the harbor. The food is superb, the choice of specialty cocktails and beers enticing, and the service exemplary. You are sure to be especially enchanted by their harpist's renditions of traditional Spanish and favorite contemporary songs.

Taneytown
An Enchanting Inn
May Put Love on Track

$\mathcal{D}$ue to circumstances beyond our control, this chapter has turned out to be more enigmatic than even we expected.

We were originally drawn to this part of central Maryland by two things: reports of an interesting inn and a company that offers a variety of entertaining train excursions.

You know what they say about "the best-laid plans." Between the time of our research and the time of this writing, a dispute arose between **The EnterTRAINment Line** and the company that owns the tracks on which their trains run. This had resulted in a cessation of their excursions. Whether this is temporary or permanent, it was impossible to ascertain at press time. The options they offered from their base in Union Bridge were both entertaining and unique, but at this point all you can do is call for an update on the situation before setting your itinerary.

The local inn is one of the most enchanting and romantic places we've seen. Without doubt, it is worthy of a visit; even if your only "outside activity" is a stroll around town.

Antrim 1844 – An Antebellum Country Inn is at 30 Trevanion Road, just off Route 140 (East Baltimore Street) and a few hundred yards east of Taneytown. It is easy to miss, but if you can locate the Taneytown Bank & Trust, at the junction of Route 140 and Trevanion, you'll be "warm." (The entrance to Antrim is just to the rear.) At first glance, the environment seems rather ordinary, but don't be fooled. As soon as you pull into the drive, you'll realize it's far from that. This magnificent three-story square mansion is distinguished by majestic porticoed entrances, as well as a smaller two-level addition on one side.

Once inside, you're transported back – in the twinkling of an eye – to a time of genteel grace and elegance. This inn has an authentic mid-19th century ambience that tends toward the formal. Yet it is not at all pretentious. The hosts' southern hospitality will put you right at ease, setting the tone for what will prove a relaxing weekend. Your key will be waiting for you by the door, accompanied by a hand-written card bearing your name.

If your room is one of the nine within the mansion, expect it to be large and furnished with a cozy canopied feather bed and other antiques. There will also be a fireplace and either a marble bath or a double jacuzzi. Most rooms offer a lovely panoramic view of the surrounding Catoctin Mountains, which you may enjoy as you share a glass of sherry from the waiting decanter. On the way in, be sure to introduce yourselves to James, one of a company of wooden butlers stationed outside each door. He will faithfully provide guests with fresh baked muffins, coffee, tea and a newspaper each morning. This will keep you satisfied before the formal breakfast hour, which is between 9 a.m. and 10 a.m. But don't expect a television or even a telephone. The proprietors realize that one aspect of romance is being able to concentrate totally on each other. (By the time you get back to your room you won't be in the mood for such distractions, anyway.) The room rates range between $150 and $175 a night.

The inn's five suites are located in outbuildings. Each has a queen-sized bed, a fireplace, and its own unique character. The "Ice House" next to the formal gardens has the style and quaint character of an English cottage. "The Barn" houses two rooms. Each of these has a private deck, from which you may enjoy a peaceful view of the bubbling brook as it meanders through the woods. "The Cottage," originally the office of the plantation's overseer, has a jacuzzi and private courtyard. The tariff for the suites is from $250 to $300 per night, per couple.

Once you've settled in, it is time to explore the remainder of the house and its 23 acres of cultured gardens. Hopefully, by this time you won't be in hurrying mood, as this is one experience that should definitely be savored. With a complimentary glass of wine in hand, you may lounge in the drawing room, study in the library or wander arm-in-arm through the garden. Here you will be serenaded by the trickling melody of the dancing waters running from the fountain. Do take a bit of time to explore the grounds, as they really must not be missed. You will also notice the lovely house on the opposite side of the fountain; it is the residence of the owners/innkeepers, Dort and Richard Mollett.

Perhaps by now you are in the mood for some gentle activity. Lob a few balls on the tennis court or try your hand at lawn bowling, horseshoes, croquet, or badminton. Afterwards, cool off with a dip in the unusually elegant pool and a refreshing drink from its gazebo bar.

This is all marvelous, but there is one treat yet to come. As you might expect, the evening meal is quite an event here. One half-hour before it is served, wander inside. Here you'll be met by a charming young lady with a tray of hors d'oeuvres and a little wine. You'll get used to this kind of attention – maybe too used to it – because it will never be necessary to ask for a refill. During the colder months, dinner is served in "The Smokehouse," which boasts a brick floor and large fireplaces. As delightful as this is, the summer months are nicer. During this period, you'll be seated at a candlelit table on the back veranda, overlooking both the formal gardens and the verdant Catoctin mountains. Cocktails, if you desire them, are followed by a five-course extravaganza prepared by an award-winning chef.

No part of this exquisite meal is rushed, and the experience is heightened as you watch the blazing red sun slowly ease its way towards the outreaching trees.

Before you succumb to this evocative memory, don't miss the opportunity to linger for awhile in the intimate Pickwick Tavern. Innkeeper Richard Mollett may have popped in for a nightcap, and you'll get a chance to chat. Then you will understand how Antrim came by its character.

One of the greatest compliments you can give the Molletts is to tell them that this is how you would have pictured the mansion in bygone days. It doesn't take too much imagination to visualize General Meade observing troop movements from the widow's watch during the Battle of Gettysburg (which occurred about 12 miles north). But this natural, unaffected atmosphere wasn't easy to re-create. The Mollets spent many painstaking years renovating this home to such a standard. There's no doubt that Antrim 1844 offers the perfect respite for even the most discerning travelers.

When you are ready for this experience, telephone (410) 756-6812, (800) 858-1844, or fax (410) 756-2744 for a reservation.

Annapolis
Romance Here is Much More Than Academic

There is a quaint, enchanting city on the banks of the Severn River and the Chesapeake Bay that was, for a short time, the capital of this nation. In addition, it has been the state capital for over 300 years. Walking through the streets, you will be transported back in time; unusual road patterns and an even more unusual mix of Colonial, Federal, and Victorian architecture give this city a look that is quite distinct. Then there is the water. It was this city's strategic position – at the mouths of the river and the bay – that gave it commercial importance and made it the ideal site for one of the nation's leading military academies. These days, Annapolis is known primarily as the sailing capital of the U.S. and the home of the United States Naval Academy.

Annapolis was named in honor of England's Queen Anne. The first settlers arrived here in 1649. Before the end of the century – 1694, in fact – the town's rapid growth made it a natural choice as the capital of Maryland. The very unusual street layout – two major circles, with streets radiating from them – was designed the next year and is still in use today. By the mid-18th century, Annapolis had developed into a thriving colonial seaport and a commercial center, with tobacco being the chief cash crop and the currency of the province. In 1772, work began on a new state capitol building, but it was not until after the Revolutionary War that it was finally completed. In 1845, the nation's first naval school was established by Secretary of the Navy George Bancroft. Initially, there were just 50 students, four officers, and three civilian professors. Five years later it officially became the United States Naval Academy. Except for a period during the Civil War (when it was relocated to Newport, Rhode Island), Annapolis has been home to this world-famous institution ever since.

The dominant feature of this city is a magnificent narrow dome topped by an unusual tower and an observation deck. This belongs to the **Maryland State House**, set at the highest point in the city in the middle of the imposing State Circle. It has its fair share of historical interest as well. Completed in 1779, this is the oldest state capitol in continuous legislative use in the country. Between 1783 and 1784, the old senate chamber was the seat of the Continental Congress. Thus, it has the honor of being the only state house ever to have functioned as the nation's capitol. In the same chamber, General George Washington resigned his commission as commander-in-chief of the Continental Army on December 23, 1784. The Treaty of Paris, which ended the Revolutionary War, was officially ratified just a few weeks later, with Thomas Jefferson appointed the first United States minister plenipotentiary to foreign governments on May 7, 1784. There is much to see inside as well, and tours conducted by state house guides are normally given from 10 a.m. to 5 p.m. daily. Call (301) 974-3400 for specific tour information.

To get the real flavor of Annapolis, it is necessary to ramble around State Circle and then down any – or preferably all – of those small, colorful streets sloping toward the river.

Here you will find homes both small and large, brick and wood, in all kinds of shapes, and either Colonial, Federal or Victorian in style, arranged in no particular order. The closer you get to Market Square, the more you begin to feel the maritime presence. Given the number of small specialty shops along the way, you're in for an delightful experience. Mixed in amongst these are important houses, museums, and the like; one or two brochures will assist you in identifying them. These are available year-round from the **Convention & Visitors' Bureau** at 26 West Street, telephone (410) 268-TOUR, or fax (410) 263-9591. In season, you may also obtain them from the visitor information booth at City Dock. "Annapolis: Maryland Avenue & State Circle" gives a detailed listing of everything located on what was once the most important street in the city.

When traveling to the Convention & Visitors' Bureau, pass the second of two traffic circles – Church Circle – to historic St. Anne's Church and Reynold's Tavern, both of which date from 1747. You may find it interesting to take a tour of this area and, if so, you have options. **Three Centuries Tours of Annapolis** at 48 Maryland Avenue, telephone (410) 263-5401 or fax (401) 263-1901, offers a two-hour guided tour with "The Colonials." This originates at various locations, depending upon the season. Maybe you prefer to do things on your own. If so, head for the **Maritime Museum** at City Dock, (410) 268-5576. Here history comes alive on a 45-minute **Acoustiguide** audio tour narrated by Walter Cronkite. Ghost lovers are also in luck. From April through November, beginning at dusk and again at 9 p.m., **Ghost Tours** depart from outside St. Anne's Church, weather permitting. Rain cancels the tours, but fog and mist just add to the atmosphere. Telephone (410) 974-1646 for reservations or more information. The more energetic might find it fun to cycle around town. If so, contact **Downtown Cycle**, (410) 267-7681, located just across from the museum at 6 Dock Street. This organization rents bicycles by the hour (either individual bikes or two-person tandems).

Now it's time to head down Main Street to **City Dock**, the focal point of Annapolis. A walk down this steep street will demonstrate the cosmopolitan nature of modern-day

Annapolis. Apart from the usual shops and boutiques, there is an array of restaurants you would not expect to find in a smaller city.

You will also undoubtedly encounter the midshipmen who make this city famous. As they are obliged to walk around in their distinctive uniforms, you could hardly miss them. If they pique your interest, visit **The United States Naval Academy**, just a couple of blocks away from City Dock. Originally just 10 acres, **The Yard**, as it is commonly called, has now been expanded to a huge 338-acre complex that is home to a brigade of 4,000 midshipmen and 580 faculty members. Wonderful guided tours are offered, but the schedules are both seasonal and complicated. Therefore, we suggest calling (410) 263-6933 for details. You will learn about the students' quaint customs and see Bancroft Hall which, since it is home to the entire brigade, is one of the largest single dormitories in the world. (It features no fewer than 1,873 rooms, over five miles of corridors, and 33 acres of floor space!) The academy chapel is the final resting place of John Paul Jones, the greatest of the Revolutionary War naval heroes. His remains were returned here after they were found by a U.S. Ambassador to France in a Parisian graveyard; they had been "lost" for over a century.

By now, you may be getting hungry. Take the short stroll back to City Dock, where you will find numerous restaurants and cafés, many with an appropriate nautical flavor. None, however, has a history like that of the **Middleton Tavern**, 2 Market Space, (410) 263-3323. Annapolis has more 18th-century buildings than any other city in the country, and this classic Georgian structure is of that genre. Originally constructed around 1740, Middleton was purchased in 1750 by Horatio Middleton, who ran it as a tavern. Middleton also operated a ferry between Rock Hall and Annapolis and, as the law then required ferry operators to provide lodging for travelers, the tavern became an inn. Since the ferry considerably shortened the journey between Philadelphia and Virginia, it was widely used by prominent men of the time. George Washington, Thomas Jefferson and Benjamin Franklin were all guests at the Middleton.

Since those days, the building has had a variety of uses. Now, however, it has been renovated to re-create the warmth and ambience for which it was once famous. Enjoy a drink at the piano bar, nibble from the raw bar, and afterwards select from an interesting menu which offers both traditional and innovative dishes. You may choose to have your meal served at a cozy table next to one of the two fireplaces or, weather permitting, take a leisurely lunch in the sidewalk café. Try and do the latter, as it will give you the opportunity to take in the real flavor of this charming and romantic city. Directly in front of you is the **Market Place**, where you may select fresh seafood to take home. The boats bobbing around the dock to your left will surely tempt you to take to the water. Here, too, you have plenty of options.

 Let's start with the nearest ones. **Chesapeake Marine Tours and Charters**, at Slip 20, City Dock, telephone (410) 268-7600, operates a variety of cruises between Memorial Day and Labor Day. You may choose a 90-minute cruise aboard the *Providence,* which tours around the Severn River, taking in the Annapolis Harbor and the U.S. Naval Academy. This is offered with or without lunch or, alternatively, during the "happy hour," with a complimentary glass of champagne. Two similar 40-minute cruises on either the *Harbor Queen* or the *Miss Anne* take you around the residential area of old Annapolis and the headwaters of Spa Creek. Maybe you feel like splashing around on your own? If so, any of these vessels may be chartered for a very private cruise at prices starting from $150 an hour. The same company offers another novel way of getting around − the **Jiffy Water Taxi**. This operates continuously on specified routes, or to alternate locations upon request. Telephone (410) 263-0033 to arrange this wonderfully romantic way of getting to a restaurant, or perhaps back to your hotel. The environmentally aware will delight in the 45-minute **On The Bay Ecotour**, which sets sail from the City Dock at 10:30 a.m. on Saturdays and Sundays. This trip takes you along the Severn River to explore the marsh life, and to observe the osprey nests at close quarters. These birds are so romantic − did you know there are more breeding pairs of osprey in the Chesapeake Bay than anywhere else in the world? Did you also know that the Chesapeake Bay is the largest estuary in North America, and that it supports over 2,700 different animal species? Learn these and many more bay-related facts on this special tour, which runs regularly from Memorial Day through Labor Day and may also be chartered by private parties during the off-season. For more information, call (410) 263-6041.

If you are seeking some real adventure, you may want to take your own boat trip or try a bit of fishing. Across the river in Eastport – reached either by a short walk or by water taxi – is your entrée to both. If you want to play captain for a day, **Annapolis Sportfishing Center**, located at 222 Severn Avenue, (410) 263-0990, offers a full range of brand new vessels, ranging from 14-foot motor boats to 23-foot catamarans. Of course, you will need a certain amount of safety awareness but, even if you are a novice, the center will treat you to "basic training" and get you out on the water in no time. Rates range from $139 for a half-day to $329 for a full day. You may prefer a romantic two-hour evening cruise for $89-$149, depending upon the size of the vessel. Fishing enthusiasts have choices as well. Charter a boat out into the bay or even try salt water fly fishing, a relatively new concept. For either, the rate is $250 for a half-day (about five hours), or $350 for a full eight-hour day. The season for both boat rentals and fishing runs between May 1 and mid-November. Call and ask to speak with Pete Miller; he will be happy to assist you.

If you are in the market for something different, you may customize your own cruise on a 45-foot Hunter Legend yacht by contacting **SunNSail Charters** at (410) 280-2761. Although they offer both full and half-day trips, it is the Sundown Sail that will appeal most to romantics. For $200, you will be treated to a cruise of twoanda half to three hours, setting your own course. Not only that, they will cook whatever you desire, or provide their own gourmet cuisine, served to you on board. (Liquor laws dictate they provide only mixers, so bring your bottle.) On your return to the dock, chilled champagne awaits you. This is very much an up-market experience, so give them as much advance notice as possible. Then go to 904 Primrose Road, Number 103, and prepare to be pampered. On this trip you are in charge, not just along for the ride.

Annapolis' many tourist attractions, as well as the proximity of both the state assembly and the U.S. Naval Academy, have given rise to a wide range of hotels, inns, and bed and breakfasts. Many of these are of an exceptionally high standard.

If you fancy something small, old, and very comfortable, you will love the **One-Four-Four Bed & Breakfast**. This lovely Georgian residence at 144 Prince George Street, telephone (410) 268-8053, dates from the last half of the 18th century and boasts interesting historic connections. It was owned by Dr. James Murray, a Revolutionary War patriot who is believed to have treated Thomas Jefferson in his practice here. Located in the heart of the historic district, it is just a stone's throw from the U.S. Naval Academy and City Dock. The interior is elegant but comfortable and offers you a choice of three rooms. The smallest room, renting for $90 a night, has a private bathroom but only a shower in which to bathe. The mid-sized room has a private jacuzzi and steam room, while the largest room, which occupies the entire third floor, features a queen four-poster bed, sofa, love seat, and wet bar. They both have a fireplace, and each rents for $120 a night. A full "English" breakfast is served as late as 11 a.m. – allowing you time for a comfy sleep-in! To top it all off, there is a roof garden with spectacular views of the city.

A little way across town – in a different kind of neighborhood with a different kind of atmosphere – is a gracious home from the Civil War era that has been lovingly restored. Located at 74 Charles Street, it now houses the **Charles Inn Bed & Breakfast,** (410) 268-1451. Here things are a bit less formal. All four bedrooms sport feather beds with fluffy down comforters, as well as private baths (two of which feature a private jacuzzi). It is authentically furnished throughout with delightful antiques. Included in the tariff is a full breakfast with service enhanced by fine china and crystal. Off-street parking is available, and if you don't fancy the short walk to and from town, just call the water taxi. This establishment's warm and comfortable ambience reflects the personality of its owners, John and Paula Hartman. The rates aren't bad either – between $69 and $159 per night.

If you have your heart set on a room overlooking the water there is only one choice. That is the modern **Annapolis Marriott Waterfront Hotel** at 80 Compromise Street, telephone (410) 268-7555 or (800) 336-0072. The hotel's fifth floor has panoramic windows overlooking the water. Here you may take your pick of a suite or two rooms that, besides offering the standard amenities, feature private jacuzzis. Depending on the season, the rooms rent from between $175 to $240, with the suite between $245 and $395. If you prefer to "dine in," this establishment offers Pusser's Landing, a colorful and unusually decorated combination of restaurant, bar and store. Valet parking is available.

The largest and most luxurious hotel in Annapolis – with 217 newly remodeled and beautifully appointed rooms – is also the only one that merits the AAA Four Diamond rating. This is the **Loews Annapolis Hotel**, which features large, comfortable rooms with every possible amenity – including a fully-stocked mini bar. There are king and queen-bedded suites, as well as a Presidential Suite. The price range is $135-$200 a night. You may enjoy relaxing in the spacious central atrium, or in the Weather Rail Lounge and Seafood Bar. The Loews offers another surprise, something not generally found in larger hotels: an excellent award-winning restaurant called **The Corinthian.** Many years of traveling experience have taught me that hotel restaurants seldom offer the best fare. The Corinthian is very much an exception to this rule. The food is well-prepared and attractively presented, while the service is superb, the wine list thorough, and the atmosphere delightful. All told, a pleasurable dining experience – but don't forget to make a reservation. The hotel also offers a small on-site fitness facility, concierge service, and valet parking. You'll find the Loews a few hundred yards past Church Circle and the Visitors Bureau, at 126 West Street, telephone (410) 263-7777. It is a short distance away from the historic area and City Dock, but don't let that put you off. The complimentary in-town shuttle service will take you anywhere, and bring you back whenever you wish.

If you're looking for something historic, you will want to consider the **Historic Inns of Annapolis,** an organization with a novel concept. Their offices are located at 16 Church Street, telephone (410) 263-2641 or (800) 847-8882, but they own not just one but four historic buildings which have been renovated to house top-class hotels. To their credit, these still retain their own unique character.

The most unusual of these is the wedge-shaped **Maryland Inn**, located on Church Circle. This inn dates from 1776 and was advertised in a 1782 issue of the *Maryland Gazette* as a "house of entertainment." From the outside, it oozes character; the inside is even better. Each of the 44 rooms and suites – most of which have queen-sized beds – has been carefully restored and beautifully furnished. No two look anything alike, and they come in different shapes and sizes. You may have a quiet drink here in the Drummer's Lot Pub, relax while listening to live jazz in the 1784 King of France Tavern, and enjoy traditional meals (including the area's famous cream of crab soup) in the Four-Star **Treaty of Paris** restaurant.

Around the corner – and around State Circle – are the other three hotels. These are as different from each other as they are from the Maryland Inn. The oldest of these, the c. 1727 **Governor Calvert House**, is actually comprised of two restored Colonial and Victorian residences into which 55 charming rooms have been incorporated. There are only 29 rooms in the **Robert Johnson House**, which is actually a clever integration of three individual houses built around 1765. The **State House Inn** is the youngest, dating from 1820. Its nine suites outfitted with jacuzzis will appeal to the young at heart.

The rooms at these hotels range from $125 to $185, with the suites upwards from $295. An excellent value is the **Nifty Weekend Vacation** package, which includes lodging on Friday and Saturday night, chilled champagne upon arrival, a candlelight dinner for two on Friday night in the Treaty of Paris restaurant, same-evening admission to the King of France Tavern, a Continental breakfast on Saturday, and Sunday brunch – all for $360, including tips and gratuities.

It would be inappropriate to discuss accommodation in Annapolis without offering some options with a nautical flavor. To start with, how about a real lighthouse? About six miles out of town – and none too easy to find – is the **Chesapeake Bay Lighthouse Bed & Breakfast**, at 1423 Sharps Point Road, (410) 757-0248. It is a full-scale replica of a typical lighthouse, such as the one still active at Thomas Point. It is also a U.S. Coast Guard-sanctioned private aid to navigation. The light here, which is in full view of the south anchorage point for the port of Baltimore, has been flashing nightly for two years. Due to zoning regulations, only three of the rooms may be rented. Each offers luxurious accommodation, with a full-sized private bathroom, queen-sized bed, and a spectacular water view. A Continental breakfast is included in the rates, which vary from $85 to $105, depending on the quality of the view. There are three acres of shoreline to explore, giving guests ample opportunity to study a variety of wildlife up close. If you need more exercise, climb to the upper lightroom/lookout deck and enjoy the panoramic view which encompasses the Bay Bridge, the Thomas Point Lighthouse, and the entrance to Annapolis Harbor. Here are the directions: Take Route 50/301 east to Exit 28. Travel south along Old Mill Bottom Road to the end and make a left onto St. Margaret's Road. Follow that with a quick right onto Pleasants Plans Road, and then another right onto Cherry Road. Turn right again onto Sharps Point Road. After going around a sharp righthand bend, turn into the second driveway on the left. It sounds more complicated than it actually is, and you'll find that it is worth the extra effort.

Instead of sleeping next to the water, have you ever considered sleeping on it? You can do it, even without being on a cruise. **Harborview Boat & Breakfast**, a division of Paradise Bay Yacht Charter, Inc., offers a very limited number of yachts for this purpose. They range in size from 34 feet to 127 feet, with air conditioning, heat, refrigerator, and stereo equipment; overnight rental rates range from $125-$400 per couple, per night. You'll find them docked at the prestigious Annapolis Landing Marina, number 980 Awald Drive. Two options can make this an absolutely unforgettable experience. The first of these is on-yacht catering (with 72 hours' notice) for hors d'oeuvres, lunch or dinner. The menus are imaginative, wide-ranging, and can include alcohol. Secondly, for $200 extra, you may arrange for a captain to take your boat out on a three-hour cruise. Just imagine, three hours on the bay at sunset, after which you dock for an on-board dinner under the stars. If you want to say an extra-special "I love you," have the folks at Harborview arrange to have a dozen roses waiting in your cabin, or, if you like, a single rose on the pillow. Then let the sound of the water lapping against the hull gently lull you to sleep. Remember, though, supply is limited and demand is high; so book early at (410) 268-9330. (In addition, be sure to ask for detailed directions.)

Annapolis is a sophisticated and cosmopolitan town. As is usual in such circumstances, there are a great many restaurants catering to almost any taste.

At the bottom of Main Street — number 100, to be exact — you will find the family-owned and operated **Buddy's Crabs and Ribs**, (410) 626-1100. You won't find pretentiousness here — just a large buffet-style restaurant with a happy, bubbling atmosphere. There is great foodand plenty of it, especially seafood; also all kinds of all-you-can-eat deals at very reasonable prices, and 22 large windows affording a picturesque view of the City Dock.

At the other end of Main Street, up the hill and on the far side of Church Circle, is a restaurant of a decidedly more formal style. William Reynolds purchased the land and built the tavern in 1747. Here he rented rooms, served meals, and conducted his millinery business. The **Reynolds Tavern** subsequently underwent numerous changes in ownership and was used for a variety of purposes until the mid-1980s, when the building was painstakingly renovated to its original 18th-century condition and reopened as an old-time tavern. Located at 7 Church Circle, telephone (410) 626-0380, it offers traditionally elegant dining rooms, beautifully landscaped gardens for fine or casual dining, highly acclaimed creative cuisine, and a fine wine list. For those just wanting to sample the atmosphere, the Franklin Street Pub offers a public hour with complimentary hors d'oeuvres. A combination that shouldn't be missed, even if you are merely sightseeing!

If you still have the time or energy for entertainment, an equally eclectic selection awaits you. Annapolis boasts a number of resident theater groups, as well as an opera company, a ballet company, and a symphony orchestra. Then, of course, there are the sporting activities of the midshipmen. The atmosphere at the fall football games is not quickly forgotten. The choice is yours, and the visitors' bureau can provide you with up-to-date details on schedules.

Throughout the year, many interesting events are scheduled in Annapolis. The **Annapolis Spring Boat Show** and **Annapolis Waterfront Festival** are held at the end of April. In May, you may participate in the **Mid-Atlantic Wine Festival**, the **Annapolis Rotary Crab Feast** (the world's largest) and, of course, the city's own **Fourth of July** celebration. August's offerings are especially interesting. At nearby Crownsville, the **Maryland Renaissance Festival** attracts over 200,000 people and has a 5,000-seat jousting arena. The weekend after Labor Day kicks off the **Maryland Seafood Festival,** and in late September there is the Afro-American ethnic **Kunta Kinte Heritage Festival**, as well as the **United States Sailboat** and **Powerboat Show**s. October is time for the **Anne Arundel Scottish Highland Games**. In late November and all of December, there are the **Christmas in Annapolis Celebrations**.

Maryland's Eastern Shore

St. Michaels
The Town that Fooled the British

Numerous charming, historic small towns dot the coastline of the Chesapeake Bay, but you will be hard-pressed to find one more pleasing than St. Michaels. The initial land grants for this area were given in the middle of the 17th century, but the town derived its name a couple of decades later from the Episcopal Parish of St. Michael the Archangel, established here in 1677. Shipbuilding and tobacco were the earliest major industries, but active growth did not start until the Revolutionary War. Then, and during the War of 1812, St. Michaels was an important center for the building of privateers, blockade runners and naval barges. Inevitably, this brought unwelcome attention from the British naval forces. It was during an attack that St. Michaels earned its nickname, "The Town That Fooled The British." On August 10, 1813, a number of British barges shelled the town, but the residents had been forewarned. They cleverly raised and secured lanterns to the masts of ships and the tops of trees. As a result, the incoming cannon balls overshot the buildings. So effective was this ploy that only a single house was struck; to this day, it is known as the "Cannonball House."

When St. Michaels was incorporated in 1804, it was re-surveyed and laid out in three square areas grouped around the harbor. This served the town well, since St. Michaels' most successful commercial endeavors were the boat-building industry and the harvesting and processing of crabs and shellfish. The advent of the railroad in 1890 opened the town to visitors; seafood and local produce were then carried by steamship and sold in the busy markets of Annapolis and Baltimore.

Today, tourism prevails as the town's most lucrative industry; and it easy to see why. Few places offer such easygoing charm. A visit to St. Michaels is a welcome respite from the pressures of modern life, and the goal of your stay need be nothing more than relaxation. Stroll around town, enjoying the curious mix of architectural styles—Georgian, Federal, "Tidewater telescope" Colonial, Queen Anne, Edwardian and Victorian. Stop to watch as the boats sail in and out of the harbor. Shop at a delightful array of specialty shops and boutiques that would not be out of place in far larger towns. Dine at your choice of any number of fine restaurants and take to the bay on one or more cruises. You won't be disappointed.

There is no shortage of choice when it comes to accommodation, either. A number of inns and bed and breakfasts have been established in response to the growing tourist trade. Some of them will truly surprise you, in terms of both style and price. Just beyond the town limits – at 308 Watkins Lane in the direction of Tilghman Island – sits a beautiful Colonial mansion set in an enviable location and surrounded by well-groomed lawns that run right along the bay. Built in 1812, this now houses **The Inn at Perry Cabin**, telephone (410) 745-2200 or (800) 722-2949 and fax (410) 745-3348. The Laura Ashley name is known worldwide, but not generally for its hotels. Sir Bernard Ashley, co-founder of the Laura Ashley Company, sought to change this when he took over The Inn at Perry Cabin. His concept was to combine the luxury and atmosphere of an English manor house with the warm informality of a hospitable American inn. He has certainly succeeded in this, the first Ashley Inn in America. Everywhere you wander – in any of the 41 private bedrooms or in the numerous public rooms – you will find a stylish mix of English and American antiques complemented, of course, by the elegantly understated fabrics of Laura Ashley. The total effect is one of luxury, with comfort built in – not an ostentatious place, but rather one that encourages you to

relax as if you were in your own sitting room. Each bedroom features a private bathroom, remote-controlled color
cable television, direct-dial telephone, and individual heating and air-conditioning controls. Mineral water and fresh
fruit are complimentary. There are four different styles of
room from which to select. House rooms rent for $175-$275;
state rooms, for $295-$345; studio rooms, for $395-$475;
and master suites, which run $525. These tariffs are per
room, per night, exclusive of 8% taxes; they include a daily
newspaper, full English breakfast and afternoon tea.
There are also a top flight restaurant; an indoor pool; and
a health facility with exercise room, sauna and steam
room. Outdoor sporting enthusiasts will enjoy golf, tennis,
sailing, fishing and hunting. In addition, there are 25 acres
of grounds to explore – perfect for those leisurely walks. In
its seventh annual readers' survey, *Condé Naste Traveler,*
one of the world's most respected travel magazines, rated
the Inn at Perry Cabin the fifth-best resort in the mainland
United States (and the 26th best overall travel experience
in the world). The inn has also played host to ABC's *Good
Morning America,* as well as luminaries like former British
prime minister Margaret Thatcher. The rates here are
considerably higher than many other options in the area,
and some of these rooms fall short of spacious. Nevertheless, the ambience and amenities combine to make this a
marvelous place to spend a really romantic weekend.

Those who prefer a more modern style and a harbor view
will gravitate towards the **St. Michaels Harbor Inn &
Marina,** 101 North Harbor Road, telephone (410) 745-
9001 or (800) 955-9001 and fax (410) 745-9150. Innovatively designed to hug the harbor front, this inn features
two wings built at right angles to each other, with boat
moorings running the length of the shore-front sides. An
open-air, harbor-side pool and bar are set in a large wooden
deck at the junction of the wings. Romantically minded
couples will find two of the four categories of rooms particularly appealing. The large one-room Captain Suites offer a
king-sized bed, wet bar, refrigerator and one of three options: a private balcony, a patio, or a large Palladian window for those spectacular harbor views. If you need more
space, choose one of the two Admiral Suites; these feature
a king-sized bed, a commodious living room, a wet bar, a
refrigerator and a private balcony overlooking the harbor.

Though the seasonal tariff here is complicated, weekend rates vary between $109-$379 a night, with a two-night minimum stay on weekends from May through the middle of October. The rates include complimentary newspapers and magazines, as well as bicycle rentals. There is also an impressive array of weekend packages. From February through April, a Romantic Getaway Package is offered. This includes two nights' accommodation, with a champagne welcome and special gift; a gourmet dinner for two in the inn's magnificent waterfront Lighthouse Restaurant (known for its extensive wine list); breakfast for two; and admission to the Chesapeake Bay Maritime Museum – all for $319 per couple. Other possibilities include the inn's Winter Wine Weekends, its Winter Waterfowling Weekend and the intriguing Just For The Fun Of It Weekend.

A few blocks away at 204 North Talbot Street sits a late 1860s colonial house that has been transformed into one of the most romantic bed and breakfasts I have ever seen. Innkeepers Jim and Lin Barrett understand the allure of romance, and everything they do is geared towards creating and maintaining that magic mood. Even in much larger places it is not all that common to find rooms with both a jacuzzi tub and fireplace; moderately-sized **Barrett's Bed & Breakfast Inn** has five "romantic rooms" that fall into this category. Each features a queen-sized bed adorned with a handmade quilt and feather comforter; a private bath with double jacuzzi tub; a fireplace; and Oriental rugs. A small bottle of champagne welcomes you upon arrival. The rate for these rooms is $190 a night. Three "cozy rooms" are also available. These offer similar amenities – excluding the jacuzzi – and the tariff is only $130. When you venture out of your room, you may enjoy chatting with the other guests in the common room. This last is invitingly decorated with Oriental rugs and antique furniture; it also has a fireplace, a library and a dining area, and is perpetually embellished with fresh flowers. Breakfast includes a hot entrée, home-baked bread served with jams and jellies, fresh fruit and cheese, as well as coffee and a specially blended tea. If you wish, it may be served in your bedroom between 8:30 a.m. and 10 a.m. There is a two-night minimum stay on weekends.

During some holidays, a three-night minimum stay is required. Telephone (410) 745-3322 for reservations.

Your best option for dinner is conveniently located within walking distance – in fact, almost next door. **208 TALBOT**, (410) 745-3838, is considered one of the finest restaurants in town. The atmosphere here is casually elegant. The frequently changing menu, though relatively small, offers innovative cuisine finely balanced between seafood and traditional American dishes. Not only has this restaurant been featured in numerous magazines, chef and co-owner Paul Milne has appeared on the Discovery Channel's *Great Chefs Of The East.* To avoid disappointment, always make a reservation. Dining here is not inexpensive; the fixed price meal on Saturday evenings is $43 per person, exclusive of alcoholic beverages, while an à la carte meal for two – with wine – is in the region of $120. Nevertheless, this is an occasion when spending dollars makes sense.

Having checked in to your choice of hotel, what do you do next? Given St. Michaels' location, most activities are oriented around the water and many are seasonal, as well. One place that is open year-round is the **Chesapeake Bay Maritime Museum**. Located on Mill Street at Navy Point, it is immediately recognizable by its lighthouse. This last was constructed in 1879 in the "screwpile" design; its place of origin was down the bay at Hooper Strait. In the mid-1960s, it was scheduled for demolition, modern technology having rendered it obsolete. Thankfully, The Maritime Museum – established in 1965 and still in its fledgling stages – had other ideas. Considering this ideal for incorporation into their facility, they arranged for the octagonal structure to be dismantled and shipped to St. Michaels in two main sections. With the main body on one barge and the roof on another, the journey must have been a strange sight indeed. From these small beginnings, the museum has grown into an 18-acre complex. It is now considered one of the finest of its kind on the East Coast. Apart from preserving the cultural heritage of the Chesapeake Bay, exhibits such as decoy and firearm displays, model ships, and a reproduction of 18th-century docks trace the history and traditions of the area. The *Rosie Parks* is a Chesapeake Bay skipjack; the *Edna Lockwood,* a century-old two-masted bugeye that still races; and there are many more examples of every imaginable type. As an added bonus, the museum hosts numerous special events throughout the year. To find out what's going on during your stay, phone ahead at (410) 745-2916 .

Seeing all these seafaring vessels may whet your appetite for the water. The 65-foot steel *Patriot* is appropriately painted red, white and blue. It sails four times a day between the months of April and October from its dock next to the Maritime Museum. This narrated one-hour cruise along the Miles River includes many stories about the history of Talbot County; it will also give you a glimpse of both the wildlife and the watermen who call these waters home. The lower deck is climate-controlled with large panoramic windows; for those preferring to feel the breeze, there is a canopied open-air upper deck. You may slake your thirst at the bar, which serves both alcoholic and non-alcoholic beverages. This ship is handicapped-accessible and the fare is $8 per person. Call (410) 745-3100 or fax (410) 745-3100.

Approximately 11 miles from St. Michaels, along Route 33, you will come across unspoiled little **Tilghman Island**. First charted by John Smith as early as 1608, it wasn't until 1775 that it was named in honor of its then-owner, Matthew Tilghman. It sits at the northern entrance to the Chesapeake Bay's largest river, the Choptank, and just off the southern end of the Bay Hundred Peninsula. The name "Bay Hundred" originates from the early division of Maryland into "hundreds," a practice dating to Anglo-Saxon times. The island is today, as it was then, inhabited by fewer than 700 people. Many of these make the Chesapeake Bay seafood business their livelihood. Tilghman's future seemed uncertain after it suffered costly losses of resources and property at the hands of the British in the War of 1812. In 1890, however, a steamboat service was established here; it lasted well into this century. This leisurely and efficient means of access opened the island to vacationers, who were lured by its superb fishing and genteel accommodations. In those days, travelers were escorted to and from their destination by horse- or ox-drawn vehicles. Today, Tilghman is reached via a drawbridge. But once over it, little else has changed. You'll be greeted with a quiet, warm hospitality that has become the island's trademark. One main road runs from north to south over the three-mile length of the island; other roads feed off of it, taking you to the waterside or other points of interest. Accommodations are available, the details of which follow; but even if you decide not to stay on the island, it is a place that deserves a visit.

Of the few inns and B&Bs here, only two are of the same style and standard as those found in St. Michaels. Situated on Dogwood Harbor, home of the last working skipjack fleet, both establishments are exemplary and deserving of your consideration.

The Lazyjack Inn, located on the edge of Dogwood Harbor at 5907 Tilghman Island Road, (410) 886-2215 or (800) 690-5080, is a delightful 160-year-old house owned and personally operated by innkeepers Mike and Carol Richards. The setting is idyllic for a bed and breakfast, and also affords "Captain Mike" proximity to his other business venture, the *Lady Patty* (more later). Of the four available rooms, the Nellie Byrd Suite is perhaps the most romantic. It enjoys unsurpassed views over the harbor and Choptank River, features a king-sized brass bed stacked with cozy heirloom quilts, as well as cushiony Oriental carpets. The Victorian sitting area is a perfect spot in which to settle down and reflect on the day's events. Before retiring, relax in the two-person whirlpool tub or, if you prefer, steam up the bathroom's three-sided glass shower. The rate for this room is $175 a night. In the oldest part of the house is the East Room, which features a double bed and a private bath. Look, too, for pine floors and exposed beams, furniture from the 1930s, and two overstuffed chairs. The large West Room has yellow pine floors, a king-sized bed covered with a patchwork quilt, a sitting area, private bath, and lovely garden views. The tariff for each of these is $120 a night. The fourth choice, the Crews' Quarters, is a little more innovative. But since the only sleeping arrangement is a double-bed sleep sofa, it may not prove so desirable. Each morning a full breakfast is served in the Harbor Room, so named because of its delightful view overlooking the harbor. If you have special dietary needs, now's the time to mention them. These are addressed as an added service, if advance notice is given. After your meal, no need to rush away. Rather, sit and savor the atmosphere in a rocker on the old-fashioned porch. Later you might want to set sail on the Chesapeake Bay and the Choptank River in the aforementioned *Lady Patty,* a 54-foot bronze and teak bay ketch that was built in 1935. If you are in the mood for company, join a two-hour group cruise that accommodates up to 16 people at $30 per person. For a really romantic treat, spend $100 on a private sunset cruise for two. Flutes are provided, so don't forget your champagne. Once out of the harbor, the engine is turned off and gentle classical music mixes with the sound of the wind as it whistles through 900 feet of working sails. All in all, an enchanting and unforgettable experience. You may opt to make this your outing for the evening, even if you are lodging back in St. Michaels. For reservations, call Mike at the number for The Lazyjack Inn.

Built in 1890, the **Chesapeake Wood Duck Inn**, (410) 886-2070, (800) 956-2070 or fax (410) 886-2263, has had an interesting and varied past. It was originally designed as a boarding house but was transformed into a bordello during the heyday of the steamboats on the bay. It was subsequently redeemed by a waterman for use as his family residence. Having left their hectic positions in Atlanta, Dave and Stephanie Feith were searching for a place to open their "dream inn" when they came upon this home. Recognizing its potential, they carefully restored and lovingly decorated it – with their own personal collection of antiques, Oriental rugs, fine art, and classic treasures. The resulting atmosphere reflected the island's warmth and charm; it opened, appropriately enough, on Valentine's Day, 1992.

There are now six beautiful bedrooms, each a testament to Stephanie's flair for interior design and her dedication to southern hospitality. With private baths, sitting areas and water views, these offer intimate and gracious accommodation for as little as $115 per night. The public rooms are memorable, too; relax in the parlor by the fireplace while listening to the Victrola, or stretch out in either the bright sunroom or screened porch. Breakfast is always a wonderful experience at the Wood Duck, whether served in the formal dining room or on the wicker-filled screened porch. Dave is a gourmet cook, and not only is the food exquisite, it is a definite departure from the usual bed and breakfast fare. The menu – which changes often – includes such delicacies as sherried crab quiche, or a puff pastry filled with a ham-wrapped omelet topped with key lime mustard sauce and garnished with edible flowers. Whatever the main course, it is usually accompanied by some variety of seasonal fruit and freshly baked sweetbreads. The presentation is just as important to Dave and Stephanie as the food. Just to insure you'll feel properly pampered, they will serve you at a table adorned with fine china, crisp linens, fresh flowers and Stephanie's grandmother's Depression glass. Bicycles and fishing gear are available, as is access to the nearby Harbortowne Country Club, which offers swimming, tennis, a fitness center and golf. In the summer of 1995, the AAA elevated the Chesapeake Wood Duck Inn to Three-Diamond status, a rare honor for a bed and breakfast. Don't hesitate to call (410) 886-2070 or (800) 956-2070 and fax (410) 886-2263 for your reservation.

Your curiosity will no doubt be aroused by the strange old wooden sailing vessels moored in the harbor. Called skipjacks, their survival is due to a hundred-year-old Maryland law that permits dredging for oysters only under sail with a sailboat that displaces fewer than 10 tons of water. About 20 skipjacks remain, and their average age is 80 years. One of these continues to dredge for oysters each winter, moonlighting part-time as a cruise vessel. The *H.M. Krentz* was built in 1955 by master shipwright Herman Maston Krentz, of Harry Hogan, Virginia. It is operated today by Captain Ed Farley, who has been sailing skipjacks for the past 21 years. It sails daily from midday to sunset, accommodating either individuals or groups. Half-day, full-day, or overnight cruises are also available on request. For further details, give Captain Ed a call at (410) 745-6080.

Harrison's Chesapeake House, (410) 886-2121, has been an institution on Tilghman Island for more than 110 years. They are old-fashioned to a fault, and proud of it. In fact, they don't want to be anything else, which is part of the attraction. No chrome and glass here, just old-style decor and a great atmosphere. The restaurant is as full of character as the island it inhabits. Massive in size, it's comprised of several rooms lined with photographs of the many famous personalities who have enjoyed – and often return to enjoy – this inviting family atmosphere. The fare is mostly seafood, and highly rated. The house specialty, fried chicken and crab cakes, is particularly delicious. In the summer months, you may eat outside on the deck overlooking the water, where the aroma of pit beef and pork roasting on the grill mingles with bay-scented breezes. With all this sensory input, you may be tempted to order two entrées. Dining isn't all this establishment offers. Over the decades, the Harrison family has built up the largest privately-owned sport fishing fleet on the bay. That means 15 boats, each of which can accommodate up to six fishermen. They set sail at 7 a.m. and return between 3 p.m. and 4 p.m. during the many different fishing seasons between the end of April and the middle of November. All bait and tackle are provided, along with a healthy box lunch and beverages, for $60 per person ($70 during the rockfish season). Naturally, they reserve the right to fill the boat. For a few extra dollars, your catch will even be cleaned and packed! Perhaps you fancy hunting instead? If so, no need to go elsewhere. Harrison's also offers seasonal **Goose Hunting** at $300 and **Sea Ducking** at $200, with prices based on a party of one or two people. Whatever the reason you came to Harrison's, you will leave with its image imprinted indelibly in your mind.

There is no visitors' center or tourist information office in St. Michaels. The nearest one is run by the Talbot County Chamber of Commerce in Easton, and is only open during business hours, Monday through Friday – not very convenient for weekend travelers. However, they will be more than happy to answer any queries if you phone them at (410) 822-4606 or fax them at (410) 822-7922. Information is available until 9 p.m. on Fridays (and between 9 a.m. and 5 p.m. on Saturdays and Sundays) at the Talbot County Community Center, 10028 Ocean Gateway, Easton, MD 21601.

 The island hosts three celebrations annually. The **Tilghman Island Seafood Festival** in June features live music, arts and crafts, a fireman's parade, a crab race, and even a crab-picking contest. The island's newest event, a **Jazz Festival**, is held in September. On **Tilghman Island Day** in October, you'll enjoy waterman exhibits, skipjack races, music, boat docking contests, and plenty of Chesapeake Bay seafood.

Ocean City
Good Food, Good Fun & a Beach Blanket for Two

*N*o romantic weekend guide would be complete without a chapter extolling the virtues of the sea. Ocean City, Maryland offers much in the way of seaside entertainment – during any season. In fact, its growing popularity draws such large crowds during the summer, and on holiday weekends, that visiting out-of-season may be preferable. It's true that sunbathing would not be an option and many of the more traditional activities are seasonal, but these are easily traded for the charm of walking across an empty beach with the waves thundering around you.

When visiting Ocean City, you will be faced with an unexpected problem: finding interesting and unique places to stay. Not that Ocean City lacks hotels. Mile after mile of all varieties span the coastline. Most of them, though, lack those romantic little touches that transform the ordinary into the extraordinary.

If there's one exception to that rule, it's a complex with two hotels and a restaurant so special it could hold its own anywhere in the world. In fact, it is one of those rare hotels that is worth visiting simply for its own merits, regardless of location or nearby attractions. The **Fager's Island Hotels** are at 201 60th Street, telephone (410) 723-6100 or (800) 767-6060, fax (410) 524-9327. Surprisingly, it isn't along the ocean. It features a more tranquil venue across the Coastal Highway on the Isle of Wight Bay. The larger of the two hotels is the British Colonial-style **Coconut**

Malorie. From the moment you enter the lobby, you will be impressed. Spacious and elegant, it features clusters of tables and chairs where couples may sit and enjoy the gentle splashing of the indoor waterfall in concert with tunes from the grand piano. Bright and colorful paintings contribute to the hotel's Caribbean theme. These original paintings from Haiti adorn not just the public areas, but the rooms as well. The tower, with its spectacular views over the bay, houses a Haitian art gallery and library perfect for browsing through on a lazy morning.

It's fair to say that each of the Coconut Malorie's 85 suites – four of which have handicapped facilities – can be recommended. Though varying in size and facilities, they are all light and modern with custom-designed furniture. The rates for these range from $69 to $219 per night, depending on the day and season. However, if you really want to pamper yourselves, you will reserve one of the two corner "concierge" suites. Of the many rooms we have researched for this guide, these are among our favorites. They are large, with living/dining room, bedroom, kitchen, all-marble bathroom with a romantic double shower and jacuzzi, plus a balcony. To make dinner even more romantic, you may have your meal brought directly from the restaurant and served in your private dining room. The rates for this luxury start at $89 to $249 a night.

Connected to the Coconut Malorie by arched footbridges and sitting literally in the bay is her totally different sister hotel. It is obvious why this two-level, innovatively designed building—encircled by balconies and topped by a cupola – is named the **Lighthouse Club Hotel.** This unique structure houses 23 pie-shaped suites which are entered from a multi-story atrium-styled "lobby" with an unusual staircase and huge suspended fish "swimming" through the air. Each suite is luxuriously furnished with custom furniture and intimately secluded, with a private deck affording unparalleled views of the bay, the wetlands and Ocean City's glorious sunsets. Depending on your choice of room, you may end the evening – or begin it – with a soak in the double jacuzzi. In the winter, get toasty and warm while cuddling in front of your private fireplace.

Not to be missed is **The Fager's Island Restaurant & Bar**, renowned throughout the area for its award-winning wine cellar. Featured are imported private label wines from Burgundy, Bordeaux and Champagne, as well as Blue Dog Ale, which is brewed exclusively for the hotel.

After dinner, share a glass of wine and a quiet moment in the gazebo built out into the bay. In season, you may wish to take a dip in the open-air pool, with its unusual bar and exotic cocktails. This hotel also offers a turndown service with a difference. When you return to your room for the evening, the curtains are drawn, your room is bathed in gentle candlelight, and soft music accompanies the sound of the Isle of Wight Bay lapping outside your window.

All of this is available for $89-$249 a night. To further entice you, Fager's Island offers Murder Mystery, Valentine Island and Island Getaway packages for couples. It is no surprise that Fager's has been awarded Mobil Four-Star and AAA Four Diamond ratings.

Thirty blocks further north, at 91st Street on the ocean front, is **The Princess Royale Oceanfront Hotel and Conference Center**, telephone (410) 524-7777 or (800) 4ROYALE, and fax (410) 524-7787. This hotel is typical of such resort areas, but offers more varied, better quality and much newer facilities. A unique feature is the huge, four-story atrium with a large pool sauna; whirlpool baths, hot tubs and the Palm Court Atrium Café, where you may enjoy a sunrise breakfast or sit by the pool and sip a frozen cocktail. There are 340 well-appointed rooms overlooking the Atlantic Ocean. But it is the nine honeymoon suites – with their heart-shaped jacuzzis – that will interest most couples. These cost between $149 (weekdays) and $269 (weekends).

There are those who equate ruffles and lace with all that is romantic. For lovers of things Victorian, this area offers two enticing options.

At 28th Street and the ocean, just one block north of the boardwalk's end, is the **Dunes Manor Hotel**, telephone (410) 289-1100 and (800) 523-2888, or fax (410) 289-4905. The unusual, modern facade belies an interior that takes you straight back to the 19th century. Exemplifying this tradition is the complimentary afternoon tea, poured from a sterling silver tea pot into china cups. It's often served to you by the owner herself – 81-year-old Thelma Conner, honored as Maryland's Independent Hotelier of the Year in 1994. All rooms face the ocean, but we'd recommend one of the 10 king-bedded rooms with a private balcony and Victorian-style wrought iron furniture. These have a small fridge which you may stock with your favorite beverages, and a microwave for fixing late-night popcorn. The rates are between $59 and $190 a night, depending upon the season. There are 150 other rooms – eight of them equipped for handicapped guests – with rates between $44 and $185. The Victorian Room restaurant has an intimately warm decor, the Zippy Lewis Lounge has an ocean view and, during the season, kick off your shoes and enjoy the Barefoot Bar and Grill on the lower porch overlooking the beach.

Some people enjoy the attractions of a resort, but prefer staying out of town. For these types there is the perfect place just seven miles away at Berlin. This town's main street was originally a path connecting local Indian tribes. Later, in colonial times, it became the main trade route between the shore and points north and west. During this period, it was renamed the Philadelphia Post Road. By the early 1900s, Berlin boasted more hotels than nearby Ocean City, but after World War II it suffered a period of decline. Today the town has made an effort to regenerate itself, wisely building on its past. As a result, a substantial area has been designated a national historic district. Berlin offers a perfect antidote to the hustle and bustle of the beach. Just strolling around brings back the tranquility of another age. For those interested in more area history, brochures and walking tour guides are available from the **Berlin Chamber of Commerce** by writing P. O. Box Berlin, MD 21811, or calling (410) 641-4775.

At 2 North Main Street you will find one of the town's most prominent buildings. Unusually shaped due to its corner position (and with a porch opening onto the sidewalk), it was built in 1895 and used as a hotel during the Victorian era. Today it has been lovingly restored to its former elegance and grandeur. Operating now under the name **The Atlantic Hotel Inn & Restaurant**, it has received the following accolades: a Mobil Three-Star rating, an AAA Three-Diamond rating, a Great Inns of America designation, the 1989 Maryland Historical Trust Preservation Project Award, and inclusion in the National Register of Historic Places in 1980.

Each of the 16 rooms is individually decorated with furniture, fabrics and colors of the Victorian era, but with the conveniences of modern bathrooms, air conditioning and direct-dial telephones. Rates include a country breakfast; depending on the day of the week, the season, and the room's location, they range $55-$135 per night.

Consistent with the ambience of the hotel (and equally special) is its restaurant. The intimate and formal dining room offers some of the finest international cuisine on the Eastern Shore. Fans of Spanish food will know that the Basque regions of both Spain and France are renowned for their cuisine, the influence of which can be seen on this restaurant's menu. This restaurant's wine cellar has also won the Wine Spectator Award of Excellence. For reservations at The Atlantic Hotel, call (410) 641-3589 or (800) 814-7672, or fax (410) 641-4928 for a reservation.

After settling into your room, it is time to start enjoying yourselves. When planning your stay, remember that many activities are seasonal, which generally means they're available only between May and September. Unless otherwise noted, this is true of the following.

Not surprisingly, many activities take place on the water – either the ocean, the bay, or a combination of the two. And there is something to suit most everyone's taste. For the ecologically minded, take an offshore nature cruise aboard the high-speed cruising yacht *O.C. Princess*. Leave shore at 4 p.m. Tuesday through Saturday, headed for the sparkling clear waters beyond the shores of Ocean City. Here, you will spend three hours being introduced to Atlantic bottlenose dolphins, sea turtles, pelicans, osprey, and other rare and endangered species – as well as migrating whales, if you're lucky. A side-trip takes you to Assateague Island in search of the wild ponies. This is a real value at just $18 per person. For a variation on the same theme, try a one-hour cruise through the restful inland waterways, harbors and bays in and around Ocean City, aboard the *Bay Queen*. This affords an unparalleled opportunity to see both the bird sanctuaries and wild ponies, as well as the fishing fleet unloading their bountiful catches of lobsters, fish, scallops and clams. All of these are destined for local restaurants. Who knows, maybe you're looking at your evening meal! If you feel adventurous, you might try your hand at catching your own supper. The *O. C. Princess,* which is powered by triple turbo diesel engines, leaves every morning at 7 a.m for deep-sea fishing. For $30 per person, plus $5 rod rental, you might return to the pier with sea bass, tautog, bluefish, sea trout or mackerel. Don't forget to rub each other down with sunscreen so you'll be getting a tan, not a burn. Tickets for any of the above may be purchased from the **Shantytown Lighthouse Pier**, located in the Shantytown Village & Marina at Route 50 and Shantytown Road. For reservations or information, call (410) 213-0926 or (800) 457-6650.

Those who thrive on speed can sit back and hold tight for a unique 50-minute ocean ride aboard the *Sea Rocket*. This 70-foot vessel, which sports jet-propelled, turbocharged General Motors V-12 engines, is certified for over 150 passengers. Its home dock is at the end of South Division Street. Rides are $8 per person and reservations may be made by calling (410) 289-5887. Wear casual clothes – or better still, a swimsuit.

Water sports enthusiasts who prefer to pilot their own craft will find Ocean City an absolute paradise. No company is better equipped to meet your needs than **Watersports Unlimited**, (410) 250-2777, located at the 142nd Street Marina next to Harpoon Hanna's. Try para-sailing at 400, 600 or 800 feet (the price ranges $40-$60, according to the height). There are also the Kawasaki jet skis at $45 per half-hour, or any type of pontoon, fishing, crabbing, power or ski boat. They're all here, at competitive prices, plus a deposit, of course. The really adventurous may choose the **Bay-Air Package.** This consists of one half-hour jet ski rental, followed by a 400-foot para-sail ride, at a much-reduced combination price of $60. For a more peaceful ride, sail off into the shallow, protected back bays in a catamaran or windsurfer. These are available (with lessons, if necessary) from **Sailing Etc.** at 54th Street and Coastal Highway, telephone (410) 723-1144.

You've seen things from sea level; now it's time to get a bird's-eye view. Take Route 50 to 611 and travel two miles south to Ocean City Airport, where **Sky Tours**, operated year-round by Greg von Rigler, allows you to "touch the clouds, skim the seas and set your imagination free" while gaining a fresh understanding of the fragility of the barrier island ecology and wildlife. You can choose a day, sunset or night flight. At Christmas time, and the fourth of July, the night sights are particularly special. Maybe you'd rather sieze the opportunity to become members of the "mile high club." Whatever your intentions, call Greg at (410) 289-TOUR to book your 15-minute ($19 per person) or 30-minute ($35 per person) flight.

The really brave among you might try returning to earth under your own power – by skydiving! Kevin Gibson runs the **Skydiving Center** at the Ocean City Airport. Dives may be made any time from 9 a.m. to sunset, seven days a week between mid-April and Halloween. Just pop by in athletic-type clothes (no boots) and after a half-hour training session with your instructor, you are ready for your tandem jump. The pilot will relax you with a scenic flight over Ocean City beach and the boardwalk in a specially-configured Cessna. You'll then ascend to 9,000 feet. When everything is ready, the door will be opened and you and your instructor will free-fall together for about half a minute. Spread below you will be the panoramic Atlantic Ocean with its islands, inlets and, of course, Ocean City. Your instructor will point out the sights. When he activates the parachutes, you'll experience a kind of peaceful serenity only skydivers enjoy. The cost for this enchanting and memorable experience is $195, including lessons, equipment, follow-up materials and even a certificate. Only a few restrictions apply. You must be at least 18 years of age, weigh less than 275 pounds, and have steady nerves! For an extra $22, you can soar even higher – to 12,000 feet – for an extra long free-fall. If space is available, a non-jumping partner may accompany you for $28 more. To capture the experience for perpetuity, you may arrange to have a mini-movie made of your jump. This will be professionally edited and enhanced by a musical soundtrack – provide your favorite compact disc, if you wish. You might consider having this done "on the sly" and surprising your partner with it at an upcoming special occasion. A clever and unusual gift for $60. Although reservations are helpful, they are not absolutely necessary. For more information, call (410) 213-1319.

Now turn your attentions to a different type of harness. **Delmarva Downs**, just minutes from Ocean City at the junction of Routes 50 and 589, is an exciting place to spend an evening trying your luck on 12 harness races. You can h ave a full-course dinner served at a private dining table overlooking the finish line. For information on racing dates and post times, call (410) 641-0600.

No trip to Ocean City would be complete without a visit to **Secrets**, located on the bay at 49th Street, telephone (410) 524-4900, and open year-round. This bar/restaurant has a very romantic Jamaican environment. In the warmer months it is especially fun to visit the indoor/outdoor bar. Rafts and inner tubes are anchored to its own private beach. Here, time appears to stand still as you and your special someone float dreamily around, sipping exotic cocktails. The restaurant is open between 11 a.m. and 2 a.m. for both lunch and dinner, seven days a week

Information about events and activities in Ocean City is available through the **Visitors' Center**, in the Convention Center, 4001 Coastal Highway. Hours are 8 a.m. to 5 p.m., Monday through Friday, and 9 a.m. to 5 p.m on Saturday and Sunday between October and April .Visit between 8 a.m. and 6:30 p.m. any day of the week during the summer. Alternatively, call (800) O-C-OCEAN.

Numerous local events take place throughout the year. Of particular interest are: **St. Patrick's Parade & Festival** in March; the **White Marlin Festival & Parade** in May; two July 4th celebrations (the **Jamboree in the Park/Fireworks,** located uptown at Northside Park and 125th Street, and the **Beach Concert/Fireworks,** by the boardwalk); the **White Marlin Open Tourney** in August; the famous **Sunfest** in September; and throughout December, the **Winterfest of Lights**.

Western Maryland

Cumberland
Romancing the Rails
& Closing the Gap

Squeezed between Pennsylvania and West Virginia, in a scenic valley adorned by numerous church steeples, is a town of much historical interest and considerable charm. This area, known as "The Gateway to the West," was first settled in 1709 by Thomas Cresap, an English immigrant who established a trading post in what is known today as Oldtown. In 1749, a stockade called Fort Mount was erected in a strategic valley a little further west, at the confluence of Wills Creek and the Potomac River. Six years later, British general Edward Braddock decided this was a perfect base from which to launch attacks against the French and Indian forces at Fort Duquesne (now Pittsburgh). Braddock enlarged the fort and renamed it Fort Cumberland to honor his friend, the Duke of Cumberland, who was commander-in-chief of the British Army and the son of George II. George Washington, a young colonist familiar with the American wilderness, was appointed as an aide to General Braddock. In fact, he began his military career here, in the same spot where he would end it many years later. It was while stationed here that Washington conceived the idea of a "national road" to lead from the nation's capital westward into the unexplored continent. After the Revolutionary War, his work assured that this became a reality. Construction also began on the C&O Canal. This would follow the Potomac from Washington to Cumberland, which had been incorporated as a town in 1787.

Though the advent of the railroad short-circuited the canal's completion, it brought its own brand of prosperity to Cumberland. The area became a center for trade, commerce and transportation that was second only to Baltimore in terms of growth and expansion during the 19th century. Allegany County's good fortune continued well into the 20th century but, like many other places, began to fade rapidly during the 50s, when de-industrialization began. The change from an industrial to a service-based economy has not been easy. Yet Cumberland has somehow managed to retain an atmosphere that is only a dim memory in most cities. Coming to this town is like stepping back into the 60s and 70s, which, though not always attractive, is certainly one of its main attractions. Much emphasis has been placed on the development of tourism. Indeed, there is much of interest here, even if the attractions are more subtle.

Don't expect many interesting places to stay or eat; the area's tourist industry hasn't come that far yet. There is, however, one inn that could hold its own anywhere. The **Inn at Walnut Bottom**, at 120 Greene Street, (301) 777-0003, offers 12 elegantly comfortable rooms and suites, two parlors, and game and televisions rooms. The bedrooms are set either in the 1820 Cowden House or the 1890 Dent House and are furnished with a unique mix of antiques and period reproductions. You'll pay $65 a night for one with a shared bath, $75 for one with a private bath and $85 for a deluxe room. Private car parking and mountain bike rental are available, and both breakfast and afternoon tea – served with cookies – are complimentary.

Also owned and operated by the inn are the **Haystack Mountain Art Workshops.** Between June and November, famous artists come here to teach their crafts. If you are creatively inclined, call for more information about the weekend packages, which include accommodation, meals, and workshops with the artist of your choice. Two other special weekend packages are worth investigating. Each one includes two nights' lodging, breakfast for two each morning, one dinner for two and a pair of tickets for either the Cumberland Theater (Western Maryland's only regional professional theater) or the Western Maryland Scenic Railroad. The cost is $285 and they are available between the middle of June to October and May to December, respectively.

The inn also houses the **Oxford House Restaurant,** which is far and away the best in town. Owners Jaye and Bill Miller believe that dinner is an experience to be savored; they ensure that the food is prepared with care and attention to detail. The menu is innovative, and although there is a fish and seafood emphasis, other tastes are more than adequately accommodated. Not only is the food delicious, it is well-presented and served in one of three intimate dining rooms. The atmosphere is enchanting, too, and given the lack of restaurants in town, this makes for a very pleasant surprise. Jaye and Bill are really to be congratulated. Be sure to call ahead at (301) 777-7101 for a reservation; you wouldn't want to miss this opportunity.

There is one more restaurant that merits discussion. Because it seems incongruous with the area, this one is even more of a surprise. Travel a few miles to the west, where you will come to the small and otherwise unprepossessing town of Frostburg. It is there, at 86 East Main Street, that you will find **Au Petit Paris Restaurant Francais,** which has been operating for over 35 years and is considered to be western Maryland's finest restaurant. In this intimate environment, chef/owner Louis St. Marie generally prepares at least nine appetizers, two soups, seven salads and over 25 entrées. The latter feature steak, fresh seafood, poultry, veal and succulent lamb. As a fitting finale, they offer at least 10 mouth-watering desserts and six coffees. An outstanding selection of European and domestic wines adds the finishing touch to a truly memorable dining experience. Another surprise for a town such as Frostburg is the cost. It is not inexpensive, with some entrées priced well over $30. This, however, doesn't hinder trade; the restaurant's clientele comes from far and wide. Indeed, the Au Petit Paris has served clients from almost every country in the world, including Russian cosmonauts. Now that the Washington Redskins have chosen Frostburg as their summer camp site, the restaurant can look forward to even more business.

Au Petit Paris' success is due largely to the unity of vision inherent in a family venture. Louis' wife Jeanne is the hostess, his daughter Jeanine is the bar manager, and his son Louie is the maitre d'. The story of how they happened to relocate from Texas to Frostburg is fascinating. We won't spoil the surprise here; ask one of them to tell you. The lounge opens at 5:50 p.m., and dinner is served in the restaurant from 6 p.m. to 9:30 p.m., Tuesday through Saturday only. Reservations are absolutely essential; call (301) 689-8946 or (800) 207-0956.

 On the way there, while traveling along Route 40, stop at the **LaVale Toll Gate House.** This unique seven-sided building dates from 1836 and is the only remaining toll house on Maryland's historic national pike. Over the course of the toll house's history, an estimated $10,000 was collected from over 20,000 travelers. These are final figures, as the only thing you need to pay here now are your respects.

The best way to see Cumberland is on foot. You won't need to walk very far, and it is the only way to ascertain the real flavor of the town. Ask at the inn for three brochures: "Walking Tour, Historic Downtown Cumberland," "Cumberland's Victorian Historic District," "Washington Street, A Self-Guided Walk Into History," and "Fort Cumberland Walking Trail and George Washington's Headquarters." If their supplies are depleted, make your way to the **Allegany County Visitors' Center**, (301) 777-5905 or (800) 50-VISIT. This is housed in the Western Maryland Station Center, just a short walk from The Inn At Walnut Bottom on Canal Street. Simply go out the front door and turn right, then go left at the lights and follow the train tracks to the station. The center is on the lower level. Hours are from 9 a.m. to 5 p.m. Monday through Friday, or from 10 a.m. to 6 p.m. on Saturday.

The station, originally constructed in 1887 and replaced by the present structure in 1913, is also the headquarters of the **Scenic Western Maryland Railroad**, (800) TRAIN-50. This is home to the *Mountain Thunder*, a 1916

Baldwin steam locomotive aboard which you may take a three-hour "Steam Through History" round-trip excursion to Frostburg. This 32-mile journey boasts spectacular scenery, takes you over an iron truss bridge, passes through the 1,000-foot Brush Mountain Tunnel and allows for a 90-minute layover at The Old Depot in Frostburg. This Cumberland and Pennsylvania train depot was built in 1891 and completely transformed 92 years later into an exciting complex that includes a restaurant decorated in the railroad theme, interesting shops, and a scenic railroad turntable. There is just one train daily, May through September and November through December. It leaves at 11:30 a.m. at a fare of $13.75 per person. As demand is particularly high during the fall foliage season, two trains run daily in October, departing at 10:45 a.m. and 3:30 p.m. The fare during this period is $15.75. Special trips are offered from time to time throughout the year; these include a murder mystery and buffet dinner. Train journeys are always romantic, and these are something to get truly steamed up about.

Back in town, take a stroll around the downtown area. The first guide will teach your untrained eye to focus on the interesting architectural and historical aspects of the buildings here. Guide number two will give you insight into a much more intriguing area. From the inn to the visitors center, your attention is bound to have been drawn to a small log cabin at the end of Greene Street. Closer inspection will reveal that it served as George Washington's headquarters in 1755. Except for the trenches, it is the only structure remaining of Fort Cumberland. Built in a strategic location, and seemingly well-defended, the fort never came under a large-scale attack. But higher hills nearby gave the aggressors some advantage; therefore, duty here was considered hazardous. It was from this site that General Braddock led his ill-fated expeditions against the French and Indians. Ignoring Washington's advice on a strategy to fight the Indians, Braddock marched his redcoated forces out in full sight and straight into lethal ambushes. The fort was garrisoned until 1765. In 1793, President George Washington returned to this site to suppress the Whiskey Rebellion in nearby Pennsylvania.

Washington Street – which used to encompass the stockade on its eastern end – is now a historic district in its own right. (It was named to the National Register of Historic Places in 1973.) Guide number three is helpful here, but the elegant buildings alone should tell you that this was the town's pre-eminent residential area during Victorian times. Indeed, it still is – and rarely will you come across a more delightful thoroughfare in any town. Beginning at the foot of Baltimore Street (the pedestrian shopping center), press on up the steep hill, which is dominated by the Emmanuel Episcopal Church. This structure dates from 1849/50, and was modeled after the Gothic St. Paul's Church in Brighton, England. Of particular interest are three beautiful Tiffany stained glass windows.

Past the court house and public library are four blocks' worth of houses with styles and characters so disparate that in many other environments, they would appear unseemly. Here, however, they are quite charming. In fact, it would be difficult not to want to live on a street like this. You'll surely want to spend some time at number 218, **History House**, run by the Allegany County Historical Society. This dignified Victorian dwelling is home to hundreds of items of local and national significance, with an emphasis on antiques and domestic items from the 19th century. The nursery is filled with late-1900s cribs, dolls, toys and even a hand-made doll house. There is also a magnificent turn-of-the-century bathroom. Tours are given on the hour from 11 a.m. to 3 p.m., Tuesday through Saturday, and at 1:30 p.m. and 4 p.m on Sunday during the months of May through October. To get back to the inn, simply make any left and stroll down the hill to Greene Street.

It's time now, perhaps, to take one of those mountain bikes and explore the C&O Canal towpath. Go as far as you like, but remember to save enough breath to pedal yourselves back. There is another option for cycling enthusiasts. **Appalachian Valley Bicycle Touring**, (410) 837-8068, offers a bed and breakfast weekend based around Cumberland. On selected weekends in May, July, September and October, you may spend Saturday exploring the wilderness of the Savage River Park and Sunday following the C&O Canal and visiting the engineering wonder of the Paw Paw Tunnel. The cost is $330 per person. This includes accommodation, meals, taxes and gratuities, tour leaders, a support van, maps, and even a souvenir AVBT T-shirt and water bottle. If you don't have bikes, don't worry; they will rent you those as well.

Cumberland is not as easy to reach when traveling from the north or south. But Interstate 68 – which runs on an east/west axis, and roughly parallels the old national highway – allows much better access when coming from the vicinity of Washington D.C. and Baltimore.

This area may not have many of the more traditional attractions. Nor is it a likely choice when planning a romantic weekend. That would, however, be dismissing it too easily. Cumberland has its own brand of charm, and the surrounding countryside is splendid, particularly in the fall. And how many opportunities do you get these days to travel on a train pulled by a steam engine? There are also numerous events scheduled throughout the year. The three most likely to interest visitors are the **C&O Canal Boat Festival** in July, the **Maryland Rail Fest** from the end of September through the beginning of October, and the **Victorian Christmas at History House** during the first two weeks of December.

Deep Creek Lake
From Slope to Shore:
A Sporting Proposition

You have decided to take a romantic weekend holiday. Where will you go? Perhaps you have been trying to choose between one of the delightful year-round resorts and a lakeside retreat. In the far western portion of Maryland, there is a place that offers the best of both of these options – Deep Creek Lake. Admittedly, though, it isn't the easiest place to get to. It's best to take Interstate

68 west and then Route 219 south – but few will be disappointed by the destination. What you'll find is Maryland's largest fresh water lake – man-made, at that. A full 12 miles long, the lake covers over 3,900 acres and has 65 miles of shoreline. At this point in time, it hasn't been over-developed. This adds considerably to its charms, but presents a problem with accommodation.

To the northwest – squeezed between the lake and the mountains, and next to the small town of McHenry – there is the **Wisp Resort.** This is truly a place for all four seasons. In the winter, you'll enjoy an extensive network of 23 slopes and trails, totaling 14 miles over 80 acres of ski-friendly terrain. The maximum elevation is 3,080 feet, with a 610-foot vertical drop. The Wisp's slopes, rated 20% beginner, 50% intermediate and 30% advanced, are serviced by two triple-chair lifts, three double-chair lifts and a poma lift. These get you back to the top quickly, so you can spend your time skiing – not waiting in line. Night skiing and snowboarding are also offered, as are rentals of the very best equipment. If you need lessons, they have that covered, too; the Wisp Ski School, operated by Austrian instructors, is PSIA-certified. And don't be concerned about a lack of snow; Wisp uses a 100% airless snow-making system that can cover 90% of the slopes in four days.

During the warmer seasons enjoy the resort's 7,122-yard, 18-hole championship golf course, one of the top 10 in Maryland. Before teeing-off, you may practice on the driving range and putting green. Mountain bikes are on hand to facilitate your enjoyment of this beautiful location; just make sure you avoid the groundhogs and steer clear of the resident bears. (That is one kind of hug you can do without!) As a new feature, in-line skates are now available for rent. And you may take advantage of the Olympic-sized indoor pool any time of year.

If all of this activity makes you hungry, you won't need to go far. The Wisp Food Mall offers you four choices: the **Pizzazz,** for pizza of all kinds; the **Bavarian Room Restaurant**, with a cozy old world atmosphere; the **Sweet Street Bakery**, to satisfy your sweet tooth; and the **McHenry House Cafeteria**, open during the winter only.

The on-site hotel offers a terrific Romantic Retreat Weekend, where for $206 per couple you get a room with turndown service, video rental, romantic bath amenities, photo album, champagne, massage discounts, a valuable coupon book and $50 in WISP dollars. If this interests you, call (800) 462-WISP for information and reservations.

If you prefer to be closer to – and overlooking – the lake, try the Wisp's sister company, **Will O'The Wisp.** Just five miles south on Route 219, this seven-story building has its own 700-foot private lakefront beach, as well as condominiums of various sizes. These are furnished with up-to-date facilities, including a kitchenette. Many have fireplaces and each has either a patio or a balcony, allowing you unobstructed views of the lake. On-site is the delightful Four Seasons Dining Room. This has an indoor/outdoor flavor, with marvelous views over the lake from windows on three sides, and an impressive 570-square-foot mural on the remaining wall. If you don't fancy swimming in the lake, you may still take to the water in the large indoor heated pool. Between dips, try the neighboring whirlpool and sauna. If you desire more strenuous exercise, handball or racquetball are available as well.

The tariff schedule is a bit complicated; the prices differ between the two seasons and the different styles of room. It may be helpful, however, to think in terms of $80-$134 a night for a one-bedroom condo. A wide array of popular packages are also offered, some of them oriented towards golfing and skiing, and therefore linked to the Wisp. There is an extra charge for these, the amount of which depends upon the facilities you wish to use. All told, however, the rates are less than normal. Prepare, too, to be "wowed;" some of these packages include WOW money which, we surmise, is equivalent to WISP dollars. So call the Will O'The Wisp at (301) 387-5503, extension 2206 for reservations, or 2201 for general information.

Although there are several bed and breakfasts in the area, none of them really attracted us. However, there is one scheduled to open by the end of 1995 that certainly sounds interesting. Deep Creek Lake was created in 1927, as a result of construction by Pennsylvania Electric. At this time, a right of way was designated for pedestrian use all around its shoreline. There was, however, one exception: a century-old farmhouse (estimated to be the oldest in the area) that found the newly-formed waters nearly lapping at its doorstep. Of all the houses on the shoreline, it is still the closest to the water. During our research, it was undergoing renovation to transform it into an eight-room bed and breakfast dubbed the **Lakepointe Inn – A Bed & Breakfast**. (At this printing, no telephone number has been assigned; if you like the sound of this place, get it from the information operator.) Each of the medium-sized rooms will have a private bath and a bed outfitted with a down comforter. The estimated tariff, as of July 1995, was between $75 and $150 a night. This will include a full breakfast and use of bikes and canoes. Proprietor George Pettie is considerate of all circumstances; in compliance with the Americans with Disabilities Act, he has even designed one wheelchair-friendly room.

For the best selection, book a private home or condominium from one of the area realty companies. There are numerous options, many of which front on the lake. These are often attractively appointed and feature all-modern facilities (sometimes even a jacuzzi). Outside of July and August – when there is often a weekly minimum – they're ideal for a romantic weekend. After all, as enticing as a hotel is, the atmosphere and privacy is nothing like that of a home. There are two companies we recommend. **Mountain Lake Rentals & Property Management**, (800) 846-RENT, offers special romantic packages known as "Just for Us – Two-Night Escapes," which include a $25 dinner certificate for the Silver Tree Restaurant, as well as complimentary wine and flowers. Offering a wider selection is **A & A Realty**, (800) 336-7303. This company is in the process of developing a "romantic package" of its own, which is expected to be in place by late 1995. A & A's properties are of varying sizes. Depending on both season and demand, it is difficult to project an exact price range. Most probably, it will fall between $150 and $450 – depending largely upon what you want, and when you want it.

Those who come here for the warm weather activities will be itching to get out on the lake. There is certainly no shortage of options – especially when it comes to boat rentals. Here, there are almost as many kinds of vessels as there are companies to rent them. If you are at McHenry, or close by, then consider **Deep Creek Outfitters**, (301) 387-6977. This company can be found on Deep Creek Drive, which runs parallel to Route 219. Canoes, fishing boats, runabouts, inboard/outboard ski boats, and even a five-man Torpedo water sled are available. Prices range from $5 an hour up to $260 for a full day. You must be over 21 years of age and, if born after July 1, 1972, comply with the Maryland Boating Safety Certificate Law. Be aware that when renting boats, you assume responsibility for the craft, as well as any personal injury or property damage resulting from its use. Also for rent are water skis and knee-boarding equipment, while fishing tackle and bait may be purchased. Just make sure you catch something; we don't want any fishy stories about the ones that got away! This company also has the largest boat on the lake. Called *The Evening Star,* she cruises at 2 p.m. each Saturday and Sunday, taking on passengers at $6 a ticket. On a limited number of Saturdays between May and September, dinner cruises are also offered. For $25 per person, you can enjoy both a four-course meal (prepared by McClives Restaurant & Lounge) and the beautiful scenery of Deep Creek Lake, Maryland's best-kept secret.

If you are staying at – or near – the Will O'The Wisp, a walk next door will take you to **Crystal Waters**, (301) 387-5515. Here you may rent canoes, pedal boats, fishing boats, pontoon boats or runabouts. These cost anywhere from $6 an hour up to $140 per day. Crystal Waters also offers a lake cruise aboard one of its pontoon boats. This leaves five times daily (between 10 a.m. and 6 p.m.) and costs $6 per passenger.

Water-skiing is quite popular here and watching the action may inspire you to try your luck. If so, head for High Mountain Sports a half-mile south of the Route 219 bridge (beside Trading Post at Traders Landing), for a water-skiing lesson from Greg Rouse. The cost is $50 for the first person, and $10 for each additional person in the party. After an hour and a half, you should be ready to tackle the waves on your own. But take it easy; you don't want an accident to spoil your weekend. Be advised that reservations are definitely required. They may be made by telephoning (301) 387-4199 in advance. Should you feel inclined to cling to *terra firma,* you may want to rent a pair of mountain bikes. These are available as well, at rates of $25 for a full day (eight hours), $18 for a half-day, or the minimum rental period of two hours, at $12.

Things on the surface may be fine and dandy, but you're probably wondering what's going on underwater. To find out, call **Breathe Deep S.C.U.B.A.** at (301) 387-8035. Here, you will receive individual attention – including an above-ground lesson and approximately one hour of underwater instruction – for $45 per person. You will need a wet suit, which is easily rented for $10. Call well in advance for a reservation but remember, don't get "tanked up" before you get there. Alcohol and water sports do not mix!

For those of you who prefer something a little faster-flowing, there is always whitewater rafting. Water is released from Deep Creek Lake into the Upper Youghiogheny (try and pronounce that correctly the first time!), making for hair-raising rafting trips through one of the last remaining wilderness canyons in the eastern U.S. **Precision Rafting**, (301) 746-5290 or (800) 4-PRE-RAF, is based in Friendsville. This is just a few miles north of McHenry on Routes 219 and 42. If you are in good physical condition and possess the required swimming skills, an expert guide will accompany you on either a raft or kayak for a thrilling day on the river. The $105 fee includes hot sandwiches and cold drinks. There's usually a video, too, through which you may relive your memories of an exciting day.

By this time, most of you will be glad to get two feet back on the ground – unless you prefer four, that is. If this is the case, turn onto Mayhew Inn Road (which is just to the right, off of Route 19). Half a mile later, the road diverges from the lake. Simple follow it around to **Western Trails Riding Stables**, (301) 387-6155 or (301) 387-6890. There are horses here to suit anyone's tastes and abilities, from beginner to expert. The cost is $15 per hour, or $45 for a half-day (three and a half hours). If you want to spend more time in the saddle, a full day (five and a half to six hours) will cost you $80. If you choose the latter, be sure to take a packed lunch. They will keep this in the fridge and deliver it to you – along with complimentary soft drinks – at lunch time.

On the subject of food, let's discuss some other attractions. **The Point View Inn**, located between the Will O'The Wisp and McHenry, is situated in an absolutely delightful location. Sitting out on the terrace during lunch (moor your boat there if you like), you can imagine yourself on either the Swiss or Italian lakes.

While in a Continental state of mind, we mustn't leave France out of the equation. Although its location at 21311 Garrett Highway (a.k.a. Route 219) is not so hot, the concept behind the **French Café Bakery**, (301) 387-8504, is both simple and clever. On the ground floor is a bakery with a delicious array of croissants that rivals that of any French town. There's also a grocery store stocked with all of your French favorites, from fondues to escargots. Be sure to take something back with you to your hotel. Add a chilled bottle of champagne, and you'll swear you're dining in some outdoor café on a Paris boulevard. You may also eat in the restaurant upstairs. Though not large, the room is light and airy, with a lake view and a rather eclectic menu. (Try Le French Beret for lunch.) The wine list is small but growing. Definitely a fun place, not to be missed.

If you fancy seafood to go with your French goodies, **Dr. Willy's Great American Seafood Co.**, (301) 387-7380, is the only game in town. You will find it off of Route 219 on Quarry Road, behind Garrett National Bank and the Deep Creek Baptist Church. Be sure to read up on "The Legend of Dr. Willy," which is printed on the back of their brochure. It may or may not be true – but it's certainly entertaining.

One more thought...

There is one idea that is so unusual and exciting that we knew it had to be included in this guide. But, as it only takes place once a year in Virginia and Maryland (and then sometimes in different locations) it doesn't really fit into any chapter.

Most everyone has seen footage of fighter planes in combat. Who hasn't wondered what it would be like at the controls? Well, now you don't have to wonder any more. Air Combat U.S.A actually allows you (accompanied by an instructor, of course) to fly one of two Marchetti SF 260 NATO air combat trainer planes. You'll don your flight gear, go through a briefing, fly in formation, take part in an aerial dog-fight, be de-briefed and then be able to relive it with a video tape of your "mission." Imagine the thrill as you watch the "enemy" plane you've been tracking take a vertical dive, the telltale smoke billowing from it.

So call (800) 522-7590 to give your partner a real thrill. Since nothing is simulated, this is one experience no one will ever forget!